Man's
Knowledge of Reality

AN INTRODUCTION
TO THOMISTIC EPISTEMOLOGY

Frederick D. Wilhelmsen
Associate Professor of Philosophy
University of Santa Clara

Englewood Cliffs, N. J.

PRENTICE-HALL, INC.

1956

To

Ronald Mentasti

Sacerdos et Amicus

Preface

At one time, epistemology was taught as a discipline following logic and preparing the student for metaphysics and the other philosophical sciences. This intermediate study, often called "criteriology," was designed to answer the critical problem, demonstrate to the student's satisfaction that he had a body and that he lived in a real world, prove to him the trustworthiness of his instruments of knowledge, and—perhaps—teach him a little about the methods proper to the sciences and something concerning deductive and inductive reasoning. Fortunately, "criteriology" is dying out today in American Catholic colleges and universities. This happy demise is largely the effect of the work of Etienne Gilson, who has shown us that such a "science" not only violates the realism of St. Thomas, but violates reality itself.

The resurrection of the metaphysics of St. Thomas within the last quarter century has taught us all at least one thing: if we would be faithful to reality, we must begin philosophy with the concrete, sensible being grasped by man in judgment. This is the common evidence; we begin here or we do not begin at all.

Therefore it seems that an epistemology integrally Thomist would be a theory of knowledge having the theory of judgment as its center and perfection. This book is nothing more than an essay towards such an epistemology.

The prospective teacher has a right to know just where the author of a textbook in philosophy stands. I am a Thomist—but Thomism is an ambiguous term. I, for one, do not deplore this. It bespeaks both the freedom and the fruitfulness of those who have made St. Thomas their master. To make my position as clear as possible at the very outset, let me state that my Thomism is not necessarily that of the classical Commentators. With all Thomists, I owe them a great debt of gratitude. Nonetheless, I part company with them on a number of issues because they seem to have parted company on these issues with their master, but principally because I think their master was right and they were wrong.

There are Thomists today who hold that the act of judgment is a linking of concepts within the mind followed by a comparison of this complex apprehension with reality. There are Thomists who hold that the pre-cognitive informing of the intellect by the intelligible species is preparatory to an act of simple understanding that can be distended subsequently into a judgment; that a completed act of simple understanding necessarily precedes every judgment. There are Thomists who hold that the intellect in judgment is actualized by two formally distinct intelligible species. I do not hold these positions, nor—as far as I can determine—did St. Thomas.

In evaluating my effort, I ask only two considerations of my readers: that their judgment be measured, first, by reality, and, second, by the extent of my faithfulness to the philosophy of St. Thomas.

Although an introduction, the book is not a simplification. It presupposes some study in the philosophies of man and being. A Thomistic epistemology—as we understand epistemology today—is necessarily a composite discipline, combining the psychology and metaphysics of knowledge. The book is divided into three sections: the first attempts to state the Thomistic reasons for rejecting the critical problem as raised by Descartes; the second, and most important, section takes up the theory of judgment; the third is a broad introduction to the epistemology of the speculative sciences.

The book is not a complete epistemology. I have chosen only those questions that seemed most important theoretically and most timely for the man of our day. A complete epistemology would go far beyond the limits usually granted for academic study, and for this reason I have not dealt explicitly with practical, artistic, aesthetic, and historical knowledges.

Because I presuppose some understanding of the nature of man and his operations, and some understanding of the basic ontological structure of being, I have not written down to the reader. I have taken his maturity for granted and assumed some background in philosophical discipline and terminology.

The last section and chapter is nothing but an introduction to the epistemology of the speculative sciences. The suggested texts for reading, which accompany many of the chapters, are not in any sense complete: they were selected simply because they seemed typical of the reasoning of St. Thomas on one or more doctrinal issues discussed in the body of the chapter. Nor are the bibliographies complete: they only include English and American works that the reader might consult with profit, and works in other languages that have shaped my own thought in some special manner and to whose authors I feel indebted.

I extend my deepest appreciation to the Rev. George V. Kennard, S.J., for introducing me, many years ago, to St. Thomas' theory of judgment. To those friends and former students who suffered with me through the formative stages of the work; to the Rev. Joseph Milunas, S.J., who encouraged me at a crucial point in my research; and, most especially, to the Rev. Ronald Mentasti, who heard the whole business through to the end—my gratitude.

FREDERICK D. WILHELMSEN

Table of Contents

‹ I ›

Metaphysical Realism

‹ 1 ›

The Meanings of the Word
Epistemology

"Epistemology" is a derivative from the Greek words meaning the "science of knowledge." Presumably, a study of epistemology would be an exploration of that science. But the presumption is somewhat deceptive because there is no such thing as a single "science of knowledge." Science, in the Thomistic sense of the term, means an understanding of things through their causes, but the causes of knowledge are many. These causes, in turn, are located within sciences distinct from any supposed "science" of epistemology. Knowledge is a way of existing: as a way of existing, knowledge is properly considered by metaphysics. Knowledge is a psychological operation: as a psychological operation, knowledge is properly investigated by the philosophy of man. But if knowledge is treated adequately by both metaphysics and psychology, what then is left of the supposed "science of epistemology"?

There is no distinct science of epistemology in the Thomistic sense of science.

From one point of view, the above reasoning is infallible. But although infallible, it is irrelevant. Although it is certainly true that there is no distinct science known as "epistemology," it does not thereby follow that there is no such thing as a philosophical investigation which is properly epistemological in nature. Epistemology can mean more than a nonexistent science. The term has at least five meanings, one historical and the others doctrinal. Among these five meanings, the historical and two of the doctrinal are valid; the remaining two doctrinal meanings are without any real significance.

Although not a science, "epistemology" has a number of valid meanings.

3

The burden of this introductory chapter is the explanation of the meanings of the term "epistemology" and the application of these meanings to the three sections making up the following study.

Historically, epistemology has come to mean the way men answer or confront the critical problem; this confrontation involves one's whole position on knowledge and its relation to things.

Historically, the term "epistemology" has come to mean the ways in which philosophers have met the so-called "critical" or "epistemological problem." Very briefly, we can describe the critical problem as follows: How does the mind move from an understanding of itself and its own operations, to an understanding of things? How does the mind know that it really knows things, not simply its own knowing? The ways in which men meet that issue, the reasons they advance, the conclusions they draw, have been unified by the modern mind under the term "epistemology." Whether philosophers accept the question as stated and attempt to answer it one way or another, or whether they reject the very statement of the question are considerations irrelevant to the historical meaning given epistemology. If you ask a scholar what was the epistemology of Leibniz, he will answer in terms of what Leibniz held on the relations between the mind and reality; he will not answer you in terms of what Leibniz held on free will or the laws governing the motion of bodies. If you are asked to describe your own epistemological position, you are expected to state what you believe to be the relations between man's knowledge and reality; your answer will include—either explicitly or implicitly—a rejection or an acceptance (whole or partial) of the so-called critical problem. Thus the community of learning has come to designate as epistemology the position any given philosopher maintains on the nature of human knowledge and its relation to the real world.

Epistemology can mean: (a) the metaphysics of knowledge and truth; (b) the psychology of human knowledge. There seems little justification for retaining the term in these senses.

"Epistemology" has at least four other possible meanings within the body of Thomistic philosophical doctrine: two of these meanings are invalid, two valid.

"Epistemology" can refer to the simple metaphysics of knowledge and truth, and "epistemology" can refer to the psychology of knowledge. Taken in the first sense, epistemology is nothing other than the metaphysics of knowledge; it is that part of the philosophy of being which investigates the act of knowing and the conditions proper to that act in the light of its very existence. Although we are free to call this investigation "epistemology," we are really talking about nothing other than the metaphysics of knowledge. Taken in the second sense, epistemology means the psychology of knowledge; it is that part of psychology which investigates the origin, the nature, and the processes of human intellection. Once again, although we are free to call this "epistemology," we are really talking about psychology. These two senses of the term "epistemology" do not designate anything other than the sciences of metaphysics and psychology.

"Epistemology" can also mean, and principally should mean, an investigation linking the metaphysics of knowledge and truth with the psychology of knowledge; this is not a distinct science of philosophy as, for instance, ethics is a distinct science. It is, nonetheless, a distinct way of organizing the matter in question. Epistemology, in this sense, is a philosophical penetration of the nature and conditions of the act of human knowledge *as such*. It prescinds from whether or not that act be scientific or nonscientific, poetic or historic, practical or speculative. Epistemology, as defined, investigates what is uniquely proper to human knowledge to the degree to which that knowledge is related to the metaphysics of being and truth; since it looks to human knowledge, it belongs partially to psychology: it investigates the origin, processes, and conditions of human understanding; since it looks to human *knowledge*, it belongs partially to metaphysics: it investigates the act of knowledge and truth. Epistemology is neither the one science nor the other, but is both of them together.

"Epistemology" can also refer to a discipline—metaphysical and psychological in character—that investigates the conditions proper to the many diverse kinds of human knowledge. In this sense of the term, epistemology is not one discipline; it is many. What is proper to scientific knowledge as scientific? What is proper to historical knowledge as historical? These are epistemological questions. In this sense of the term, there are as many valid epis-

Epistemology can mean: a study linking the psychology of knowledge with the metaphysics of knowledge and truth.

Epistemology can also refer to the philosophy of the unique kinds of knowledge; there are as many valid epistemologies as there are valid ways of understanding.

temologies as there are valid kinds of knowledge. This last way in which the term can be taken is dependent on, and derivative of, the previous consideration. That which is universally common to human knowledge underlies and conditions that which is proper to this or that kind of knowledge. It follows, therefore, that this final valid meaning of the term is less ultimate and less crucial than the second. An exhaustive analysis of all the possible "epistemologies" would entail a philosophical reflection on every distinct kind of knowledge exercised by man.[1]

In conclusion, we can sum up this introductory discussion by stating that epistemology has three valid meanings: (a) the historical—the first section of this book is given over to epistemology in this sense of the term; the first section of the book will state our position in reference to the critical problem; (b) the doctrinal—an investigation of the relations between the metaphysics of knowledge and truth and the psychology of knowledge, and this, which is the most important meaning of epistemology, is discussed in the second and largest section of this study; (c) the doctrinal consideration of the distinct kinds of human knowledge—this last is as varied as human knowledge itself, and the third section limits itself to certain kinds of human knowledge, namely, the speculative.

[1] The vast scope of such a task is beyond the economy of a book of this nature. The third section of this study investigates only one kind of knowledge, that is, the scientific in its speculative "parts."

A complete epistemology should include, ideally, the nature of practical knowledge; knowledge by connaturality; artistic knowledge; poetic knowledge; historical knowledge; and knowledge by Faith. Such an undertaking would entail not only an understanding of the philosophical principles and disciplines involved but of the objects of the diverse kinds of knowledge. An epistemology of art, for instance, could not be written by a man who was nothing more than a philosopher; he would need an intimate knowledge not merely *about* the arts but *of* the arts. The same principle holds true for the epistemological penetration of historical knowledge.

Bibliography

Gilson, Etienne, *Le Réalisme Méthodique, dans Philosophia peren-
nis* (Regensburg: Melanges Geyser, 1930).

—— *Réalisme Thomiste et Critique de la Connaissance* (Paris:
J. Vrin, 1947).

Maritain, Jacques, *Distinguer pour unir, ou les degrés du savoir*
(Paris: Descleé de Brouwer et Cie., 1946), pp. 138-145.

Van Steenberghen, Fernand, *Epistemology*, tr. by J. W. Flynn (New
York: Wagner, 1949), *passim*.

The Birth of the Critical Problem

---

(1) THE METHOD OF DESCARTES

Critical problem in its modern form stems from Descartes.

The critical problem, as we know it in the modern world, was raised by René Descartes in the seventeenth century. Since epistemological considerations have dominated western thought since Descartes, it is not an oversimplification to call him the father of modern philosophy.

The Cartesian program: a method universally applicable to all the sciences; a methodic doubt maintained until dissolved by the method.

Disgusted with the lack of certitude and with the confusion in philosophy as he knew it, wearied of the endless disputes between philosophical factions, Descartes resolved, therefore, to rebuild philosophy from the very foundation. His intention was to think through the whole of philosophy from its origins to its final conclusions. The instruments of the Cartesian reform were twofold: a method which Descartes thought to be universally applicable to all the branches of philosophy and science, and a universal doubt of the truth of all things and principles hitherto accepted by him. The method was used to dissolve the doubt.

Cartesian method: (a) natural habits of reasoning; (b) principles of logic; (c) methods proper to mathematics.

The Cartesian method had three antecedents: "common sense" habits of reasoning which are innate and which are the common property of all men, be they learned or not; the principles of scholastic logic; and the methods of reasoning proper to mathematics.

"Good sense," wrote Descartes in his *Discourse on Method*, "is, of all things among men, the most equally

8

distributed." [1] Natural, untrained intelligence spontaneously moves towards the truth in all men who use their reason. All men understand the meaning of thinking, feeling, doubting, existing. There is an innate power within the mind that impels it forward to grasp the meaning of these operations, operations which are one with itself. Not only are these operations open to all men who think at all, but all men use the same method or technique for arriving at the truth. Commencing with more simple problems, they move to the more complex. Confronted with an unknown complexity, they break it down into its simpler elements, understand these, and then return to grasp the complex meaning in its very complexity. It does not require education to exercise the reason in this manner because the reason is one with man himself.

"Good sense," untrained natural intelligence, understands the meaning and nature of its own operations, and spontaneously proceeds to the truth by moving from the simple to the complex.

The principles of scholastic logic, wrote Descartes, agreed with the processes of simple, informal reasoning. Scholastic logic taught nothing that contradicted the method all men use to reach the truth. Scholastic logic merely organized informal reasoning around certain laws and rules which were drawn from that very reasoning itself.

Scholastic logic was in agreement with "good sense."

Nonetheless, scholastic logic failed to measure up to its claim to be an instrument leading the mind to an understanding of philosophic truth. This contention of Descartes was little more than the shrewd conclusion of a man who had been exposed to the actual state of philosophical thought in the early part of the seventeenth century. Platonists, Scotists, Thomists, and others disputed endlessly about issues whose resolution seemed as far away as ever. To the mind of Decartes, the scholastic philosophers had reached nothing more than a high degree of probability in the most crucial philosophical issues they confronted. But probable knowledge is not *certain* knowledge, and only certain knowledge—knowledge that no man can doubt—is worthy of the name of science.

Nonetheless, scholastic logic failed to lead the mind to philosophic truth.

Descartes then turned to mathematics as the science

1 Rene Descartes, *Discourse on the Method of Rightly Conducting the Reason, and Seeking Truth in the Sciences,* tr. by John Veitch (La Salle, Ill.: The Open Court Publishing Co., 1946), p. 1.

that alone had succeeded in achieving a marked degree of certitude. There were no mathematical sects. Mathematical demonstrations could not be doubted by any mind that understood them. Therefore, concluded Descartes, the method that functions within mathematics, the method yielding absolutely certain conclusions, must be disengaged from mathematics and applied universally.

Only mathematics yields absolute certitude. Descartes decided to apply this method universally.

The method included two "moments"—one intuitive and one deductive. Initially the mind cleared itself of the sensible and imaginable. The mind drew in upon itself, so to speak. Confronted there by a world of intelligible objects—"ideas"—the mind proceeded to reduce these objects, to "analyze" them, down to their most simple elements. An object is grasped as such when it is intuited as an intelligible reality "clear" and "distinct" in kind.[2] A clear idea is an idea seen by the mind in such a fashion that the idea depends on nothing else for its comprehension and penetration by the act of intuition. The clarity of an idea, therefore, includes both the act of intuition and the object intuited. A mind only half attentive, a mind cluttered with the objects of sensation and imagination, cannot grasp an idea in its clarity as an object. Only the mind attentive and attuned to the object presented in the idea can see it as such. Thus the clear idea is one which is evidently itself and which is known in this act as being evidently itself. The distinction of the idea is the negative side of its clarity: If an idea is evidently itself, then it excludes every other idea. This is what Descartes means by distinction or distinctness.

The method involved two "moments": (a) intuition; (b) deduction. Intuition consisted in reducing an idea to its most simple elements and intuiting it in its clarity and distinction. An idea is clear when it is evidently itself and is intuited as such; an idea is distinct when it excludes every other idea.

Once an order of clear and distinct ideas is grasped, an order of "simple natures" in the language of Descartes, the mind can proceed to deduce from those ideas everything implicitly contained within them.

Thus intuition furnishes the mind with a set of ideas whose objectivity cannot be doubted. Deduction is the tool whereby the mind expands its knowledge by moving rationally from the ideas to every truth implicitly contained within them.

Deduction follows on the intuition of clear and distinct ideas.

[2] *The Principles of Philosophy,* tr. by John Veitch (La Salle, Ill.: The Open Court Publishing Co., 1946), I, 45, p. 152.

(2) THE RELATION BETWEEN IDEAS AND THINGS

The relation between *things* and *ideas* according to Descartes is not without importance in understanding the second element of his program; that is, the *methodic doubt*. The *object* is that which is intuited in an *idea*. The object, in turn, is the very intelligibility or rationality of the thing. My idea of a triangle, for instance, includes the "objectivity" of triangle, namely, its very "triangularity." Whatever is true of the nature of triangle, as understood in the idea of triangle, is true of every single existing triangle. Thus the movement of the mind, according to Descartes, is from the idea to the thing, from the mental to the real. *But mathematical objects do not include their own existence.* Although I can be absolutely certain that my idea of triangle corresponds to a real triangle, I cannot—by that very fact—conclude that the real triangle *exists*. Thus the method, when restricted to the mathematical, leaves untouched the question of actual existence. It is possible, therefore, for the mind to doubt the real *existence* of mathematical objects, even though the mind cannot doubt their reality (that is, as objects of the mind).[3]

What can be said of the idea can be said of the thing. Mathematical objects do not include their own existence. Man can doubt the existence of these objects.

(3) THE METHODIC DOUBT

This raises the whole question of the methodic doubt. The mind, says Descartes, is capable of doubting, not alone the extra-mental existence of all things thought, perceived, imagined, and sensed; but the mind can doubt its own ability to understand the truth as such. The mind can conceive the possibility that it is being deceived in all its operations, as well as in the reality of the things grasped in those operations.

It is necessary, therefore, to raise this doubt to the position of a methodic principle. Unless the doubt can be dissolved by the method, philosophy cannot be built on

Man can even doubt the existence of all things, as well as doubting his own ability to understand truly.

Methodic doubt the starting point of philosophy.

---

[3] *Ibid.*, I, 1-7, pp. 130-2.

solid grounds. *This methodic doubt of Descartes became, in time, the critical problem.* Philosophy must begin not with a fact—as in Aristotle—but with a doubt. It is possible, wrote Descartes, to doubt all the principles, conclusions, and axioms of science; it is possible to doubt the extra-mental existence of all objects; it is possible to doubt the ability of the mind to reach reality. Thus Descartes began philosophy by applying the doubt universally. "I will consider myself as without hands, eyes, flesh, blood, or any of the senses, and as falsely believing that I am possessed of these; I will continue resolutely fixed in this belief." [4] "Resolutely fixed," that is, until the method of reduction to the clear and distinct can dissolve the doubt.

(4) THE COGITO

"I think; therefore I am"; a truth (including its own existence) so clear and distinct that it cannot be doubted.

His second step consisted in finding an idea so clear and distinct that he could not doubt it. This idea had to involve the element of existence. In short, it had to be a nonmathematical idea. He fastened, finally, upon his own existence as a thinking principle: *Cogito ergo sum;* "I think; therefore I am." If I doubt that I am, I must be, because doubting is thinking and thinking is being. If I am deceived by some evil spirit into thinking that I exist, then I exist truly because being deceived is thinking (even if thinking falsely), and thinking is existing. [5]

(5) THE EXISTENCE OF GOD

The idea of God includes existence; since I possess the idea, God must exist.

Having established his own existence as a thinking principle to his satisfaction, Descartes cast around for a second application of his method. He could not move to the existence of material things because the idea of matter is one with the idea of extension: but extension, as a conceptual content, does not include its own existence. Descartes needed a second existent before he could reach the existence of the world. He fixed upon the idea of God:

[4] *The Meditations of Descartes,* tr. by John Veitch (La Salle, Ill.: The Open Court Publishing Co., 1946), p. 28.
[5] *Ibid.,* p. 30.

There is an idea which I think, the idea of an absolutely perfect being; this being must exist in reality beyond my thinking because the idea of a perfect being includes the idea of existence. A nonexistent perfect being would not be perfect. But I have the idea of the perfect; therefore He exists. To deny His existence is to deny the clarity and distinctness of the idea of God; but this cannot be denied, because the clear and distinct idea in question is, in fact, thought by me.[6]

(6) THE EXISTENCE OF THE WORLD

Only then did Descartes move to the existence of things outside his own mind. The mind possesses a *passive* power within itself, a power capable of receiving impressions which are not one with its own active power of thinking. This passive power reports the existence of a body that perceives and senses things beyond itself, as well as the existence of the things perceived and sensed. All men spontaneously judge this to be the case, and if their reasoning runs into a watershed of nothingness, if there really are no material things behind my sensations and causing them, then it follows that God Himself must be causing them. But if God were causing my sensation, He would be in the impossible situation of permitting the whole human race to be deceived about a piece of perfectly sensible reasoning. God, being a perfect being, is perfect truth. He could not permit such a massive lie to be perpetuated through history.[7]

The mind possesses passive powers which report sensations and things sensed. There must be a cause of these sensations, namely, extended, material existing things.

The Cartesian critique moves from the existence of the self as a thinking principle to the existence of God, and, from both of them, to the existence of the material order. The certitude I possess about things is dependent on the certitude I possess about myself as a thinking principle. Apart from the clarity and distinctness of my own thinking operations and self, the truth about God and the truth about things fade away into the doubtful world of folklore.

If I were deceived in this reasoning, God would be causing my sensations and would be thus deceiving me concerning their origin. God, perfect Truth, could not do this.

6 *Ibid., V Med.,* pp. 78-79.
7 *Ibid., VI Med.,* pp. 84-104.

(7) DESCARTES AND THE CRITICAL PROBLEM

Such, very briefly, was the program of Descartes. We have no intention in this study of subjecting the Cartesian position to a close analysis. There are flaws in his reasoning, but these flaws are actually irrelevant to the epistemological issue. This issue is Descartes' insistence that philosophy must begin *in* and *from* the mind and proceed to things; that the first unshakeable truth known to man is the existence of himself as a thinking principle; that everything else known to man is dependent on this first of truths; and that, consequently, whatever is known about the world is critically dependent on what is first known about one's own knowing. If a man accepts Descartes' initial principle, he is forced immediately to ask the following question: If I am philosophically—that is, critically—certain of only one thing at the outset of my philosophizing, and if this one thing is the existence of myself as a thinking principle, then how am I able (if I am able at all) to move from this primitive certitude to a knowledge of other things, and, most especially, to a knowledge of the existence of the extra-mental world, of things existing independently of my own understanding? This is the famous "critical problem" that has plagued thinkers since the time of Descartes.

(8) CRITICAL EPISTEMOLOGY

There are only two fundamentally distinct philosophical positions with reference to the critical problem: a "critical" and a "noncritical" position. Those philosophers who maintain, along with Descartes, that philosophy must begin with the certitude possessed by the mind thinking and that therefore philosophy must answer the critical problem, are called in this book "critical philosophers." These men hold that the mind must begin by reflecting on its own operations. Some critical thinkers agree with the whole Cartesian program, some agree in part and disagree in part. Some maintain that the mind can never reach external reality, that the external world is unknowable; others maintain that there is no external world, that reality is the product of the mind. But despite their diverse conclusions, these men are all critical thinkers because their point of departure is the mind understanding and knowing with an absolute certainty its own existence and operations.

(9) METAPHYSICAL REALISM

Those philosophers who disagree not only with the conclusions of Descartes, but with his point of departure, are "noncritical" thinkers. They hold that philosophy must begin with something other than the certitude men possess about their own existence as thinking principles; they hold that philosophy must begin with *things*, with *being*. For this school of thought, the first and ultimate principle and truth of philosophy is the judgment, "Being is." We call this school of thought "metaphysical realism"; *realism*, because it holds to the real existence of things in independence of men's thinking or knowing them; *metaphysical*, because it holds that this truth is the first and ultimate principle of philosophy, a truth independent of any critique of knowledge.

The author of this study rejects not only the conclusions, but the point of departure of Descartes; he holds that the "critical problem" need not be answered, because it ought never have been raised. But he also holds that a philosopher must give an account of his rejection of the critical problem. In short, the author is a "metaphysical realist," a realist in the tradition of Thomas Aquinas. The following two chapters set forth the reasons for maintaining this position.

Bibliography

Collins, James, *A History of Modern European Philosophy* (Milwaukee: Bruce Publishing Co., 1954), pp. 138-199.

Descartes, René, *A Discourse on Method*, Veitch's translation (La Salle, Ill.: The Open Court Publishing Co., 1946); *The Meditations*, Veitch's translation (La Salle, Ill.: The Open Court Publishing Co., 1946); *The Principles of Philosophy* (La Salle, Ill.: The Open Court Publishing Co., 1946).

Gilson, Etienne, *The Unity of Philosophical Experience* (New York: C. Scribner's Sons, 1937).

Maritain, Jacques, *The Dream of Descartes*, translated by M. Anderson (New York: The Philosophical Library, 1944).

‹ 3 ›

Metaphysical Realism

---

(1) POINTS OF DEPARTURE

Epistemology, in the historical sense of the term, is essentially a quarrel about the first principles of philosophy, a quarrel resulting from Descartes' raising of the critical problem. Philosophers cannot ignore the challenge of Descartes. Even if they disagree with his point of departure, they must give an account of their disagreement. If they think that philosophy should not begin in the mind but that it should begin in things, they must state their reasons for thinking as they do. Epistemology, as pointed out in the opening chapter, is the name given to that philosophical investigation which looks to the origin and the first principles of all philosophy as they are related to the metaphysics and psychology of intellection.

As indicated, there are only two fundamentally opposed positions on the first principles or truths from which philosophy should begin and upon which philosophy should be grounded: Philosophy must seek its point of departure in the mind or philosophy must seek it in things. We have called these positions "critical" and "noncritical." The critical philosophers—following the program of Descartes—attempt to subject the instruments of knowing to a searching analysis in order that they might establish (if possible) the reliability of human knowledge itself; once they have established this reliability to their own satisfac-

17

tion, they turn to other philosophical issues; they begin
with the evidence of thought; they terminate (perhaps)
in the evidence of being. The noncritical philosophers—
the metaphysical realists—begin with things and, in the
course of their speculations, they explain knowledge in
terms of what they know about the being of the things
that are. The first principle of critical epistemology is the
truth that "thought is," either thinking in general or my
own thinking. The first principle of noncritical epistemology—of metaphysical realism—is the truth that "being is"
or "beings are."

The noncritical thinkers are in the tradition of Aristotle
and St. Thomas Aquinas. The existence of things in and
for themselves is evident to all men, and this evidence is
the first truth known to man and it is the first truth known
to philosophy. Everything else that is known by man is
known in the light of this first truth about being.

The critical philosophers do not present such a united
front as do the metaphysical realists. They disagree widely
among themselves on the ultimate nature and meaning
of reality. The *critical idealists,* for example, maintain
that even though things may exist beyond our knowing
them, their existence would be irrelevant to our speculations.[1] We know what is contained within human reason,
and whatever is within reason has come forth from reason
and obeys its laws. The *absolute idealists* maintain that
nothing exists beyond the order of thought; being is a
function of the mind; the act of thinking creates its own
object and beyond that act there are no objects. (*Absolute*
idealism is divided into *subjective* and *objective* idealism:
The former maintains that whatever exists has being only
within the mind of the individual thinker; the latter maintains that all reality is the creation and object of spirit
and that whether that "spirit" be yours or mine is irrele-

[1] The terms "critical idealist," "absolute idealist," and so on, are used
in a somewhat arbitrary fashion in the text. They do not necessarily correspond to the names the philosophers in question give their own systems. The names used in the text are nothing more than dialectical
terms designating logically distinct positions with reference to the critical problem. Thus Kant and Brunschvicg can both be called "critical
idealists" because both held that the real is that which is organized by
the mind and by the sensibility of man.

vant to the issue.)² The *critical realist* teaches that although things do exist beyond our thinking them, although we do know the things that are, the philosopher must begin speculating with the data of thought; once he has established that we cannot doubt the evidence of our own existence as thinking or knowing principles, he can move to a consideration of things existing beyond the intelligence.³ The critical philosophers are really agreed on only one point: Philosophy must begin in the mind, not in things. Their agreement on this one point sets them together in one camp in opposition to the metaphysical realists, to the men who maintain that philosophy must begin with the evidence of being.

The men holding critical philosophy in any of its many forms accuse the realists in the tradition of Aquinas of simply assuming that a world of things exists in and for itself. The Thomistic realist, so goes the complaint, is a man who merely pounds the table and asserts flatly that things exist without justifying his assertion in any way. He is a naïve realist, a man who refuses to take into account the past three hundred years of philosophical speculation, a philosopher whose philosophy amounts to little more than the spontaneous affirmations of the man in the street. The Thomistic position, according to the critical epistemologists, is really no position at all; it is nothing but "common sense," uncriticized, unpenetrated by philosophical analysis. When Boswell asked Dr. Johnson to refute the idealism of Bishop Berkeley, Johnson kicked a

Critical school accuse the metaphysical realists (that is, Aristotelians and Thomists) of merely assuming an existing order.

² Bearing in mind the above qualifications, we can call Fichte, Schelling, and Hegel absolute idealists in an objective sense: that is, there is a real world beyond the individual subjectivity of the existing knower, but this real world is the objectification of absolute spirit or mind.

³ Critical realism is not one school of thought; it is many. The United States has given birth to the most significant critical realisms in the twentieth century: for example, the systems of D. Drake, A. O. Lovejoy, J. B. Pratt, A. K. Rogers, G. Santayana, R. W. Sellers, and C. A. Strong. Their program was published in: D. Drake *et al.*, *Essays in Critical Realism: A Cooperative Study of the Problem of Knowledge* (London: Macmillan, 1921). The Neo-Realists, headed by John Wild, seem much closer to the basic metaphysical position of St. Thomas: that is, they are more fully aware than their predecessors of the need to link epistemological considerations to a metaphysics of being; compare, John Wild (ed.), *The Return to Reason: Essays in Realistic Philosophy* (Chicago: Regnery, 1953).

stone on the street. This, say the critical thinkers, is dogmatism: unreflecting, unthinking, unenlightened. This is not philosophy: It is prejudice.

There is no doubt that Johnson's kicking the stone was not philosophy. But the Thomistic realist maintains that he can explain why Johnson kicked the stone. Johnson kicked the stone because he was certain there was a stone to kick, not because of prior convictions he entertained about the nature of the mind, but because of the stone itself.

(2) ASSUMPTIONS; POSTULATES; EVIDENCES

Assumption or postulate: a proposition that is neither proved nor evident, but which is self-coherent and noncontradictory.

Was Johnson assuming the existence of the stone? Do the Aristotelians and the Thomists *assume* an existing world? This is the charge of the critical philosophers, and in order to understand the charge we must know exactly what is meant by an *assumption*. In English, the word is synonomous with the word "postulate." Both mean any self-coherent, noncontradictory proposition someone is asked to accept as true even though its truth is neither evident in itself nor capable of proof. I might assume or postulate, for instance, that the Republican Party will win the national election in 1980. Since I am writing these words in advance of that time and since I possess neither internal evidence nor proof for the proposition I set forth, it is clear that the opposite could be advanced with equal force; that is, the Republicans will not win in 1980. Another example of the postulate, taken from the past, is the assumption of many military historians that the German Army under Von Kluck would have taken Paris in 1914 had the right wing been strengthened. Perhaps; perhaps not: I possess no compelling evidence on the issue. A postulate, therefore, is something of a "neutral" proposition: it is not proved to be true; it is not proved to be false; it is not a contradiction; but it is not evident in itself.

It should be clear from the above that the very meaning of the term "assumption" or "postulate" is dependent on the meaning of the terms "evident" and "proved." A postulate is a proposition neither evident nor proved. In order to talk sense about postulates a man must know that he means when he uses the terms "evidence" and "proof," since he defines a postulate in opposition to these two terms.

In the English language an *evident proposition* means a proposition whose truth is grasped as soon as a man grasps the proposition itself; the truth of an evident proposition is seen once the proposition is seen. Such a proposition cannot be denied or doubted once it is understood. I need no prior information in order to know that the proposition expresses the truth: It stands on its own two feet. A *proved proposition,* on the contrary, is a true judgment whose truth depends on propositions that are prior and better known than itself. I know, for example, that "John is capable of reasoning," because I know that "man is capable of reasoning," and that "John is a man." The two latter truths ground the truth that "John is capable of reasoning." Therefore, a proved proposition is one whose evidence rests in the evidence of other propositions. I could not know its truth simply by grasping the meaning or elements of the proposition itself. I must refer it to propositions previously understood by me to be true and from which I infer the truth of the proposition in question.

To sum up, there are three fundamental types of possible propositions (other propositions can be reduced to these three): *postulated* or *assumed*—a judgment that makes sense but whose contradictory could make equally good sense; *evident*—a judgment whose truth is seen once the proposition is seen; *proved*—a judgment whose truth depends on prior propositions, better known than itself, grounding the truth of the proved proposition.

Now let us return to the issue: Do the metaphysical realists, the philosophers in the tradition of Aristotle and Aquinas, assume that a universe of things exists beyond thought? Is the judgment "things exist beyond my knowing them" a postulate or is it evident? (We can eliminate the possibility of the judgment being a proof, because if

An evident proposition is one whose truth is contained totally within itself; it cannot be doubted, and, because evident, it cannot be proved.

A proved proposition is one that is true, but the evidence for its truth is found in previously understood and better-known truths.

The existence of things is evident to a Thomist, assumed by a Platonist.

it is a postulate it cannot be proved and if it is evident it need not be proved; only if the existence of the world were neither evident nor postulated would we have to attempt the Cartesian method of proving the existence of things.) If the question is really put to a Thomist, he will answer in terms of evidence. But, if the question is put to a philosopher implicitly or explicitly holding a Platonic theory of man, he must answer in terms of assumption; he cannot, if he be true to his position, answer that the existence of things is evident to man.

(3) THE PLATONISM OF CRITICAL EPISTEMOLOGY

Critical epistemology entails a Platonic theory of man.

The introduction of the Platonic psychology is by no means irrelevant to the issue at hand, because, as shall be indicated in due course, the critical philosophers implicitly presuppose a kind of Platonism when they accuse the Thomists of assuming that things exist independently of the human mind.[4] The Thomistic position would be an assumption on critical terms, and the critical thinkers assume that their terms are the only ones possible in philosophy.

Platonic man is two things: soul and body; what the soul knows is separate from what the body knows.

What is the Platonic conception of human nature? Plato and those following him do not look upon man as a unity in being. Man is not really one thing; he is two things: a soul and a body, neither of which is joined to the other in the unity of existence. In Platonism—as has often been said—the soul stands to the body as a helmsman stands to the ship; as there is neither an existential nor essential union between helmsman and ship, there is neither an existential nor essential union between soul and body. There is no existential union between helmsman and ship because the one is not the other: the helmsman is one thing; the ship is another thing. Neither is there an essential union between them: the nature of a ship does not include as one of its elements the nature of the helmsman. The union is accidental. The helmsman could re-

---

[4] The split of man into body and soul has been brilliantly traced by Etienne Gilson in his *Unity of Philosophical Experience* (New York: C. Scribner's Sons, 1937), *passim*.

main a helmsman without a ship. The ship could exist without the helmsman (there is such a thing as a ship in port without a crew). So, too, with the soul and the body: they happen to be united together in this life; perhaps their union is due to some primitive calamity; in any event, the union is not the congenial union between principles acting together to make up one thing; it is the union of two things, essentially separate in nature.

Because the soul and the body are not essentially united, there is no essential connection between what the soul knows and what the body knows. Plato's soul knows a world of abstract principles, universal essences and laws, spiritualized forms; his body senses a shadowy world of sensible qualities. Plato's man really lives two lives. One is the life of the contemplation of pure forms or essences, the ideal world of "the Good, the True, and the Beautiful." This is the realm of science and certain knowledge. The other is the life of sensation, the life lived by the body in its contact with the shifting kaleidoscope of material things as they collide with the senses, impinging themselves on the body as they pass through history on the road to oblivion. This is the realm of mere opinion, a world of which we can have absolutely no certain knowledge at all.

Platonic soul knows the abstract order; the Platonic body senses the material order.

Because the only possible *source of evidence* for the existence of material things beyond the human mind would be sensation which alone contacts materially existing things, and because sensation belongs to the body and is therefore cut away from intellection which belongs to the soul, the Platonic intellect cannot take into account the data of sensation. Only an intellect can judge. *But if the intellect has no essential contact with the body, it could never judge things to exist with any degree of certitude.* It could never get at the evidence. The existence of a world of things would be neither evident to such an intelligence, nor would it be susceptible of cogent proof. The intellect might well assume or postulate that a world exists; it could just as well assume the contrary. "Things exist beyond my knowing them"; "things do not exist beyond my knowing them": both propositions are reason-

Plato's soul is cut away from the source of evidence for the existence of things; therefore, his soul could only assume that things exist; it could just as well assume the contrary.

able possibilities to the Platonic soul, cut away as it is from the body.

Critical school is implicitly Platonic.

This digression into Platonic psychology has not been made to convict the critical philosophers of any conscious adherence to the Platonic theory of man. Most critical philosophers are not Platonists in any strict, formal sense. Nonetheless, their critique as well as their attack against Thomistic realism implies a Platonic notion of man. In order to mount the barricades of critical epistemology, man must mount as a Platonist. This is not only a logically necessary deduction from the first principles of critical thought, it is also an accurate historical description of the modern philosophical temper.

Philosophical thought since Descartes has been implicitly Platonic about the nature of man; therefore, it has been critical about the existence of things beyond our knowing them.

Since the time of Descartes, philosophers outside the Aristotelian and Thomistic traditions have been extremely reluctant to admit that there is any such thing as a man. With Plato, they think that man is two things, not one. On the one hand, he is a center of sensation and perception: a body. On the other hand, he is a center of abstract laws and judgments: a mind. What the mind knows is not related directly to what the body senses, and what the body senses is not really known by the mind. From this follows the widespread refusal (shared by all within the critical camp, with the exception of the critical realists) to admit that men can be sure about any*thing* whatever. My mind, for example, can be certain about the laws governing the relationships between triangles, but my mind cannot really know whether there are any such *things* as triangles. The mind knows a world of logical relations and scientific laws; the mind has nothing to do with sensing or feeling reality. If there are any triangles, they exist in chalk upon a blackboard, or they are traced in the air by cigarette smoke, and so forth. Now chalk, wood, and smoke are realities initially *sensed,* not *thought.* Because the mind thinks rather than senses, because what the mind thinks is isolated from what the body senses, the mind cannot say anything about these realities. Men, therefore, are doomed to live an extremely curious life. They can scientifically penetrate the most abstruse of mathematical theories; they can elaborate the most complicated of logical systems; but they cannot really know any *things* at all. They can sense them, perceive them, eat them, sleep in them, talk to them, marry them, beget them, but they cannot know them; they cannot be certain that they are, that they exist.

This prevailing conviction that man is not one thing but two things, that what the mind knows is essentially unrelated to what the body feels, gives birth to two apparently contradictory systems. One philosophical faction is more impressed with the mind than with the body: it sweeps away the evidence of sensation and declares that reality is fundamentally mental or spiritual; the human spirit creates the real world, and whatever lies beyond that world is irrational and unknowable chaos (if anything does lie beyond the world at all): this is *absolute idealism.*

Idealism: the effect of the Platonic theory of man.

The other faction is more impressed with the body than with the mind: The only fact that really matters is the fact of sensible experience, but since what we sense are not things which can be known by our minds, our minds are given over to the task of ordering and cataloguing our sensations according to patterns which we impose upon the data of sensation; we do not exactly create the order of nature, but we give the law to nature: this is *Kantianism* or *critical idealism.*[5]

Perhaps our earlier example of the triangle will make the distinction more vivid: The triangle is a reality which the human spirit has generated or created, say the absolute idealists. The triangle is a bit of nothing which the body senses and which the mind organizes in this way, that is, by imposing on the sensation the form or law of triangularity, say the Kantians. These positions may seem to be opposed, but both are fundamentally the same; they come out of the same philosophical presuppositions. Both

[5] For Kant, man gave the law to nature (compare, *Critique of Pure Reason,* Preface to Second Edition, B x-xvii-i [Smith, ed.], pp. 17-23). The only proposition which was both universally necessary and which simultaneously dealt with reality was the *synthetic a priori* judgment. Perceptions were synthesized and then rendered intelligible by being subsumed under certain "categories," which were *a priori* forms of the mind which functioned as principles for the intelligible discernment of the real.

agree that there is no such thing as a triangle-being; both agree about this because they agree that there is no such thing as a man who could simultaneously sense this triangle-being with his body and know that it existed with his mind. Both positions are critical; both agree that philosophy must begin by analyzing the data of the mind; both imply a Platonic theory of man.

Critical school maintains that all truth can be doubted apart from the testimony of the "Cogito."

The critical school insists that philosophy must begin either with the act of thought itself, or with the self considered merely as a principle conscious of its own operations. What we first know and know with absolute certitude, said Descartes, is the existence of our conscious, thinking states. All other truths we know can be doubted apart from the unshakeable testimony we possess about our existence as thinking principles. For Descartes, the first of all truths was *"Cogito ergo sum"*—"I think; therefore I am." This first truth guaranteed the whole gamut of knowledge possessed by man, and without this certitude all human knowledge dissolved into an uncertain body of opinion. For Kant, the judgment *"Ich denke"*—"I think" —was a judgment transcending every other judgment because presupposed by all of them; it was the very ground and justification for the possibility of knowledge and experience.[6] As with Descartes and Kant, so too with all the thinkers who believe philosophy must begin with some critique of knowledge.

(4) THE ASSUMPTIONS OF A "CRITIQUE"

Critique of the critique: a double abstraction from the pre-philosophical situation lies behind the critical act.

But in order to begin philosophy this way, the critical thinkers must make a double abstraction or removal from things as they find them prior to the act of philosophizing. Prior to the reflective, critical act in which thought discovers itself to be thinking, the act of knowing is not an autonomous, independent state: it exists in the knowing subject, the man. Prior to the critical act, thought does not know itself as a thinking principle: Knowing is a knowing of this or that thing in the existing world. The critical philosopher first abstracts this act of knowing from

[6] Kant, *Critique of Pure Reason*, B 137 (Smith, ed.), pp. 154 ff.

the man possessing the act. Secondly, this abstracted act
of knowing turns about and finds it can throw into doubt
both the existence of the man who has the act of knowing
and the existence of the thing known in the act of knowing. In short (and here one needs what Kierkegaard called
"the sense of the comic"), this strange act of thinking,
living its own life in a void, doubts both the existence of
the man without whose existence there would not even
be an act of knowing and doubts the existence of the
thing known without which it would not even be an act
of knowing, because, of itself, it is a knowing of *this thing.*

In order to grasp the point more concretely, concentrate for a moment on the fact that you are here and
knowing this piece of paper before your eyes. The situation involves three elements: (1) the piece of paper (2)
being known (3) by you. Now suppress the first and third
elements; that is, the fact that there is a piece of paper
and that you—a flesh and blood human being—know the
piece of paper. Retain only the act of knowing, without
referring that act to the thing known or to you—the subject—exercising the act. Once you have done this, you are
in the position of the critical philosopher after he has established the starting point of his critique of knowledge.
You and what you know have dropped out of the picture. There remains only pure knowing or thinking, knowing or thinking itself to be knowing or thinking.

The critical school drops both the thing known and the knower; it retains only pure knowing or thinking.

The man of common sense, unencumbered by what has
become a latter-day philosophical prejudice, might tend
to react against all this the way Hilaire Belloc's Sailor re-
acted to the idealist metaphysician: He baptized him with
a pint of beer in the name of the five senses. The reac-
tion would certainly clear the air, but it would leave the
issue as clouded as before.

How does the critical thinker get himself into this exceedingly curious situation? He gets there, as indicated,
by assuming implicitly that man is the kind of thing Plato
thought him to be. For the purposes of his critique, he
assumes that knowledge is cut away from things and
men. He assumes that he can doubt the existence of an
external world and that he can doubt his own existence

as a concrete flesh and blood man, even though he cannot doubt his existence as a thinking principle. He assumes that he must try to prove that a world exists and that he exists within that world. He insists on beginning philosophy with the naked certitude possessed by a disembodied principle of pure thought understanding only itself and its own laws. Most of the critical thinkers eventually conclude—quite sensibly—that they cannot get outside of the mind; the attempted "proof" that a world of things exists in independence of the mind collapses. The men become idealists. A few of the critical thinkers believe they can establish a bridge leading pure thought into the world of reality. In any event, philosophy has been established only by cutting the mind away from things and from the body. This is Platonism.

The existence of things could only be a postulate on critical terms.

The critical school would dismiss this analysis as a psychological rather than an "epistemological" (that is, critical) discussion. The attack is perfectly valid. It *is* a psychological analysis, and the whole point is made when one sees that the critique of knowledge depends on making this double psychological abstraction of the mind from the concretely given situation. The mind has been artificially dissected from things and from the body. Once this operation has been made, it follows that the critical thinker cannot judge things to exist in themselves with any degree of certitude. He must restrict philosophy to an analysis of the purely abstract "objects" intrinsic to the mind. To assert that material things exist in and for themselves would be a sheer assumption. And so it would —for the critical philosopher!

But the Platonic presuppositions of the critique are not the only framework within which a man can philosophize.

(5) THE THOMISTIC POSITION

Existence of things concretely present to man is evident.

Suppose our original question is asked a metaphysician in the tradition of Thomistic realism: Are there things existing in independence of the act of knowing them? He will answer that, beyond the least shadow of a doubt, the independent existence of things is evident to all men when they act as men. It is not evident in exactly the same way in which axioms or first principles of, let us say, mathematics are evident. The latter are evident because they cannot be thought of as being in any other way than the way we think them; for example, "the whole is greater than the part" is a truth that is evident in itself (self-evident) because I cannot conceive the opposite proposition being true even if I try; for all time and even into eternity a whole will always be, must always be, greater than any of its parts. It is certainly true that I can conceive of the things around and about me as nonexisting; for example, I can very readily grant that the typewriter I am using at this moment might someday not exist. Nonetheless, it is impossible for me to judge that the typewriter does not exist at this very moment, because at this moment it does exist. And I know that the typewriter exists—not as a body knows or as a mind knows—but as a man knows. The existence of the typewriter is evident to me because I sense the typewriter at this moment and know with my intellect that what I am sensing actually exists: that it is being, a hard core of reality that is not created by me, not constructed by me, but that is simply given me as existent.

The extra-mental existence of things is not evident to an intellect functioning in a void, because an intellect cut away from sensation would have no contact with things. It could only know essences or natures in a state of abstraction from the singular, material existence they enjoy in themselves. The human intellect, as a human intellect, could know only the de-existentialized natures of things. An inspection of our concepts reveals the truth of the above statement.[7] Our concepts do not tell us *that* things are, they tell us *what* things are; they reveal nature or essence, not existence. "The existence of things is outside the order of concepts," wrote St. Thomas in the thirteenth century.[8] The same thing was said in the eighteenth century by Immanuel Kant when he pointed

Existence escapes the conceptual order.

[7] Future chapters indicate the psychological reason for this fact.
[8] *De Veritate:* 3, 3, ad. 8.

out that my idea or concept of a hundred dollars does not add one cent to my pocketbook.[9] I can think of a fortune all day long and my thoughts do not entail or conjure up the actual existence of the fortune. This may be a tragedy; it is, nonetheless, the common lot of all human concepts.

Sense knows sensible qualities, not existence as such.

If the intellect, by itself, only knows concepts expressing essences abstracted from their actual existence in things, it is also true that the existence of things is not evident to mere sensation. The senses cannot judge or affirm anything; they just sense. And although sensation is genuinely knowledge, it is knowledge that bears on sensible qualities, not existence. Existing things thrust themselves upon the senses, but the senses know them, not precisely as existing, but as colored, tasted, heard, touched, and felt. The senses sense things that are; they do not judge them to be.

Existence known to man as a body-soul unity. This truth is evident to man.

That things exist, therefore, is known neither by the intellect nor by the senses. This is true, but it is also profoundly irrelevant: strictly speaking, there is no such thing as an human intellect "by itself"; nor is there such a thing as brute sensation "by itself." Man is neither one nor the other. He is both of them joined in that unity of being we call man. *It is only as a man—as a body-soul unity—that he knows things to exist, and he knows this truth as neither postulated nor demonstrated, but as evident.*

Man knows what he senses, and senses what he knows.

We men know that things exist because we sense and perceive them. Sensation meets existing things; sensation does not know them as existent. Sense senses red, but does not know that the red thing exists. Intellect, alone, could know the essence of the red thing, but it would not know the existence of the red thing. Man, taken as he is—body and soul together—knows what he senses and senses what he knows.

This truth is so powerfully ingrained in human nature that absolutely no sane man doubts the existence of the things round and about him. Not even the critical philos-

[9] Kant, *Critique,* Transcendental Dialectic, Bk. II, Ch. 3, Sect. 4, in *Kant's Selections,* ed. by Theodore Meyer Greene (New York: Scribner, 1920), p. 268.

opher doubts for an instant that an external world exists, when he acts outside his private world of critical philosophy. When he builds his critique of knowledge he artificially sets aside the evidence presented to his mind by his senses. He pretends that he has no senses or that he must, for the sake of his critical reasoning, doubt their validity, or that, although he does have senses, they are irrelevant to philosophical discourse. He is free to think this way if he wishes, but when he does so think he is no longer asking whether or not existing things are evident to man.

To sum up: *Man knows there are things because he senses them.*

(6) THE PROBLEM OF FALSE PERCEPTIONS

At this point the idealist and the skeptic (whose position on this issue parallels that of the idealist) usually advance the problem of hallucinations, pathological sense states, and dreams. Because there are false perceptions such as hallucinations, so goes the objection, I could never be certain there were any true perceptions.[10] How can I know that what I perceive really does exist and that I am not dreaming or imagining, etc. This position, the common coin of skepticism, is advanced everywhere today by the partially educated as a final objection against realism; and yet the objection is a painful sophistry. How can I even speak of false perceptions unless I can measure their falsity by a true perception?

Etienne Gilson has likened the sophistry to the reasoning of a man who would maintain that because there are sound hearts and unsound hearts a physician could not tell in advance which heart was sound and which was not. Obviously he could not tell in advance of an examination! And if he does detect a diseased heart, he

Problem of "false" perceptions. How can I be certain a perception is true?

10 Strictly speaking, as shall be shown in the chapter on Truth, perceptions always represent what is perceived. Falsity results from faulty judgments made about the perception. Common speech, however, permits us to call those perceptions "false" which do not represent material things as they actually exist in the real world. It is in this popular sense that we speak of "false" perceptions in this chapter.

knows that it is diseased because it does not sound like a healthy heart, and he knows *that* because he knows what a healthy heart sounds like when he hears one.[11]

*Skeptic and
idealist
treat real
order as
though it
were the
logical.*

The idealist and his skeptical ally have invented a logical or mental category of sense perceptions that do not exist and they have proceeded to treat the real order as though it were the logical. In the mind, we group concepts according to genera and species; but genera and species do not exist as such in the real world. In the mind, there is a class of perceptions which is neither true nor false, a class that can be determined by the species "true" and "false"; so, too, with hearts. In the mind, perceptions as well as hearts are either true or false, sound or unsound. There is a genus or class "heart" under which fall the species "sound" and "unsound"; there is a genus or class "perception" under which fall the species "true" and false." Therefore, in the mind a heart is either sound or unsound, a perception either true or false. But *in existence,* one heart beats soundly and another does not; one perception is true and another is not. In existence there are no "either-or" situations; in existence there are no genera, no perceptions that are either true or false, no hearts that are either sound or unsound. If there were, I would have to define a sound heart as one that would be unsound if it were not sound; a true perception as one that would be untrue if it were not true. Thus idealists often speak of true and false hallucinations. When they have reached this stage they have given up the game in all but words. If I did not know that some of my perceptions accurately reported reality, I could not know that some other of my perceptions did not accurately report reality. The fact that I can even raise the problem of false perceptions indicates that there are true perceptions and that I know them to be true. The false can only be measured by the true.

*False per-
ceptions are
known to
be false
only
through
comparing
them with
true per-
ceptions.*

Man, through his intellect, can test this or that sensation or perception by referring it to other sensations or perceptions. More accurately, he can refer a doubtful

[11] E. Gilson, *Realisme Thomiste et Critique de la Connaissance* (Paris: J. Vrin, 1947), pp. 197-200.

sensation to what he already knows with certainty about things. A man who has a peculiarly vivid dream in which an old friend stands before his bed and warns him of impending disaster can be so shaken that he might be inclined to believe his dream to be truth indeed; he is reassured on the morrow when he recollects that his friend has been dead now for a quarter of a century. He weighed his dream and reality found it wanting. This is the normal way in which we men shake off illusions and exorcize phantoms. When a man no longer distinguishes reality from appearances, he no longer functions as a normal human being; he has lost "insight" into reality; this is the very definition of a mentally sick man. The idealist and his allies would have us accept as a first principle that in order to philosophize a man must put himself in the condition of the insane. The idealist fails to give us any reasons why we should.

(7) THE SENSE SKEPTICISM OF A "CRITIQUE"

The fundamental Platonism behind critical philosophy is perhaps best revealed in its thoroughgoing *sense skepticism*. By sense skepticism, we do not mean doubtfulness or skepticism about this or that given sensation. We mean a radical refusal to grant any intrinsic truth value to sensation as such; we mean a complete, universal distrust of sensation and of the data presented by sensation. The critical school throws into doubt the whole sensorial order and then it seeks to find some purely intellectual or mental set of principles through which this doubt can be dissolved; the ability of the senses to validly carry reality to the intellect is set aside, and the intellect tries to find something *within itself* that might act as a criterion for sensation as such.

A complete skepticism about sensation is behind the critical approach to philosophy.

A criterion for sensation is impossible and, even if it were possible, it would be superfluous and illogical to attempt to fashion one.

It is impossible to subject sensation to a critique because the critique, being the work of reason, would not

An a priori criterion for sensation is impossible, and, even if it were possible, it would be superfluous and illogical.

be sensation itself; it would be logically prior to sensation, acting as a framework within which sensations could be tested and validated. This is impossible because sensation *is not* intellection. The mind cannot deduce or prove, prior to sensation or apart from sensation, that sensation can deliver reality to the intellect, any more than the owner of a horse can deduce, prior to the race, that his horse will win the race. If the horse wins, the owner can only gratefully accept the victory. If sensation delivers the goods of existence to the intellect, the intellect can only accept the existence delivered. *To see this is to see that sensation is a first principle in human knowledge.*

A critique of sensation would be superfluous, because an intellectual criterion for sensation would be a criterion for sensation in general, for sensation in the abstract, and there are no sensations in general, there are no sensations in the abstract. "Sensation" is a concept in the mind. In reality, sensation is always the concrete sensing of this or that thing.

The critique, finally, would be illogical, because, in order to doubt the validity of any one sensation or any class of sensations, we would have to judge the sensation —to test it—by comparing it to other sensations known to be valid, the way in which we reject the apparent fact that parallel train tracks meet on the horizon by walking down the track and thus *seeing* that they really do not meet.

In conclusion, we can do no better than repeat with Newman [12] that man cannot bargain with his powers of knowledge. He is not outside of them. They are part of his being. He can only use them as he finds them, as they are given him. And if he uses them as they are, he finds himself in a world of being. And he knows all this, not because of something else that he might know, but because it is evident to him.

[12] John Henry Newman, *Grammar of Assent* (London: Longmans, Green and Co., 1887), pp. 346-49.

Suggested Texts for Discussion

Some, as the Platonists, held that the forms of sensible things existed apart from matter and so were actually intelligible. According to them, real individuals come about through the participation by sensible matter in these forms, and the human mind has knowledge by sharing in them. Thus, these forms are the principles of generation and knowledge, as the Philosopher says. But the Philosopher has adequately confuted this position by showing that sensible matter in general is necessary for the understanding of physical forms, just as there is no snub without nose.

For this reason, others, bypassing separated forms of sensible things, demanded only intelligences, which we call angels, and made separated substances of this sort the sole source of our knowledge. Accordingly, Avicenna holds that just as sensible forms are not received into sensible matter except through the influence of the agent intelligence, so, too, intelligible forms are not imprinted on human minds except by the agent intelligence, which for him is not a part of the soul, but a separated substance. However, the soul needs the senses to prepare the way and stimulate it to knowledge, just as the lower agents prepare matter to receive form from the agent intelligence.

But this opinion does not seem reasonable, because, according to it, there is no necessary interdependence of the human mind and the sensitive powers. The opposite seems quite clear both from the fact that, when a given sense is missing, we have no knowledge of its sensible objects, and from the fact that our mind cannot actually consider even those things which it knows habitually unless it forms some phantasms. Thus, an injury to the organ of imagination hinders consideration. Furthermore, the explanation just given does away with the proximate principles of things, inasmuch as all lower things would derive their intelligible and sensible forms immediately from a separated substance. (St. Thomas Aquinas, *On Truth*, Q. 10, a. 6, translated by James V. McGlynn, S.J. [Chicago: Henry Regnery Co., 1953], Vol. II, pp. 26-27.)

Judgment does not depend only on the reception of the species, but also on the examination of the matter to be judged with reference to some principle of knowledge, just as we judge about conclusions by analyzing them back to principles.

Therefore, when the exterior senses are bound in sleep, the interior powers are, as it were, free from the bustle of the external senses and can better perceive the internal impressions made on the understanding or the imagination by a divine or angelic light, or by the power of the heavenly bodies, or by anything else, just as it seems to one who is asleep that he is eating something sweet when thin phlegm flows across his tongue. But, since the senses are the first source of our knowledge, we must in some way reduce to sense everything about which we judge. Hence, the Philosopher says that the sensible visible thing is that at which the work of art and nature terminates, and from which we should judge of other things. Similarly, he says that the senses deal with that which is outermost as the understanding deals with principles. He calls outermost those things which are the term of the resolution of one who judges. Since, then, in sleep the senses are fettered, there cannot be perfect judgment so that a man is deceived in some respect, viewing the likenesses of things as though they were the things themselves. However, it sometimes does happen that one who is asleep knows that some of these are not things, but the likenesses of things. (*On Truth*, Q. 12, a. 3, ad. 2, translated by James V. McGlynn, S.J. [Chicago: Henry Regnery Co., 1953], Vol. II, pp. 120-1.)

Bibliography

Aristotle, Metaphysics, IV, 4, 1005 b 35–1006 a 5, *The Basic Works of Aristotle,* Richard McKeon, ed. (New York: Random House, 1941), pp. 747-8.

St. Thomas Aquinas, *S.T.,* I, 86; *II Sent.,* 3, 3, 3, ad. 1; *IV Sent.,* 50, 13; *S.C.G.,* I, 65; *III De Anima,* lect. 8, n. 710 *seq.; Q.D. De Anima,* aa. 5, 20; *Quodl.,* VII, 1, 3; *Quodl.,* XII, 8, 11; *De Veritate,* X, a. 6, XII, a. 3, ad. 2.

Gilson, E., *Realisme Thomiste et Critique de la Connaissance* (Paris: J. Vrin, 1947), especially pp. 185-212; *Réalisme Méthodique* (Paris: P. Téqui, 1935). These works by Gilson are unquestionably modern classics of Thomistic realism. The reasoning in this chapter owes much to these books. Students who can read French are urged to study both of them carefully.

Smith, Gerald, "A Date in the History of Epistemology," in *The Maritain Volume of the Thomist* (New York: Sheed and Ward, 1943), pp. 246-255. A brief, brilliant account of the basic realism of St. Thomas.

Wild, John (ed.), *The Return to Reason: Essays in Realistic Philosophy* (Chicago: H. Regnery, 1953). A significant collection of essays by nonscholastic realists, most of whom are aware of the basically metaphysical character of realism.

‹ 4 ›

Critical Realism or the Ghost of Descartes

---

(1) THE POSITION OF CRITICAL REALISM

Critical philosophy, beginning as it does with an abstraction of the act of knowing from the thing known and from the man knowing, ends logically in a self-professed idealism. If the act of thinking thinks in a void, it follows that what it thinks is intrinsic to itself. As the German philosopher Fichte well put it, what is other than the Ego is the Ego's own thought of itself. The only being that the critique could reach would be the being of the act of thought itself.[1]

Nonetheless, this reasoning has been challenged by a formidable school of thought within the scholastic tradition; this school of thought, being scholastic, is realist; but it is also critical. The *critical realist*[2] maintains that

Critical realism: being is, but philosophy must begin with the certitude of knowledge.

[1] Gerald Phelan, "Verum sequitur esse rerum," *Medieval Studies*, Vol. 1, No. 1, 1939. Although primarily a discussion of St. Thomas' theory of judgment, it contains a brief but excellent analysis of the impossibility of getting out of the mind once a philosophy begins in the mind.

[2] Scholastic critical realism stems from the pioneering work of Cardinal Mercier. The school is largely, although not exclusively, associated with the University of Louvain. Among the more notable critical realists, we might mention: L. Noel *(Notes d'épistemologie thomiste*, Louvain-Paris, 1925; "La methode du réalisme," in the *Revue Neoscholastique de Philosophie*, 1931; "Réalisme méthodique ou réalisme critique?" in *Bulletins de la classe des Lettres de l'Acad. royale de Belgique*, 5e série, t. XVII, (1931), pp. 111-129; *Le réalisme immédiat*, Louvain, 1928. G. Picard, *Le problème critique fondamental (Archives de Philosophie*, vol. I, cahier 2, Paris: G. Beauchesne, 1923). R. Jolivet, *Le Thomisme et la critique de la connaisance* (Paris: Desclée De Brouwer, 1933). M.-D. Roland-Gosselin, O. P., *Essai d'une étude critique de la connaisance* (Paris: Bibliothèque Thomiste, XVII, J. Vrin), 1932. Van Steenberghen, Fernand, *Epistemology* (New York: Wagner, 1949). J. Maréchal, *Le point de départ de la métaphysique*, cahier V; *Le Thomisme devant la philosophie critique* (Paris: F. Alcan, 1926).

the philosopher knows being, that a universe of things exists independently of the human mind, but he also advances the theory that these truths must be established by some critique of knowledge, by some set of judgments or principles whose truth is prior to, and more certain than, the truth about being itself. I am certain, says the critical realist, that there is a world of things beyond my thought, but I must subject this certainty to criticism; I must establish the truth that I really know being. Although man begins with things, *philosophy must begin with the mind's knowing things.* The intellect, reflecting on its own operations, comes to know that this operation is genuinely true, that it really does put man in touch with things as they are. Apart from this critical reflection on the certitude man possesses concerning the existence of things, philosophy builds on sand. Epistemology, therefore, is a critique and this critique is logically prior to metaphysics as a science.

The critical realist points out that the existence of the world *can* be doubted; that it was doubted by Descartes; that modern philosophy, so far as it is in the tradition of Descartes, continues to doubt the independent reality of the world. Any truth that can be and has been doubted by so many and for so long a time is not up to the task of acting as the first principle of any solid philosophy. I cannot, says the critical realist, presuppose as a truth what the whole idealist tradition dismisses as a prejudice. I must establish my position on principles which cannot be doubted by anyone, even idealists. But that which nobody doubts, not even idealists, is the evidence of the being and activity of mind itself. Therefore, it is in the mind and in its activities that I must seek my first principles of philosophy. I must beat idealism at its own game. Descartes says *Cogito ergo sum.* I say *Cogito ergo sum.* I think; therefore I am; but that which I think, that which I know, that which I am conscious of, is the world itself. Beginning with thought, philosophy moves to things. Beginning with a critique or reflection on the act of knowing, philosophy proceeds to a certitude about being—a certitude that is properly scientific.

Reasons advanced in favor of a critique.

A Thomistic realist has no need to follow the fortunes of critical realism as it attempts to "bridge the gap" between the mind and things. The Thomist refuses to admit any gap between mind and things. Therefore, he refuses to build a bridge where there is no need for one. He refuses to separate sense knowledge from intellectual knowledge because he finds them together, not separate.

The impossibility of critical realism is rooted in a fundamental self-contradiction within the very system itself.

(2) THE MEANING OF REALISM

Realism means the position holding that the truth about being is the first of all truths; if this is rejected, the first truth will be some truth about the mind, about knowledge.

Realism *means* the following position: Being is, and the truth about being is known immediately by all men to be evident. The truth about being is the first of all truths, the bedrock upon which all sound philosophy must be built. This is what one means by a realist philosophy. But if the truth about being is not strong enough to act as the foundation of philosophy, if it is not evident, if it needs a prior truth to guarantee it, then the absolutely first principle of philosophy will not be the truth about being; it will be some other truth. The first principle will be the critique of knowledge that reflects on the judgment "being is" and that critically justifies that judgment. Critical realists dispute among themselves precisely how this critical judgment should be formulated: "I know that being is"; I am conscious of my own mental states and these mental states present realities other than themselves"; "I am certain that being is and is other than myself knowing it to exist"—these are among the most popular candidates for the critical judgment that is supposed to be the first truth of all philosophy.

If being can be doubted apart from a critical judgment by a critical realist, then he is not really a realist.

(3) CRITICAL REALISM A CONTRADICTION

There is no question here about the *truth* of these judgments: they are all true and they are all evident. What is questioned here is the claim that a critical judgment enjoys the privilege and right of being the first incontrovertible self-evident beginning for all philosophical speculation. If the critical judgment plays this role, then the truth that "being is" does not play the role; it is not the absolute beginning, the first principle of philosophy. But if being does not play the role of the first of all principles, then being, apart from the critique, can be doubted. But if being can be doubted, then it means that realism can doubt the existence of things. To dispel the doubt, it is then necessary to begin with the *Cogito* of Descartes (or with some variation of the *Cogito*).

It follows, therefore, that a "critical realism" is a contradiction in terms. Either the truth that "being exists" is first among all evident truths, or it is not. If it is not, then realism is not realism; that is, realism is not that doctrine which holds that being is the absolutely first truth known to man and to philosophy. The "critical" swallows up the "realist" in a philosophical comedy in which metaphysicians attempt to justify what they say lies beyond all need of justification.

A critique is not a contradiction for an idealist. It is the only way he can possibly begin to philosophize, because he postulates thought as the only indubitably given datum. A critique is only a contradiction within a realism.

Let us face the issue squarely: Either the first truth is "being exists," or the first truth is some variation of the *Cogito*. If the latter is first, then being could never be reached by the philosopher, or, to speak more technically, the only being he could ever know would be the being of his own knowing. If, on the contrary, being is first among all truths, then the *Cogito* and the positions dependent upon it collapse.

The realist's position must be built on the evidence of being or it never will be built at all.

Bibliography

Gilson, E., *Le Realisme methodique* (Paris: Tequi, 1935); *Realisme Thomiste et Critique de la Connaissance* (Paris: J. Vrin, 1947), esp. Ch. VI, pp. 156-184.

Henle, Robert J., *Method in Metaphysics*, The Aquinas Lecture of the Aristotelian Society of Marquette University (Milwaukee: Marquette University Press, 1951).

Phelan, Gerald B., "Verum sequitur esse rerum," *Medieval Studies*, Vol. 1, No. 1, 1939.

Regis, Louis-Marie, O.P., *St. Thomas and Epistemology*, The Aquinas Lecture of the Aristotelian Society of Marquette University (Milwaukee: Marquette University Press, 1946).

‹ 5 ›

The First Principle of Being and Knowledge

---

(1) THE PRIMACY OF BEING

It is characteristic of the ingrained idealism of Western thought since the seventeenth century that when philosophers think of "first principles" they tend to think of laws of the mind to which reality must correspond in some fashion. Thus, men will say that things must be as they are because we cannot think of them as being in any other way. Logicians will justify the principle of contradiction by insisting that things do not contradict themselves because we cannot think of them as contradicting themselves. Mathematicians will insist that a whole must be greater than any of its parts because we cannot conceive of a part as being greater than the whole. The latent idealism is contained in the "because": if things are as they are *because* I must think them so, then it follows that things are dependent on thought for their very intelligibility; reality would then obey the necessities of reason. This way of understanding principles makes good sense within a professed idealism; it makes no sense at all when advanced by a realist.

Principles are first in the mind: Idealism.

A realist finds principles in things, and the magnificent harmony between the intellect and the world arises from the fact that the intellect, by its very nature, knows the world as it is; that the intellect is totally faced toward

Principles are first in things: Realism.

the things that are and has its life by assimilating them to itself. Principles are consubstantial with being and, *because* they are one with being, they are known by the intelligence which is the faculty of being. First principles, true enough, cannot be thought of as being other than the way in which they are thought, but this is so because being cannot be other than being. This is a realism of principles.

(2) MEANING OF PRINCIPLE AND ORDER

Principle is that by which an order is established.

By principle, we mean that from which something proceeds. Principle, therefore, is bound up with the meaning of order, because whenever something proceeds from something else, there is an order between them.[1] Order, in its turn, is a relation of priority and posteriority, of "before" and "after"; whatever orders the order renders what comes "before" prior to what comes "after": this is the principle of the order in question. For example, "fatherhood" is the principle of the order existing between a father and his son; the proportion between one-and-two is the principle of the order the mathematician discovers between two-and-four and four-and-eight; "loyalty" is the principle the historian finds in the order that bound together the medieval vassal and his lord. The essence of the issue is understood when we see that wherever there is a relationship between things of any kind, a given order between things, there is a certain something governing the relationship; this "something" is what we mean by a principle.

(3) BEING: FIRST PRINCIPLE AND FIRST ORDER

Being is the most fundamental of all orders, and the principle of that order is being or existence itself.

When we seek the first of principles, we seek the first of orders. That order is the order of being. Nothing can be more fundamental because apart from the order of being there simply can be no other order. There would

[1] For an analysis of St. Thomas' philosophy of order, compare: Brian Coffey, "The Notion of Order According to St. Thomas Aquinas," *The Modern Schoolman*, Vol. XXVII, No. 1, pp. 1-18.

be nothing to be ordered. Therefore the order of being is the order of orders, and the principle of that order must be the principle of principles. This principle can be nothing other than being itself: A, B, and C are in the order of being because they exist, because they share in being itself. To seek anything more fundamental would be to seek a principle beyond being, and beyond being there is absolutely nothing.

This first principle in reality is also the first principle in understanding. Whatever the intellect knows, it knows as being, as existing or as capable of existing in some order.

Being is the first principle in the order of knowledge.

We need not be conscious of the first truth or principle. A man can finish the course of his life without formally placing before his mind the first principles of being and knowledge. A man does not have to be a metaphysician. But he does have to be a man: everything he knows is being, and as he advances through life and adds to the things he knows, his knowledge progresses from a knowledge of being to still further knowledge of being. Outside of being he knows nothing, because beyond being—once again—there is nothing to know.

Should he turn to philosophy during his lifetime, he will consciously express this principle in a judgment, the first of all metaphysical judgments: "being *is being*." This judgment is a reflection upon the fundamental law of reality and of the mind. Although there are many different concrete avenues to this metaphysical judgment, it will perhaps suffice to note that this judgment follows a reflection upon the content revealed in all judgments. If the specific meaning of the subject and the specific meaning of the predicate of every judgment is suppressed, and if the mind simply focuses its attention on what is analogically common to all judgments, it discovers that the possession of being is revealed in each and every instance:

1. "Man is rational."
2. "Softness is a quality."
3. "Triangle is a three-sided two-dimensional magnitude."
4. "Justice is a virtue."

5. "Napoleon I was Emperor of the French."
6. "This is a beautiful day."
7. "Suffer fools gladly."

These judgments differ radically in what they say: No. 1 has nothing to do with No. 2; the meaning of "rational" is involved in the meaning of "man," but neither meaning has anything essentially in common with "softness" or with "quality"; No. 3 is mathematical and is nothing at all like No. 4 which is ethical; No. 5 is historical and the essential meaning of every term differs from the intelligibility given in No. 6 which bears on the physical world; No. 7, finally, is a scriptural injunction and thus differs from the above six.

An exercise of existence is present in all judgments.
What these propositions have in common is the fact that they *are* judgments and that *they declare a given subject to exist in such and such a way:* "man" is that kind of thing possessing rational being; "triangle" is a way in which quantity exists; "justice" is a way of existing virtuously; "Napoleon" existed as Emperor, and so on. The possession of existence in some order—past, present, or future; actual or possible; necessary or contingent—is the content common to all judgments. The metaphysician, discovering this truth, enunciates, consciously, a judgment declaring "being *is being*."

This first judgment can be formulated negatively: "A thing cannot be and not be at the same time and under the same aspect." This negative formulation of the principle, known as the principle of contradiction, simply repeats the structure of being itself. "Being is not nonbeing." If being could both be and not be, what is it that is not? If it is, it is being; if it is not, it is nonbeing or nothing at all. The principle of contradiction is also the first principle in the order of demonstration or proof; every conclusion must issue eventually from being itself. If the conclusion to a process of reasoning can be shown to violate the principle of contradiction, then the conclusion declares something to exist that does not exist. A scientific conclusion must be traced back to being before the intellect can assent to it with certitude; if the conclusion is grounded in reality, then the opposite of that conclusion has no reality whatever.

Curiously enough, this clearly obvious principle has been denied in the history of Western thought. There are those who deny that being is being and, consequently, that the intellect lives the life of being.

(4) THE DENIAL OF THE MUTIST

The most common denial is as old as civilization, as weary as disillusioned sophistication. This is the denial of the mutist [2]—the man who says he doubts the principle of contradiction, but who refuses to give any reasons for his doubts and negations. This is not philosophy, not even false philosophy. It is a mood, a pose of despair. It is better not to talk to such men in philosophical terms because their problem is moral or theological; it is not metaphysical. The mutist fears an affirmation and he fears an absolute affirmation more than anything else in the world. Perhaps he senses vaguely that the absolute may wound him, may be a sign of contradiction mocking his way of life. The attitude of intellectual mutism is widespread in a decaying civilization.

Mutism: being is denied or doubted, but no reasons are given why.

(5) THE DENIAL OF HEGEL

The most serious *philosophical* attempt to deny the principle of being or contradiction is found in the idealism of Hegel. Hegel identified the orders of thought and existence. Being functions the way thinking functions, taught Hegel, because being is a "concretization" of absolute spirit. In thought, said Hegel, every proposition has its contradictory. Posit any judgment and you thereby posit its opposite. On this point, Hegel merely repeated a truth known to logicians since the time of Plato. Aristotle systematized this law of the mind in his well-known Square of Opposition: The proposition "every cow is

Hegel: being contradicts itself, because being and thought are one, and thought is self-contradictory.

[2] So far as I know, this felicitous term was invented by the Rev. Gerard Smith, S.J.; see: *Natural Theology* (New York: Macmillan, 1950), p. 67.

black" is contradicted by "some cow is not black"; "no academician is a fool" is contradicted by "some academician is a fool," and so forth. Hegel pushed this opposition of judgments to the order of being itself. "Being is being" is contradicted by "being is not-being." Given the first proposition, the second automatically follows. Therefore being contradicts itself, and this contradiction is the most fundamental law of the spirit.

If we grant Hegel's identification of spirit and reality, his position makes good sense. It was the only way he could account for progress in the universe, for change. If the real is basically the same thing as the rational, one of two conclusions follow: either the real is given once and for all or it is not. If we grant the first supposition, we must conclude—with Hegel—that spirit never gets anywhere at all; spirit does nothing but analytically dissect an order already given at the outset, an order of ideas and laws to which nothing new is ever added. Refuse the first supposition because of the fact of change in the world and it follows that reality could only advance by contradicting itself. Begin with a given—call it A—and assume that only A is given. How do we get from A to B, when B is not given? We move from A to B only if A contradicts itself. Fundamentally, B is nothing but A's negation of itself; B is non-A. In this fashion we can move from one point in the real order to another. We can account for change, for the advance of spirit.

If we refuse Hegel's identification of spirit and reality, if we judge his position in the light of realism, we can easily see that his error consisted in treating the metaphysical order, the real order, as though it were the logical. But the whole point about being, in reality, is that *it is being*. The contradictory to being, not in the order of ideas but in the order of things, would *be* non-being. But in reality there is no such "thing" as an existing nonbeing.

In being, there is no contradiction to being.

A man does not need an armory full of logical and dialectical weapons to understand this; all he needs is some existing thing which he can contemplate for a short time. Concentrate for a moment on the piece of paper before your eyes; formulate the proposition, "the paper exists"; now contradict the first proposition with "the paper does not exist." The two judgments contradict each other in the logical order, in your mind. The contradiction exists mentally because the two judgments can be entertained as logical opposites. Now return your attention to the piece of paper itself, not as it exists in a proposition in your mind, but as it is in itself. What is the contradictory of the existence of the paper in the order of being? In that order, the order of things as they exist beyond your thinking of them, there simply *is no contradictory* to the piece of paper. The nonexistence of the paper that exists is a metaphysical zero. To see this is to see that Hegel confused two orders.

(6) THE DENIAL OF POSITIVISM

Although Hegelian contradiction is still maintained by the Marxists, a more popular attack on the principle of being has come from the school of *logical positivism*. This school maintains that the principle of being or contradiction is meaningless. The principle is discarded for a new first principle which the positivists call "the principle of verification" or "verifiability." For the positivists, all thought is nothing but the way in which we order our sense experiences: There are no "things" in a realist sense of the term; there are only "facts" which are the data given sensation. Scientific law and all other "meaningful" discourse rise out of man's attempt to order his experience for the sake of his practical mastery over life. A statement has meaning, makes sense, only if it can be reduced to some sense experience with which it is directly or indirectly identifiable. Positivists do not mean merely that all human knowledge begins in sensation which alone confronts existing things; they mean that every affirmation and negation making sense is composed of a subject and a predicate which symbolize some sensorial data experienced or capable of being experienced. But the proposition "being is being," while including sensible be-

Logical positivism: The first principle is that of verification in sensible experience; "being," say the positivists, cannot be so verified.

ing, transcends the material order; it does not point to sensations or to "data," but to the truth that things are, that they exist. Therefore, say the positivists, it is meaningless: not false, not true, just gibberish.

Through this attack on the primacy of being, the logical positivists sweep away all metaphysical and religious discourse. The belief that there is a God is not condemned as false; it is just dismissed as nonsense, along with the atheist contention that there is no God. In this way, positivism cuts beneath the great debate about the final meaning of human existence that has engaged civilized man since the day he discovered he had a soul. Positivism is a far more popular philosophy today than idealism.[3] A popularized brand of positivism, a "two-bit positivism" as Dr. Russell Kirk calls it,[4] is already the common intellectual diet of millions of the semi-educated in the United States and Great Britain. The conviction is abroad in the great universities of both countries that if language could only be fossilized into rigid mathematical and logical symbols on the level of science, and reduced to simple statements and exhortations on the level of practical life, all our intellectual and social problems would wither away.[5]

The principle of verification is not verifiable.

If all propositions must be verified in sense experience, then why not the principle of verification itself? The principle is a complex of meaning, no element of which is identified with sense experience. "Every meaningful proposition is verifiable in sense experience." The predicate, "sense experience," is not sensible; it is an abstract, intelligible content; it is not identified with any given sense experience. "Meaningful" is not a sense experience. What is the "meaning of meaning"? Whatever it might be, it cannot be identified and understood simply by pointing at something and punching it. The whole proposition might be said to stand for the totality of sense ex-

[3] An excellent introductory study of logical positivism is found in: Donald Nicholl, *Recent Thought in Focus* (London: Sheed & Ward, 1952), pp. 107-146.

[4] Russell Kirk, "York and Social Boredom," *The Sewanee Review,* Winter, 1953, pp. 114-128.

[5] This position is consistently put forward by S. I. Hayakawa; see: *Language in Thought and Action,* (New York: Harcourt, Brace and Company, 1949), *passim.*

periences and thus to symbolize them all. If this is so, then there is a "meaning" beyond experience, and this "meaning" *is meaning itself*.

The amusing thing about positivism is that it proceeds to deny the intelligence by using the intelligence denied. It sets up an elaborate criterion to destroy the intellect, and the criterion turns out to be highly intellectual in structure. Positivism is, therefore, self-contradictory, self-destructive, a system that dissolves from within once it is seen to be what it is.

(7) THE INDUBITABILITY OF THE PRINCIPLE

In the last analysis, can the law of being be denied or doubted by a man? The fact that we have examined positions built on a denial tells us that some men do intend to deny or doubt the principle of being or contradiction. They are perfectly sincere in their contention. To accuse them of bad faith (as some realists have done) is to ignore their written and spoken testimony. The battle will never be resolved on this level. It is certainly possible to signify a denial or doubt of the principle of being; it is possible to intend such a denial or doubt. The real problem is not one of *intention* (which is a moral issue), nor is it one of verbal or written *signification* (which is a symbolic and grammatical issue). The philosophical question concerns the order of *exercise*.

Doubt and denial of being can be signified, but the signification demands the use of the principle denied and doubted.

Can a man actually exercise a doubt or denial of the principle of being? This is not, does he mean to signify a doubt or denial, *but can he really do it?* He cannot. His doubt or denial is impossible because he needs to use the very principle he is denying or doubting in order to signify his doubt or denial. The principle "being is being" is *being* doubted; it is not *not-being* doubted. We must take our opponent here very seriously and insist that he take himself equally as seriously. The man means what he says. He means or intends to doubt this given principle. But in order that this principle be doubted or denied, being must be being; in order that a doubt be the doubt that it is, in order that a denial be the denial that it is, being must be being. If the doubter or denier is right in his contention, then he is really wrong: he is not doubting or denying the principle, because his doubt or denial either is or could just as well be a non-doubt or a non-denial. If skepticism speaks the truth on this point, there can be no skepticism, because skepticism would not really be skepticism. It would be (or could be) something else —Thomism perhaps. The position cancels itself out.

Bibliography

Aristotle, *Metaphysics*, IV, 4, 1006 a 35–1009 a 8; 5, 1009 a 5– 1011 b 15, *The Basic Works of Aristotle*, Richard McKeon, ed. (New York: Random House, 1941), pp. 737-48.

St. Thomas Aquinas, *In I. Sent.*, 20, 1, 1, ad. 1; 20, 1, 3, 1; 12, 2, ad. 1; *In V Metaphys.*, lect. 1, ed. Cathala, n. 75; *S. T.*, II-II, 100, 4, ad. 1; *Q. Quodlibet.*, 5, 19; *In I Eth.*, lect. 1, ed. Pirotta, no. 1; *De Ver.*, 27, 4, sed contra 4; *De Pot.*, 7, 9.

Gilson, E., "Les principes et les causes," *Revue Thomiste*, Vol. LX, 1952, pp. 60-61.

Hegel, Georg Wilhelm Friedrich, *The Logic of Hegel, translated from the Encyclopaedia of the Philosophical Sciences*, tr. by W. Wallace, 2nd ed., revised and augmented (Oxford: Clarendon, 1894).

Maritain, J., *A Preface to Metaphysics* (New York and London: Sheed and Ward, 1948).

Nicholl, Donald, *Recent Thought in Focus* (London: Sheed and Ward, 1952).

Owens, Joseph, C.SS.R, "The Causal Proposition—Principle or Conclusion?" *The Modern Schoolman*, Vol. XXXII, No. 1-3.

Russell, Bertrand, *Library of Living Philosophers: Bertrand Russell.* (Evanston: Northwestern University Press, 1944).

6

The Grammar of Existence

(1) MAN'S EXPRESSION OF HIS KNOWLEDGE

To sum up what we have discovered thus far concerning human knowledge: (a) human knowledge, strictly speaking, is neither an act of sensation isolated from the intellect, nor is it an act of intellection isolated from the body; human knowledge is *neither* sensitive *nor* intellectual, because it is *both* in the unity of being that is man himself; (b) this truth is given man in his very knowledge of existing reality—that is, man *does* know being and this knowledge makes sense only if it is seen as a union of intellection and sensation; (c) the source of evidence for this knowledge is sensation, and, therefore, being and sensation are both first principles of human knowledge; (d) this knowledge is *judicative*—that is, man judges things to exist and to exist in the ways in which they do.

Our problem in this chapter is concerned with how man expresses this knowledge to other men, with how he voices or makes known to the world the understanding he has of the things that are.

Problem: How does man communicate his knowledge of existents?

Man's *expression* of his act of knowledge is not the same as the act of knowledge itself. I cannot express the truth I know, unless I really know the truth. Expression follows knowledge. Initially, we must distinguish two kinds of expression: an expression which is interior or spiritual, and an expression which is external and material. Every man "says" to himself the truth he knows; every man "voices," in a kind of dialogue which is paradoxically without words, all the things he knows. This interior expression of the truth, the intellectual "saying"

Human expression of knowledge is twofold: (a) interior; (b) exterior. Here we look only to the exterior expression.

to myself of that which I know, will be taken up in another chapter. Here we are concerned with another issue: the external and material expression by a man of his knowledge of existing reality, and the significance of that expression in revealing the structure of human understanding.

External expression of knowledge is one with human nature.

Should a man be reared from childhood to manhood in a jungle cut away from all contact with other human beings, from every trace of civilization, it is theoretically possible that he might never express in any articulate and conscious fashion his knowledge of the world. Yet even such a man would probably leave some sign that he had been a man. Even he, without tutoring and altogether alone in his humanity, would chisel some mark on stone, would carve some picture on the bark of a tree, would gesture to the birds and thus sign the wilderness with the imprint of his humanity. When happy he would sing. In all things essential he would be a human being. Gesture, line, and song would not be foreign to him.

Man is not merely part of nature. Man makes a world of his own— the world of civilization.

But this man in the wilderness is a fiction. Man as we really find him always exists in some civilized polity no matter how primitive, in some society that is altogether different from the merely physical world. Man does not fade into the background of nature to become part of the scenery: He steps out of the world and establishes a new order of things, the order we call civilization or culture. Human society is perhaps the most difficult of all worlds for a man to understand. It is difficult because he is part of it, because it forms the immediate stage on which he acts out his role in the theatre of existence. Man is too close to society and too much a part of it to analyze it clearly with proper philosophical objectivity. Yet the effort is worth the pain.

If the things man has made are stripped of their "meaning," their significance, civilization is rendered unintelligible.

Try to imagine for a moment what it would be like if the civilized world were simply a part of physical nature. By a supreme effort of mind and fancy eliminate every difference between the physical universe and the universe of human culture. Imagine that every cathedral and all roads, each article of clothing and every book, all flags and statues, buildings public and private, works of industry and signs of commerce, language written and spoken—imagine, if you can, that all this was simply part of brute nature as it is given us in the raw; should you succeed in your attempt you would have eliminated from civilization that which makes it human. You would have annihilated its significance, destroyed its meaning.

Nature makes sense apart from man, but the work of man makes sense only in terms of its maker. The traffic signal *means* a command to drive on or to halt; the kind of clothing we wear marks us as soldier, sailor, priest. The languages we speak, materially nothing but noises reverberating through space, are charged with significance, with intention, with the breath of spirit.

The work of man, physically part of nature, is as a product of the spirit, charged with meaning.

Civilization, above all, is an order of meaning, not as it exists within our minds—but as it exists potentially or latently in the things man has made and which is communicable to the society of other men. Civilization, therefore, is a public place in which men share what would otherwise have been knowledge uncommunicated and sealed within the privacy of their own souls.

(2) COMMUNICATION AND THE MEANING OF
      SYMBOLISM

To communicate with another is to enter into a union with someone capable of sharing that union. Men cannot enter into communication with one another in a purely spiritual fashion. They have tried to do so, but the testimony of the race is that they have not been very successful. Communication for human beings is effected in, and by, the sensorial order.

Human communication involves the sensorial order.

Men communicate by letting something material, some-*thing* belonging to the physical order, act as a vehicle or trajectory along which their thoughts and judgments, their affections and intentions, can travel to another man who is capable of "picking them up" at the other end of the road or at the far side of the trajectory. A *thing*, existing as such in the material order or fashioned by a man for the express purpose of communication, is made to *stand*

A material reality is made to stand for an act of knowledge. This reality, first sensed, then leads man to grasp the meaning it bears.

for an act of knowledge, is made to bear a *meaning* which is not its own by nature. This is precisely what is meant by a *symbol.*

A symbol involves: (a) a material thing or action (b) caused by a man to stand for an act of knowledge, or to represent some intention.

A symbol involves two aspects: (a) it is a material thing or a material action and, as such, it belongs to the physical universe; (b) it is made by one man to represent an act of knowledge which he wishes to communicate to other men who will grasp his meaning in the symbol he fashions. Thus, the symbol is arbitrary in the sense that men make symbols at will; men give meaning to things and they can take away this meaning if they desire. In one society, the handshake symbolizes friendship; in another, friendship is symbolized by a kiss on the cheek. At one time men will take off their hats to signify their respect before ladies; at another time they will bow deeply from the waist. At one moment in the history of the West, the color white signified death; in time it gave way to the color black.

Among all symbol-making acts, language is most fundamental.

The whole cultural life of the race of man is shot through with symbolism and man has so kneaded nature to his own image that the very world is charged with a new meaning, a significance human in kind. And yet this massive effort to remake the world in the image of reason, to sow in ordered sequence, to carve the human form in stone, to build with grace, to incarnate the gestures of the human spirit in the things of matter, all this symbolism is subordinate to, and is the result of, a more profound way of making symbols which is consubstantial with human nature; that is, the power to create language.

Language is unlike merely natural signification. Language not only points or designates; language formally intends, and is understood as such.

(3) LANGUAGE AND MEANING

Language is the most primitive symbolic function carried on by the human species, and although man could, perhaps, dispense with this or that particular material vehicle for communication, he could not dispense with language. Language is as natural to man as is flight to the bird. The cry of animals in pain, the bark of dogs, the mimicry of parrots—these sounds are not language; they follow naturally on some motor stimulus and, although they are *signs* of emotional and biological needs and reactions, they are not known by the animals themselves to be signs. A symbol is not simply a sign that means something (as smoke on the horizon is a sign of fire). A symbol is an action or a thing that must not only *designate* or *point* to a cause (or to an effect); a symbol must signify, must mean, and its meaning must be understood formally as meaning.

Human language begins with mimicry; the infant copies its mother. This mimicry becomes human only when the meaning of the word itself is grasped, only when communication is effected, only when a union with the intention of the other is established. A trained dog when called comes to its master; a child not only comes to its mother but a child knows formally that the call of the mother *intends* or *symbolizes* the command itself. The growth of language, experienced by all normal children, attests to this symbol-making character of human nature. Youngsters learn to delight in secret languages of their own; they discover the pleasure of making new words stand for old meanings; they transfer one meaning from its accustomed word-symbol and give it to another, and thus they learn metaphor. In time they come to know that a word can mean more than one thing, and the world of irony and sarcasm and hidden ambiguity, the world of double meaning and concealment reveal the possibilities of the lie and the hint as devices for confronting or evading existence. Man not only works with language: he plays with it. Language is one with human nature itself.

Man, therefore, not only knows the things that are; he also *signifies* or *symbolizes* this knowledge, and among all such significations or symbolizations language is the most primitive and the most congenial to his nature. The ways in which man most fundamentally signifies his knowledge of existing reality, therefore, must be sought in an analysis of language itself. This analysis will vary from language to language, from civilization to civilization, because there are no universal and necessary laws

Man's primary signification of his knowledge of being must be sought in language.

laid up in heaven according to which man *must* express what he knows. He is free to work out his own expression of the knowledge he would communicate to others.

In our Western civilization, man has let nouns and verbs and participles signify or symbolize the most important aspects of his understanding of the real order, of the world of being.

(4) NOUNS SIGNIFY THINGS IN A STATIC MANNER

Nouns sig-
nify states
of being or
essences.
They
represent
the "static"
order.

Nouns or substantives signify *states* of being; they signify the ways in which things exist or can exist: "man," for example, marks out a definable way of existing; "dog" signifies another way of existing: both of them and all nouns along with them intend or mean *essences* or the states of being, *what* things are in themselves. Nouns, therefore, signify the *static order:* nouns do not represent or symbolize actions or operations; they do not capture the flux and fluidity, the fleetingness of being; they intend or signify, not the flight of the bird through air, but the bird itself. And even when nouns do signify actions or operations, they signify them in a static way; they freeze or immobilize what in itself is mobile and restless: "flight" is a noun; it is a "static" representation of an action that can never exist in a static way: "immobile" flight is a contradiction because "flight" is always a "fly*ing*," a moving that can *be* only so long as it *be in motion.*

(5) VERBS SIGNIFY ACTIONS

Verbs sig-
nify acts or
operations
in their very
exercise or
"doing."

When we wish to symbolize an action *as action,* an act of operating here and now exercised, we do so by way of the verb. The act, the operation (or, to use a much abused term, the "dynamic"), is directly symbolized in our civilization by the verb. "The giant *growled* when Jack *ran away* with the golden hen." "Growled" and "ran away," the two verbs, symbolize two actions—not in an abstract and static fashion the way in which nouns would signify them but in the very exercise or doing of the acts themselves.

(6) PARTICIPLES SIGNIFY ACTIONS AS POSSESSED BY THINGS

But acts, as we find them here below, do not exist in a pure state: there is no such thing or reality as the pure act of "to growl" or the pure act of "to run." Jack did not cringe before a pure "to growl," a simple action of "growling"; he cringed before a giant who growled. No giant ever chased an unadulterated act of "to run." He chased Jack-who-was-running. No reader of these pages ever waltzed with the distilled perfection of waltzing. If a man dances, he does so with a lady-who-is-dancing, with a *thing* that does the act in question. Thus we find a third grammatical way of signifying: the participle. The participle symbolizes neither the thing as such nor the action as such but the action as exercised by the thing. Participles designate actions as participated in, as shared; therefore, participles combine the functions of both nouns and verbs. They symbolize actions as possessed by, or, better yet, as done by the things that are.

Pure acts are beyond the common vision of man's knowledge. Acts are done by things; participles signify acts as done by the things that do them; they signify acts as participated.

How does Western man signify his knowledge of being? How does he express verbally and communicate to others his realization that things exist? Does he do so with a noun, a verb, or a participle? Is "being" a noun, a verb, or a participle?

Does "being" signify as noun, verb, or participle?

(7) "BEING" DOES NOT SIGNIFY AS A NOUN

If "being" signifies as a noun, then it signifies a given reality in exactly the same way in which any noun designates a reality; that is, it expresses our knowledge of *what* things are in themselves, of essence or nature. To call a thing "being" would be simply another way of saying that the thing is what it is. "Hat" and the "being" of a hat would be interchangeable terms: both would express exactly the same kind of knowledge bearing on the same aspect of reality. But to interpret the meaning of "being" in this fashion is to fall into a nest of contradictions. Two of them stand out as unusually absurd:

(a) If "being" expresses our knowledge of a thing exactly the same way in which a noun expresses that knowledge—if "being" is a noun itself—then it would follow that "hat" and the "being" of a hat express the same truth. "Hat" and its "being" would be completely and absolutely identical from every point of view; the meaning of the one term would coincide with the meaning of the other term. But if the "being" of a hat and "hat" have the same meaning, then whenever I say "being" I say "hat." Let us look at the issue from a slightly different point of view: If the judgment, "The hat is being," simply means that "The hat is a hat" then it would follow that "being" and "being hat" mean the same truth. If this were so, a shoe could never be being, nor could anything be being but the hat itself. I could never call a shoe being, simply because I have already equated the meaning of "being" with the meaning of "hat." "Being" or "is," on this hypothesis, would mean "being hat" or "is hat." A shoe could never get a toehold in the order of being, because being would be nothing other than "being hat." In conclusion: If the term "being" signifies as a noun, then a plurality of beings is a philosophical impossibility. But a plurality of beings exists. Therefore "being" does not signify as a noun.

(b) If "being" signifies as a noun, if "being" means essence or nature—*what* things are in themselves—then it follows that any given essence necessarily entails its own existence. Once I am given a noun signifying an essence, I am—by that very fact—given its existence. The meaning of $100.00, to use Kant's famous example, would include the meaning of its own existence. But the meaning of $100.00 does not add one existing penny to my pocket. An essence can be given in the order of knowledge, but the existence or being of that essence is not thereby given: for example, I know *what* a dinosaur would be if there were such a creature nowadays; I know the meaning of the term "dinosaur," but this knowledge of the dinosaur's essence or nature does not involve my knowing *that* a dinosaur is being, that it exists. Once again, we are forced by the evidence to the conclusion that the term "being" does not mean or intend essences or natures, that the term "being" does not signify the way nouns signify.

If "being" does not communicate as a noun, then it must communicate as a verb or as a participle.

(8) "BEING" SIGNIFIES AS A VERB AND AS A PARTICIPLE

Participles, as shown above, signify neither as nouns nor as pure verbs; participles are oral and written symbols which signify neither our knowledge of the static—of what things are structurally or essentially, nor of the dynamic—of actions considered precisely as actions. Participles signify an action as done by a thing, an action as possessed or participated in by some thing which is the subject of the action itself; hence, the word "participle." The thing *takes part* in some act. Now the term "being," in the English language, designates precisely just such a taking part, or sharing, in an activity which is the most profound or significant of all acts: the act of existing. As the squirrel is called a "runner" because it participates in the act of "to run," so too the squirrel is called a "being" because it participates in the act of "to be." Being is not a state; it is not an essence; it is not what things are. Being is a *doing*, a doing which is not a *mov-ing*, a *chang-ing*, an *operat-ing*, but simply a *be-ing*.[1]

The word "being" signifies our knowledge of this "doing," and our knowledge of the subject or the thing which does or exercises the act of existing. "Being" implies, as do all participles, the thing exercising the act and the act exercised, the act done and that which does the act.

For these reasons we must say that the things we know —the world of beings round and about us—is a universe of participles. "Being" is taken from the verb "to be." To see the verbal and participial character of the word

> *"Being"*
> *directly*
> *signifies as*
> *a participle,*
> *as the shar-*
> *ing in an*
> *act desig-*
> *nated by*
> *a verb:*
> *"being" is*
> *a "having*
> *'to be.'"*

---

[1] The act of existing is a "doing" in the sense that existence is an act *exercised* by the thing which is being through that very act. The act of existing is *not* a "doing" in the sense in which operations are "doings." Operations are activities exercised by already fully constituted beings; therefore, operations fall within the accidental order (except in God, wherein essence, existence, and operation are one).

Logically, the verb "to be" is a copula; this copulative meaning is subordinate to its existential import.

"being" is to begin to think as a metaphysician, but, more immediately, it is to have the answer to the question we asked earlier in this chapter: How does man signify or symbolize his knowledge of existence? He does so in a number of ways, but none more profoundly than within language itself, and, within language, in the verb "to be." This verb has its own meaning; it lives its own life. True enough, it can and does act as a coupling link, binding together a subject and predicate in judgment. This is the logician's understanding of the verb "to be." This copulative or coupling meaning of the verb "to be" is, however, consequent upon its fundamental meaning which is to be a sign that we know something exists. "There is a typewriter before me" is a kind of judgment that does not directly link a predicate with a subject. The only possible predicate of the judgment "the typewriter *is*" could be the predicate "being." But "being" means nothing other than "is" itself. Even the copulative use of the term "to be" retains a hidden existential import: To declare that "man is a rational animal" is not to declare that any given man exists but to affirm that man is that kind of being to which rational existence is due.

(9) BEING AND THE ACT OF EXISTING

In conclusion, being does not express my knowledge of what a thing is; it does not symbolize nature or essence; it escapes conceptualization because concepts represent *what* things are in themselves.[2] It is reducible to no other order. It stands on its own, expressing an understanding of the truth that some *thing* actually is (was, will be,

[2] The concrete act of existing of any given thing cannot be conceptualized; it can only be affirmed in judgment. Nonetheless, the mind can fashion a quasi-concept of existence (*existentia ut significata* in the language of Cajetan: see: *Comm. in S. T.*, 1, 2, 1, ad. 2, n. VII, t. 4, ed. Leon. XIII P.M., p. 29). This construct can then function as subject and predicate of judgments, such as "Existence is a perfection." However, this "concept of existence" is not the *act* of being of any given thing that is. Finally, St. Thomas often calls judgment a *conceptio*. He means that the mind gives birth to its own expression of the truth. *Conceptio* in St. Thomas' Latin vocabulary does not mean what "concept" means in modern philosophical English. The term "concept" is used in the text, unless otherwise designated, in its modern sense.

could be, and so on), that something exists in some order of being.

Suggested Texts for Discussion

The verb *is* consignifies composition, because it does not signify this principally but secondarily. *Is* signifies primarily that which the intellect apprehends as being absolutely actual, for in the absolute sense *is* means to be in act, and thus its mode of signification is that of a verb. But, since the actuality which *is* principally signifies is universally the actuality of every form, whether substantial or accidental, when we wish to signify that any form or any act whatever actually exists in a subject, we express that fact by this verb *is*. (St. Thomas, *Commentary on Aristotle's "On Interpretation,"* Book I, lect. 5, end).

Being properly signifies: something-existing-in-act. (*Summa Theologiae*, I, Q. 5, a. 1, ad. 1).

The word *being (ens)* is imposed from the very act of existing, as Avicenna remarks, whereas the word *thing (res)* is imposed from the essence or quiddity. (*Commentary on Peter Lombard's "Sentences,"* B. I, d. 8, q. 1, a. 1).

Being means that-which-is, or exists *(esse habens)*. (*Questio Disputata de Veritate*, Q. 21, a. 4, ad. 4).

Now any designated form is understood to exist actually only in virtue of the fact that it is understood to exist. Thus, humanity or fire can be considered as existing in the potentiality of matter, or as existing in the active power of an agent, or also as existing in an intellect. But that which has the act of existing is made actually existent. It is evident, therefore, that what I call the act of existing *(esse)* is the actuality of all acts, and for this reason it is the perfection of all perfections. Nor is it to be thought that something is added to what I call the act of existing which is more formal than that very act, thus determining it as an act determines a potentiality. For the act of existing of which I speak is essentially other than that to which it is added as a certain determining principle. (*Questio Disputata de Potentia Dei*, Q. 7, a. 2, ad. 9).

Bibliography

St. Thomas Aquinas, *S.C.G.*, II, 54; *Q. Disp. de Anima*, a. 14, resp.; *S.T.*, I, 4, 1, ad. 3; I, 5, 1, ad. 1; I, 8, 1, ad. 4; *Q. Disp. de Potentia Dei*, 7, a. 2, ad. 9; *De Ente et Essentia*, c. 4; *In IV Metaph.*, lect. 2, n. 558, ed. Cathala, p. 187; *De substantiis separatis*, c. VI, in *Opuscula omnia*, ed. Mandonnet, t. I, p. 97; *In I Peri Hermeneias*, c. 3, lect. 5, n. 8, ed. Leonis XIII P.M., t. I, p. 35.

Caietani, Thomas de Vio, *Commentarius in Summae Theologiae*, I, 2, ad. 2, n. VII, ed. Leonis XIII P.M., t. IV, p. 29.

Finance, Joseph de, *Etre et Agir dans la Philosophie de Saint Thomas* (Paris: Beauchesne et ses Fils, 1945), esp. pp. 45-77, 157-173. The dynamism of being and the relation between existence and action.

Geiger, L.-B., O.P., *La Participation dans la Philosophie de S. Thomas d'Aquin* (Paris: J. Vrin, 1942). A study of what it means "to participate" in being in the philosophy of St. Thomas.

Gilson, E., *Being and Some Philosophers* (Toronto: Pontifical Institute of Medieval Studies, 1949), esp. pp. 154-217; *Le Thomisme*, Fifth Ed. (Paris: J. Vrin, 1945), pp. 43-68. Classical studies on the meaning of existence in the metaphysics of St. Thomas.

Klubertanz, George P., S.J., *The Philosophy of Human Nature* (New York: Appleton-Century-Crofts, Inc., 1953), pp. 159-161. A brief but penetrating analysis of the structure of language from the standpoint of the philosophy of man.

Maritain, J., *Formal Logic*, tr. by Imelda Choquette (New York: Sheed and Ward, 1946), pp. 61-62, 225-229, for a discussion of the existential import of the verb "to be"; "Sign and Symbol," in *Ransoming the Time* (New York: Charles Scribner's Sons, 1946), pp. 217-255, for a discussion of the meaning of symbol and sign; the appendix (pp. 305-317) contains valuable matter from the *Logic* and the *Cursus Theologicus* of John of St. Thomas.

Phelan, Gerald B., "The Existentialism of St. Thomas," *Proceedings of the American Catholic Philosophical Association*, Vol. 21, 1946, pp. 25-40.

Smith, Gerald, S.J., *Natural Theology* (New York: Macmillan, 1951), pp. 11-17, on the meaning of the term "being."

Voegelin, Eric, *The New Science of Politics* (Chicago: The University of Chicago Press, 1952), p. 27. A brief and succinct statement of the meaning of civilization as an order of meaning and its distinction from the order of physical nature.

7

The Logic of Existence

The first six chapters of our study have revealed the following truths: (a) man understands existing things inasmuch as he understands as a man—that is, inasmuch as his intellect and his sensorial powers function together in a psychosomatic unity; (b) being is the first principle in reality and it is the first principle in the order of understanding; (c) since being is grasped by man only in and through sensation, sensation is a first principle of human understanding; (d) man's attainment of existence is directly signified or symbolized—in Western languages —by the verb "to be." In turn, the word "being"—participial in structure—signifies the exercising of the act of existing by things rendered "being" through the exercise of that very act.

(1) EXISTENCE IS NOT REPRESENTED IN A CONCEPT

If the above conclusions are true, and reason testifies that they are, then we are faced with an almost intolerable paradox: If being is the first thing known by man— and by "being," once again, we mean the sharing in the act of existing—and if everything known by man is being in some order, then why have so many philosophers failed to grasp the fact? Why have so many philosophers permitted existence to slide right out of their systems?

If the truth about being is evident, why have so many thinkers failed to see it?

We have already suggested that the evidence of being is lost when philosophers artificially separate the body from the mind. Although true, this leaves unanswered the question as to why they make such an abstraction, why they should philosophize as they do. If philosophy has steadily and consistently lost its roots in being for centuries, there must be something in the very structure of human understanding prompting philosophers to act as they do.[1] We are suggesting, in short, that this error must be rooted in some truth. This is not such an intolerable suggestion as it might seem at first: All error has its roots in some truth, and there is some truth at the core of all error acting as its strength and functioning as its very body.

They have failed to see it because existence cannot be represented in a concept.

The above paradox seems to lie in the fact that although men know that things exist, when they attempt to represent this truth to themselves they lose it. In one sense of the word, nothing is clearer to man than the existence of things: man breathes an existing universe. In another sense of the word, nothing is more obscure. We have already seen this fact in another context. Man cannot *think* or *conceptualize* the act of existing of anything whatsoever: Existence cannot be conceptually represented.

Classical logic treats the extremes of judgment as concepts. But concepts do not contain actual existence.

Man grasps existence in judgment. But the extreme terms of judgment—subject and predicate—are treated in classical logic *as though they were concepts.*[2] But if the subject and predicate of judgment are concepts, or, if they are treated as though they were concepts, then it would seem to follow that the act of attaining existence does not contain the existence attained as one of its extremes. One of two philosophical positions usually follows from the above analysis: either existence is somehow "absorbed" within the conceptual elements constituting judgment or existence is banished from philosophical discourse. If the first course of action is followed, then existence becomes a conceptual construct, and philosophy labors under the impossible task of deducing existence from the essential order.[3] If the second course of action

---

[1] See E. Gilson, *Being and Some Philosophers* (Toronto: The Pontifical Institute of Medieval Studies, 1949), *passim.*

[2] This statement stands in need of serious qualifications, which are discussed in the chapters on judgment.

[3] For example, Descartes, Spinoza, Leibniz; see James Collins, *A History of Modern European Philosophy* (Milwaukee: Bruce, 1954), pp. 138-366.

follows, existence is somehow "bracketed," and philosophy proceeds along its own path by ignoring the existence of the world.[4] Both systems, however, come out of the same presupposition: namely, that whatever cannot be conceptualized escapes the human understanding. The first system—rationalism—tries to retain existence by conceptualizing it. The second system—phenomenology—realizing more fully than the first that existence cannot be conceptualized, simply turns its attention to other philosophical issues.

The issue in question in this chapter is the logic of judgment. We hope to demonstrate two things: (a) that although it is certainly true that existence is represented in neither subject nor predicate of judgment, (b) it is also true that the attainment of existence is represented within judgment by the verb "to be." In the last chapter we arrived at this conclusion from an analysis of grammar; now we shall confront the issue from the point of view of the logic involved in judgment. Our conclusion should demonstrate more vividly why so few philosophers have broken through to an existential epistemology.

Neither the subject nor the predicate of judgment signifies the act of existing:

(2) THE SUBJECT DOES NOT REPRESENT EXISTENCE

Should the subject of the proposition signify existence, it would signify: (a) existence as such; (b) the existence of a thing in such a fashion that the thing plus its existence would together constitute the complete subject; (c) an existing thing *as existing*. These are the only three possibilities: the first two are limited in that, at best, they could apply only to certain classes of judgments; the third, if true, could apply to all judgments. Nonetheless, all three possibilities must be rejected.

Point to be proved: neither subject nor predicate signifies the existence attained in judgment.

(a) If the subject signifies existence as such, it does so in propositions such as "Existence is a perfection,"

<hr/>

[4] An example would be Edmund Hüsserl; see J. Maritain, *Les Degrés du Savoir*, 4e éd., revue et augmentée (Paris: Desclée de Brouwer, 1946), pp. 195-208.

When the subject signifies existence as such, it signifies existence in the abstract.

"Existence is an act," and so forth. But the subject of this kind of proposition is not the actual existing of any *thing* whatever. It is rather a mental construct fashioned by the intelligence to symbolize existence in general, existence in the abstract. But there is no existence in general. Existence is always the existing of this or that thing in concrete reality. This is clearly seen when we realize that "existence" as subject of a judgment *is not:* "Existence" signifies nothing that actually is.

When the subject signifies a thing plus its existence, it does so validly only in the light of a previous judgment declaring the subject to be.

(b) If the subject signifies a thing plus its existence—the two of them together making up the subject—it does so in propositions of the following kind: "The existence of John is a fact," "The existence of a world crisis is a burden," and so on. In the first proposition cited, John's actual existence is, in a certain sense, symbolized by the term "existence." The word does *stand for* John's existence, but the word, although a sign of John's existence, does not signify an attainment of John's existence. We do not know that John exists by linking together the mental construct "existence" with the concept of "John." (I can link the mental construct "existence" with a whole host of things that do not exist; for example, an existing castle on the Rhine belonging to me by hereditary right, an existing silver mine in the Andes paying me a million dollars a year in cash, and the like). First we judge that "John exists," and only because we then know that he really is can we unite the mental construct "existence" with John himself. In short, existence as forming part of the subject of a proposition is a derivative of a previous judgment in which we really came to grips with the issue, a judgment in which the evidence of sensation forced the mind to judge: "This thing I call John exists." Only then can we talk about "the existence of John."

The subject of itself does not signify its own existence. If it did . . .

(c) If the subject *of itself* designates a thing *precisely in its very existing,* if this is the very role of all subjects in all propositions, as Franz Brentano maintained,[5] then once a subject is given, it follows that there would be no need to declare that the subject exists. For example, we

[5] Franz Brentano, *Psychologie du point de vue empirique* (Paris: Aubier, 1944), p. 213.

would not have to say "King Arthur exists"; merely to state "King Arthur" would mean "existing King Arthur." But if this were true, three absurdities would follow:

(i) Existential judgments would be superfluous. Once I am given the subject, I am thereby given its existence. But this is not true, because when I state a term in isolation of a complete proposition I do not mean, nor do people take me to mean, that the thing designated by the term really exists. *existential judgments would be superfluous . . .*

(ii) Negative judgments would be impossible; that is, "King Arthur does not exist" would really mean that "Existing King Arthur does not exist." This last is a patent contradiction. *negative judgments would be impossible . . .*

(iii) Judgments of identity would mean the same thing as judgments of existence; that is, "A is A" (judgment of identity) would mean exactly what is meant by "A is" (judgment of existence). Since "King Arthur" means "Existing King Arthur," and since "Existing King Arthur is existing King Arthur," it would follow that "King Arthur is King Arthur" means exactly the same thing as "King Arthur exists." But it does not! When I declare that "King Arthur is King Arthur," I do not mean that the fourth-century legendary king of Britain actually exists in reality: I do not mean that he *really is*. In the judgment of identity, I mean that a given subject (that undoubtedly exists, did exist, will exist, could exist, and so on) is identically itself. In the existential judgment, I mean that the given subject actually exists in reality, not merely that the king is one with his own essence but that he *really is in being*, that he exists as truly as I, the writer of these words, exist. *judgments of identity would be confounded with judgments of existence. But there is a clear distinction in meaning between them.*

Therefore, the subject of judgment does not signify the actual existence attained in judgment. Nor does the predicate, for reasons which we shall now discuss.

(3) THE PREDICATE, OF ITSELF, DOES NOT SIGNIFY EXISTENCE

Should the predicate, *of itself*, signify the existence attained in judgment, it would signify: (a) either an existing attribute *precisely as existing* (without referring the attribute to the subject in which it exists); (b) the existence of the subject itself (in this event, the predicate would be "being" itself). But both alternatives are dead ends.

If the predicate of itself signifies existence, then all predicates designate actually existent realities. This is not true.

(a) If the predicate signified an existing attribute *as existing*, we would be confronted with the following nonsense: "A Zombie is a fiction of a diseased imagination." The predicate, "fiction of a diseased imagination," on the above supposition, means "an existing fiction of a diseased imagination," which, in turn, can only mean: (i) "a fiction of a diseased imagination," in which case the problem dissolves because we are not *really* speaking of an "existing fiction, etc.," but only of a "fiction, etc."; (ii) "a fiction of a diseased imagination actually exists," not as a "fiction of a diseased imagination" (this is the first possibility, which we have eliminated), but exactly as the second. But to state this is to assert that what is only a fiction of a diseased imagination is not really the fiction it is said to be, but that it actually exists in reality; in short, what is imagined to exist and which does not exist, really exists! This is nonsense indeed!

If the predicate is "being" itself, it does not add any new meaning to the meaning contained in the verb "is."

(b) If the predicate signifies the very existence of the subject, the predicate would be "being" itself. If this were true, we would be forced to conclude that the judgment "John is" really means "John is being or existing." This is true, but it is irrelevant. "Existing" or "being" adds nothing to "is" in the example given. If I say "John is" and then add "John is running," I really add something new to the meaning of the first statement; but when I say "John is" and then add "existing," nothing whatever is logically added to the first proposition. If something were added, then the judgment "John exists" would really mean "John exists existingly," and this last is either bad poetry or sheer verbiage.

Therefore, we are forced, by the evidence of what we mean in the judgments we make, to conclude that neither subject nor predicate signify existence. And yet the judgment is—as our earlier investigation has clearly revealed—an attainment of existing reality.

The fact that neither extreme of judgment contains existence has prompted many philosophers, as mentioned earlier in this chapter, to conclude that existence escapes human understanding. Existence, say these men, is a fact posited by the mind or it is a datum given sensation. They fail to look to the third element in judgment, the verb "to be."

Although existence is not signified by subject and predicate, it is signified by the verb "to be."

(4) THE VERB "TO BE" SIGNIFIES THE EXISTENCE ATTAINED IN JUDGMENT

> "The verb *is* consignifies composition, because it does not signify this principally but secondarily. *Is* signifies primarily that which the intellect apprehends as being absolutely actual, for in the absolute sense *is* means to be in act, and thus its mode of signification is that of a verb. But, since the actuality which *is* signifies is universally the actuality of every form, whether substantial or accidental, when we wish to signify that any form or any act whatever actually exists in a subject, we express that fact by this verb *is*." [6]

This text of St. Thomas' captures the very essence of the logic of judgment. The verb "to be" does act as a coupling link between subject and predicate, but it acts in this fashion only because it has a more fundamental meaning of its own, and this meaning is "to be in act"—to exist. The evident fact that judgment is an existential knowing, a knowing of that which is, is signified directly by the verb "to be." When I state that "John is," the "is" designates the existing of John in reality. When I state that "John is a man," the "is" signifies the existence of humanity in John.

Existence, therefore, while escaping conceptualization, does not escape knowledge, because knowledge is always *of* being, of that which is in some order. Knowledge is *of being,* but what is the *being of knowledge?* This question leads us into the next phase of our undertaking.

[6] *Commentarium in Peri Hermeneias,* 1, 5, fin.

Bibliography

Collins, James, *A History of Modern European Philosophy* (Milwaukee: Bruce Publishing Co., 1954), pp. 138-366, for a discussion of the rationalism of Descartes, Leibniz, and Spinoza.

Gilson, E., *Being and Some Philosophers* (Toronto: The Pontifical Institute of Medieval Philosophy, 1949), pp. 190-217.

Maritain, J., *Les Degrés du Savoir*, 4e ed., revue et augmentée (Paris: Desclee de Brouwer, 1946), pp. 195-208.

Mascall, E. L., *Existence and Analogy* (London: Longmans, Green and Co., 1949), pp. 46-51.

‹ II ›

Judgment and Truth

8

Introduction to Metaphysics
of Knowledge

---

(1) THE "COPY THEORY" OF KNOWLEDGE

Words are signs of knowledge—judicative and conceptual—and knowledge is a sign of the thing known, a representation of the object understood. This truth, known to the whole race of men, has tricked scores of amateur philosophers into betraying the fundamental insight of realism; that is, things are, and man knows them to be and to be in the ways in which they are. Knowledge is knowledge *of* things and knowledge is also a *sign or representation* of things. Both these statements are true; indeed, both are profoundly true, and yet by the man of "common sense" they are often thought to be in conflict, even to the point of naked contradiction.

Knowledge is of things and knowledge is a sign of things: These two truths have often seemed, to common sense, to be in conflict with one another.

The deepest insights of the "common man" are customarily sound. They are sound because his certitudes, unsophisticated and without the burden of academic prejudice, arise from an immediate contact with things as they are. The common man turns spontaneously to reality for the sustenance of his spirit and he is right in so doing: his instincts are healthy. The common man is a realist simply because it is the nature of man to know reality. If asked "whether or not there are things" he is likely to smile at the unreality of the question; if he finds himself in conversation with a logical positivist who informs him that he exists merely in the perception of his companion as a bit of nothing organized by sensation, he may doubt the sanity of the positivist. The man of sound instinct and little theory is absolutely certain that he exists and that he exists in a world of existing things.

He reads the idealist and positivist out of court when it comes to the *conviction* that things exist. But should the idealist persist in his questioning, he will probably win the day. Any idealist who knows his business can trick the nonprofessional realist into a blatant contradiction. The man of common sense, strong as he is on judgment, is often weak on reason.

Common-sense realism declares that knowledge is a representation of the thing in the sense of being a copy or image of the thing known.

The man in the street is positively certain that things exist; his knowledge signifies the real world; his knowledge is *representative* of reality. Therefore—he is asked by the idealist—do you say that knowledge is *a* representation of reality? Knowledge—answers the realist—*must* be a representation of the thing known; knowledge, most certainly, is a copy or an image of what really exists outside the mind. And when the realist has gone this far (prodded by the skilful questioning of the idealist), he has talked himself right out of realism.

If knowledge is a copy, we could never know the real thing, because—by definition—all we would know would be the copy. We could not even be sure our knowledge was a real copy, because we must first know an original before we can know that its copy is a true copy.

Common-sense realism translates the philosophical problem of knowledge into terms proper to photography. Knowledge is thought to be a copy of the thing known. Knowledge thus becomes, on this supposition, a "little picture" of the thing: Either a material picture, as an image in the imagination and memory; or a picture purely immaterial, as an "idea" in the mind. But if knowledge is a copy of the real thing, how could a man be certain that his knowledge was a genuine copy, since—by definition—in order to know if a copy is a genuine copy you must first know the original of which the copy is supposed to be a copy? In short, you cannot know if a photograph of grandmother is a good likeness unless you first know what grandmother looks like. But since knowledge, on this hypothesis, is an act of picturing or photographing, you never really know grandmother at all. All knowledge is reduced to a gallery of portraits in which man is condemned to pace forever without seeing the subjects supposedly represented on the walls.

The reader is invited to try this experiment on an untrained but intelligent friend. Ask him if knowledge is *of* things; he will probably answer in the affirmative. Ask him *what* knowledge is in itself; he will probably answer that it is an image or picture of the thing known. Nine times out of ten, the spontaneous conviction that knowledge is *of* things is shaken when a person is led to the truth that knowledge is a *sign* of things. The "copy theory of knowledge" is a trap into which the majority of realists fall when they attempt to explain their certitudes about knowledge and being. Idealists have often accused realists, as philosophers, of falling into the "copy theory" and then they have gone on to heap scorn on realism itself. The "copy theory" deserves scorn, but realism—at least the realism of St. Thomas—is by no means linked to the theory in question, a theory which is literally as absurd as the idealist makes it out to be.

The doctrine that knowledge is an image or picture is called the "copy theory of knowledge." It is a philosophical absurdity.

The copy theory is open to two serious objections: (a) If knowledge is a copy, then we are given two worlds—a world of things and a copy world—when one world would do just as well. Why, ask the idealists, postulate a second universe, a shadowy world of deceptive mirrors, when idealism well explains the one world in terms of spirit's objectification of itself? (b) If knowledge is really an idea or image of reality and if things are not known in themselves, then the fact of error is unintelligible. If you say that Great Britain is an island, and I say that Great Britain is a peninsula, we are both judging truly; my idea of Great Britain happens to agree with my idea of peninsula and yours does not. Since there is no standard by which our mutually contradictory judgments could be tested, your statement is no more in touch with the truth about Great Britain's geographic position than is mine.

Copy theory attacked on two grounds: (a) Why a second world, when one will do? (b) Error is incapable of being explained: my judgments are of my ideas and yours are of your ideas—there is no standard by which either could be tested.

But despite these obvious absurdities there is something valid in the copy theory, even though it is obscured by nonsense. Knowledge *is* a sign or representation of the object. Common English usage attests to the fact that we all *mean* something when we call knowledge a representation. But how can knowledge be a sign of the thing

But knowledge does truly represent the thing known, knowledge is a sign or a representation: in what way?

known, be a representation of the object understood, without being a copy or mere likeness of the thing? In order to face this problem fairly and answer it on its own terms, we must penetrate knowledge metaphysically; we must look at knowledge in the light of its being.[1]

(2) KNOWLEDGE AS AN EXTENSION OF THE KNOWER

The knower is not only what he is by nature; he is also the nature of the thing he knows. Knowledge extends the self so that it possesses the other.

Knowledge, when we reflect upon it as a fact of psychic life, presents itself to us as an extension of the knower. The knower possesses both his own nature and the nature of the thing he knows. A stone, a reality incapable of knowledge, remains, throughout the whole course of its existence, nothing but a stone. A stone is chained, bound to the confines of its essence. But a man, when he knows something, is not only a man: He possesses another nature, the nature of the thing known. Knowledge liberates the knower from the confines of his own being.

(3) KNOWLEDGE AS OPPOSED TO MATERIALITY

Knowledge is a lack of restriction; matter is the principle of restriction. Therefore, knowledge is in reverse relationship to the material.

Because knowledge intrinsically bespeaks a lack of restriction, knowledge must be in reverse relation to the principle in reality that restricts or binds or limits. The thing incapable of knowledge is restricted to its nature; the thing capable of knowledge is not so restricted. Clearly, the factor in the unknowing thing restricting it to its nature will be lacking in the knowing subject just so far as it is a knowing subject. The principle of limitation and restriction in the world of nature is matter. Matter is used here in its strict philosophical sense, and although epistemology is not the discipline that investigates the nature of matter, it might be well to note in passing

[1] See J. Maritain, *Les Degrés du Savoir* (Paris: Desclée de Brouwer, 1946), pp. 217-230; George Klubertanz, *The Philosophy of Human Nature* (New York: Appleton-Century-Crofts, Inc., 1953), pp. 59-85; Yves Simon, *Introduction à l'ontologie du connaître* (Paris: Desclée de Brouwer, 1934), *passim;* Francis H. Parker, "Realistic Epistemology," in *The Return To Reason,* ed. by John Wild (Chicago: H. Regnery Co., 1953), pp. 152-176.

that matter individuates form, restricts form to *this* material substance.[2]

Pick up two pencils. Both of them share a certain formal structure—an intrinsic principle rendering them pencils rather than gardenias. What is it then that restricts the principle to this given pencil held in your right hand? It is certainly not the principle of "pencilness," which is shared by the pencil in your left hand as well. "Pencil-*ness*" is not restricted to any one pencil: there are millions of pencils in the world. It therefore follows that a principle other than "pencilness" cuts pencil down to this thing, carves it out in space and time, renders the form proper to *this* given reality at which I can point with my finger. Whatever it is that does the job, whatever it is that individuates, restricts, limits form to *this* rather than that, is the principle to which Aristotelians and Thomists have given the name "matter." Matter, understood in this cosmological sense, is the root principle of restriction in material nature. It follows that the more a thing is enmeshed in matter, the less capable it is of exercising knowledge, the less capable it is of escaping the limits imposed by its very materiality. Knowledge, in its very actuality, is a liberation from the confines of matter.

(4) KNOWLEDGE AS A NONPHYSICAL UNION

Knowledge is an immaterial act uniting the knower with the thing known. What, precisely, is the nature of this union between knower and thing known? It cannot be a physical union. By a physical union, we mean a union intrinsically involving change of some kind. When I eat a carrot, a physical union is effected after the processes of digestion have run their course: The carrot has become part of my flesh and blood and has been united

Knowledge does not involve any intrinsic change, either in the knower or in the thing known. Knowledge is a nonphysical union.

2 Matter is treated in the text solely as a principle in opposition to knowledge. For a full treatment of the Aristotelian theory of matter, see: Aristotle, *Metaphy.*, B. 5, c. 1, 1013 a 16, ed. McKeon, pp. 752-753; *Phys.*, B. 2, c. 6, 197 b 191 a 10, ed. McKeon, pp. 246-247; St. Thomas, *De Principiis Naturae* in *Opuscula Omnia*, ed. Perrier (Paris: P. Lethielleux, 1949), pp. 2-17. For a clear textbook treatment, see: R. P. Phillips, *Modern Thomistic Philosophy* (Westminster: Newman, 1935), Vol. 1, pp. 36-53.

with me by losing its own identity. Certainly this is not the kind of union exemplified in knowledge. If the knower physically became the thing known, then the knower would cease to be himself; he would be destroyed by being assimilated into the object known. Should the thing known become the knower, knowledge would be destructive of its object. It is evident that knowledge does not involve any change in either the knower or the thing known.[3] Nor is the knower united with a copy of the thing known as demonstrated earlier in this chapter.

The knower becomes the known intentionally: Knowledge or intentional existence is the act whereby the knower is the known and the act whereby the known is for the knower.

By a paradox that can be explained only on its own terms, the knower is united to the thing without changing the thing and without suffering any change within himself. To see this is to see that the knower has become the known in a kind of union defying physical analysis. That which is known is not only a thing existing in and for itself, but, as known, it is a thing existing in and for the knower; the knower is not only what he is in himself, but he is intentionally the thing known. This act whereby the knower becomes the known, whereby the known exists for the knower, is what Thomists call the act of intentional existing. This act is knowledge itself.

Physical existence: act of being; intentional existence: act of being-known—an act thoroughly relational.

Knowledge is *intentional* as opposed to what is called *physical* existence. Physical existence is the act whereby a thing is being; it is that act (symbolized by the verb "to be" as indicated earlier) participated in by a thing which is thereby intrinsically rendered being. Intentional existing does not make a thing *be;* there are no intentional beings.[4] Intentional existence makes a thing *be known.* Thoroughly relational in character, opposed to

---

[3] Certain psychological and physical changes occur in the total process terminating in human knowledge. But these changes are conditions for knowledge, they are not knowledge itself; for example, in order that I might *feel* heat, I must *be* hot and in order to be hot, my skin must be changed by some external heating agent. But the conditions involved in being hot are not to be identified with the act of feeling hot. If they were, there would be no distinction between being hot and feeling hot.

Certain kinds of scientific knowledge entail altering the thing by laboratory methods before the thing can be known by the scientist; such a thing is known *as altered,* not as it is in itself.

[4] Unless one were to consider objects existing solely within the reason as "intentional beings."

simply being in itself, it is an act whereby a knower is the other as other.

(5) KNOWLEDGE AND REPRESENTATION

We are now in a position to answer the question raised earlier in our discussion of the "copy theory of knowledge." How can knowledge be *of* things and also be a *representation* of things? We now know what knowledge is. But we cannot adequately link knowledge with representation until we understand fully the meaning of the latter term. But we do not really know what a "re-presentation" or "second presence" might mean or be until we grasp fully the meaning of "presence."

"Presence" comes from the Latin *praeesse:* "to be before," *esse-prae.* In common speech and common sense, "presence" has two distinct but related meanings. Initially, presence entails a "being before" something or someone, a "being in view"; in turn this involves being in a certain place and not elsewhere, being rooted to a given spot and thus present to that place or present to an observer (hypothetical or actual) whose field of vision takes in the place itself. Only the deer who has stopped running, who is no longer moving from place to place, but who is *in* place, *is present* to the hunter as he sights his prey along the barrel of a rifle. "Presence" is thus opposed to "absence," and as "presence" is initially "presence in space and time," so too "absence" first denotes absence from a certain place at a given time, as the delinquent workman is said to be absent from his place of work. But "being in place" is not the deeper of the two meanings common speech gives the term. To be in place, a thing must be; hence, the word points to the actual existence of a thing. Actual existence is signified in the *present* tense, which is opposed to both future and past: opposed to the future, because what will be, is not yet; opposed to the past, because what once was, no longer is. What exists no more, not only fails to be present to a certain place, as a child is said to be absent from school, but it simply fails to be—it is absent from being.

With the doctrine of intentional being as background, we can answer our earlier question; that is, how can knowledge be a sign or representation without being a copy? But first we must ask what we mean by "representation."

"Representation" dependent in meaning on "presence." In common speech, presence means: (a) being before another; (b) being in actual existence.

*Two mean-
ings of
presence
in common
usage are
related: to
be before or
in view,
a being
must be.*

Therefore the second and existential meaning of the term, its deeper significance in common usage, while seeming to differ from the first, does so only in part. To be in place is to be in view, to be before something or someone. But only the existent can be in place and only the existent can be in view, can *be before*. A non-guest cannot be *presented* to the Queen at Court. A non-rifle cannot be snapped to at the command: *"Present arms!"*

*Presence:
esse; re-
presence or
second
presence:
esse-ad—two
modes of
existence the
thing can
exercise.*

When the two meanings of presence are united, presence is seen to signify the "being-in-existence" of a thing, but "being-in-existence" not as closed in upon itself, but as open to the rest of the universe, as capable of "being before" something else. When this capability is actualized, when an existing reality stands before another being in any of the many possible ways in which one thing can be said "to be before" another, the thing in question is "re-presented" or "presented again." This second presence of being is actually a new way in which the thing exists. Even more, it is a new existence the thing exercises: *a mode of existing which is relational as opposed to the mode of existing by which a being exists in and for itself.* The act of existing by which a being is actually present to another is an act of "being to or toward or for something else": not an *esse*, but an *esse-ad*. Whatever is related to something else is present to that other, but this presence is not simply a "being-in-existence." If it were, the two beings would be confounded. It is, rather, the presence of the first being to the second in a new mode of existence, *in alio esse*.[5] It is in this fashion that what is privately a world in itself is opened and shared with the rest of the universe.

*Purely
material
things never
re-presented
to them-
selves, but
they can be
re-presented
physically to
others: (a)
by spatial
contact; (b)
by action
exercised on
the other. To
a knower,
things can be
re-presented
in signs of
themselves.
A sign is
that which
makes
known
something
other than
itself.*

Purely material things, things totally bound by the restrictions of matter, can never represent themselves to themselves. Such things are present to themselves only in the fundamental sense that they exist. A stone is physically present to itself, never intentionally. It can never stand outside itself and take a look at itself. Its presence is one of simply being. But purely material things can be

---

[5] John of St. Thomas, *Log.* II, Q. 21, a. 6, Reiser ed., (Taurini: Marietti, 1930), p. 686.

physically present*ed* to other things in a number of ways. For example, if I am hit over the head with a stone, the stone is present *to me,* not just to itself; this is a new presence of the stone which has made a second entry onto the stage of existence: At first simply being in itself, it is now being to my head. The example involves physical contact in space, but physical presence is far broader than this. A thing can be physically present to something else through action it exercises on the second thing, even though the action does not involve the spatial contact of the one thing with the other. In this way, the sun, through its light, is present to the sunbather. Finally, a thing can be re-presented in a sign of itself, and by a *sign* we mean a reality or an action which *makes known* something other than itself.

If I am walking through a woods and suddenly emerge into a clearing dominated on its far side by a hill, and if I see smoke rising over the hill I know that there is a fire beyond the crest. The smoke is not only a second way in which the fire presents itself to the world physically; the smoke involves not mere physical representation, but intentional representation as well; that is, the smoke is a sign. By knowing the smoke, I come to know the existence of the fire; by seeing the one with my eyes, I see the other with my mind. By understanding the sign *as a sign,* the reality signified is present to my knowledge, re-presented to me as a knower. The fire stands before me in a new order of existence.

The sign presents again the thing signified, presents it to a knower.

The distinction between physical re-presentation and intentional re-presentation is subtle but crucial: the fire is physically re-presented to the sky through the smoke it causes. The fire is intentionally re-presented to my mind as a result of my knowing the smoke as a sign of the fire. Under this hypothesis the fire can be said to enjoy three presences: (a) the physical presence of its being in itself; (b) the physical re-presence of itself to the sky through the smoke it has caused; and (c) its intentional re-presence to the mind of the observer, as a result of the observer's grasping the fire in the sign it has caused.

But the term "representation" has a meaning other than

the one disengaged in the previous pages. Besides designating a thing as *presented again to some other thing* (physically or intentionally), "representation" can also refer to a thing which *takes the place of something else.* In this sense of the term, a sign is a representative in the way in which an ambassador is the representative of his country, the way in which a regent is the representative of a king. The ambassador acts for his country in a foreign place wherein his country cannot act directly for itself; the regent acts for his king while the latter is in his minority and cannot act for himself. These last are substitutes for the "real thing"; they act *in place of someone or something else,* as, in the language of the stage, a "stand-in" is said to take the place of the star of the show should the latter be absent and unable to act his own role.[6]

This ambassadorial or substitutive meaning of the term "representation" *is not* the meaning of the term we have disengaged through our analysis of "presence" or "re-presence." A "representative" *takes the place of something else;* it re-places it. But a thing is presented in knowledge *by being actually present to the knower.* Knowledge does

not "replace" the thing known; knowledge "places" the thing before the knower. A sign may perhaps be an ambassador of a thing; a sign may act for a thing where the thing cannot act for itself, but when a sign acts *as a sign* it presents a thing to a knower. *Therefore, it is the thing signified which is re-presented, not the representative.*

We are here very near to answering the problem raised at the outset of this chapter: How can knowledge be a representation of the thing known and still be knowledge of the thing? The idealist, pushing the realist, insisted that if knowledge was representative of an object, knowledge was a copy or substitute for the object. The idealist accuses the realist of taking "representation" in the ambassadorial or substitutive sense spoken of above. The

---

[6] Of course, a regent symbolizes his king and an ambassador symbolizes his nation. In this sense both present again the realities symbolized. But they also *act for* the realities they symbolize; they take their place. And it is in this sense that they are "representatives" or "substitutes."

idealist insists that as the ambassador stands for his country, so too does the picture stand for the person depicted. And so does a realist theory of knowledge stand for the thing known. Therefore, concludes the idealist, the realist theory of knowledge is absurd. The idealist is absolutely correct if knowledge is a representation in this substitutive or ambassadorial sense of the term.

But is this the nature of knowledge? Most certainly not, if the reader can keep before his mind the distinction and relations between these two meanings of representation:[7] a representat*ive* *is* *not* the thing represented; a re-presentation *is* the very thing present again in a new or second presence, in an act of existing which is relational rather than substantial, in an act through which A is for B, rather than in an act through which A is. A sign, insofar as it might be a thing, is a representat*ive* of something not itself; a sign, insofar as it is a sign, re-presents the other to a knower. It is only in this last sense that knowledge is a representation. Should a man fail to grasp this, it will be due to the interference of his imagination.

A representative is not the thing represented; a re-presentation is the very thing present again. Knowledge presents again the thing known, presents it in an intentional way.

Picture-book philosophy and the imagination go together; they are *simpatico,* as the Spanish say. We see a fire, it makes a warm picture in the imagination; we see smoke rising from the fire, it too makes a comfortable picture as it curls around the imagination. Somebody tells us that smoke is a sign of fire: We agree. Somebody tells us that knowledge is a sign of the thing known: We agree. But when we agree with our words, we form another

We picture or imagine knowledge and thus turn the act of knowing into a copy of the thing known.

[7] The theory of knowledge is not the only discipline in which the ambiguity of the word "representation" causes confusion. A similar paradox occurs in the philosophy of politics. Does a "representative" in Congress act for the people in the sense of acting in their place? Or does a representative simply present to Congress the will of the people he represents? Is he elected to act for his constituents in the sense of doing the research and coming to the decisions that his constituents do not have the time, the inclination, or the talent to do themselves? Or does he merely act as a sounding board for their own convictions? Is authority really given a representative to act *for* the people? Or does authority remain really in the people, untransmitted to the government? Does a government *govern* or does it merely act as a technical instrument which carries out the direct will of the people? This is not the place to probe these issues. They are raised only to indicate to the reader that the metaphysics of representation and the ambiguities inherent in the term itself have bearing in more than one philosophical area.

little picture in our imagination. We add a Boy Scout to our campfire scene and we place in the middle of his head a tiny fire and we call it: "knowledge—of fire, a sign!" Then we meet an idealist or positivist or we read an idealist or positivist book, and the great disillusion sets in—the little fire in the head of our imagined Boy Scout is not the fire blazing outside his head. Fire-in-the-head is not fire-in-the-woods. Therefore, we ask ourselves—how can I move from fire-in-the-head to fire-in-the-woods? How can I be certain that fire-in-the-head *really represents* fire-in-the-woods? We finally conclude that we cannot go from one to the other, simply because the one is not the other. Perhaps the real fire caused the head fire, but we cannot know this with certainty. The head fire may have been caused by bad digestion or flying saucers. Knowledge, we conclude, may be some kind of sign of things, but what the sign might signify is hidden forever from the judgment of man. Knowledge becomes a hieroglyphic written by an unseen hand on the parchment of the human spirit. Knowledge, we decide, is nothing but a bad joke, a joke so bad we don't even see the point.

The trouble is rooted in the fact that we cannot imagine *acts;* we can only imagine *things.* We can picture to ourselves the order of material essence; we cannot picture existence. But knowledge is an act of intentional existing; it is not a thing. We can and do know this to be the truth, but as soon as we imagine it, we spoil the doctrine by turning knowledge—an act—into a little thing which in some manner duplicates or copies an unknown reality.

Knowledge not a thing which acts instrumentally to represent the other; knowledge is a "pure" sign, its whole "to be" consists in making known the other.

(6) KNOWLEDGE A PURE OR "FORMAL" SIGN

Knowing is not an existing thing which acts for another existing thing. Knowledge is unlike all other signs. Other signs have their own proper natures and physical acts of existing in the extra-mental order. For this reason they are called *instrumental signs.* They are things which are used as vehicles or instruments for the communication of intelligibility. Instrumental signs can be *natural* or *conventional:* If the thing signifies of itself, as smoke signifies the presence of fire, the sign in question is natural; if the thing is caused by man to act as a sign, as red and green traffic signals signify traffic regulations, the sign in question is conventional. But whether a sign be natural or conventional, it is instrumental if it exists as a being in its own right. The spoken word is not only a sound which is significative, it is also a sound; a marble bust of Hercules is not only a sign of Hercules, it is also a piece of marble; the Stars and Stripes not only signify the United States, the Stars and Stripes are made out of pieces of colored cloth. All signs, except knowledge, are two "realities": (a) they are things existing in the natural order; (b) they are signs. As signs they represent something other than themselves; as things they exist in their own right. Not only do they re-present the thing signified but they present themselves. *As things* which are signs of something, they are representatives in the substitutive or ambassadorial sense. *As signs,* i.e. as known to be signs, they re-present the things they signify.

Knowledge, to repeat the thesis, is not a thing in any sense of the word. A thing is an essence existing in some order of being. Knowledge is an act through which things are intentionally present to the knower. Thus it follows that knowledge is not an instrument of meaning, but is one with meaning itself. Knowledge signifies by being itself. When I know a horse, my act of knowing the horse has no other reality or function than that of making known the horse. A barber pole, on the contrary, is not only a "being a sign of barbers" but it is also a "being a piece of painted wood." And yet what is the being of the act of knowing a horse? Its being is nothing other than "being the horse" intentionally, nothing other than rendering present to the knower the horse itself. Knowledge is thus a pure or "formal" sign. Its whole existence is exhausted in re-presenting the thing to a knower.

Knowledge a pure or "formal" sign: Its whole esse is a being to or toward the other, a being other as other.

Suggested Texts for Discussion

We must conclude, therefore, that the material things known must exist in the knower, not materially, but in an immaterial way. The reason for this is that the act of knowledge extends to things outside the knower; for we know even the things that are outside of us. Now by matter the form of a thing is determined to some one thing. Therefore it is clear that knowledge is in inverse ratio to materiality. Consequently, things that are not receptive of forms except in a material manner have no power of knowledge whatever— such as plants, as the Philosopher says. But the more immaterially a being receives the form of the thing known, the more perfect is its knowledge. Therefore the intellect, which abstracts the species, not only from matter, but also from the individuating conditions of matter, knows more perfectly than the senses, which receive the form of the thing known, without matter certainly, but subject to material conditions. Moreover, among the senses themselves, sight has the most perfect knowledge, because it is the least material, as we have remarked above (Q. 78, a. 3). So, too, among intellects, the more perfect is the more immaterial. (St. Thomas, *Summa Theologiae*, I. Q. 84, a. 2, *resp.*)

. . . another kind of perfection is found in created things. It consists in this, that the perfection belonging to one thing is found in another. This is the perfection of a knower in so far as he knows; for something is known by a knower by reason of the fact that the thing known is, in some fashion, in the possession of the knower. Hence, it is said in *The Soul* that the soul is, "in some manner, all things," since its nature is such that it can know all things. In this way it is possible for the perfection of the entire universe to exist in one thing. . . .

Moreover, the perfection of one thing cannot be in another according to the determined act of existence which it has in the thing itself. Hence, if we wish to consider it in so far as it can be in another, we must consider it apart from those things which determine it by their very nature. Now, since forms and perfections of things are made determinate by matter, a thing is knowable in so far as it is separated from matter.

For this reason, the subject in which these perfections are received must be immaterial; for, if it were material, the perfection would be received in it according to a determinate act of existence. It would, accordingly, not be in the intellect in a state in which it is knowable, that is, in the way in which the perfection of one thing can be in another. (*On Truth*, Q. I, a. 2, *resp.*, tr. by Robert W. Mulligan, S.J. [Chicago: H. Regnery Co., 1952], pp. 61-62).

Bibliography

Aristotle, *On the Soul*, B. III, c. 4-5, 429 a-430 b, *The Basic Works of Aristotle*, ed. by R. McKeon (New York: Random House, 1941), pp. 589-592.

St. Thomas, *In I Sent.*, d. 19, 5, 1; *S. C. Gentiles*, I, c. 53; *De Veritate*, II, 2; *De Potentia Dei;* VIII, 1; IX, 5; *S.T.;* I, 16, 2; I, 84-88; II-II, 183, 2; *Q. Quodlibet.;* VII, 4.

Caietani, Thomas de Vio, *Commentarius in Summae Theologiae*, I, Q. 14, a. 1; ed. Leonis, XIII P.M., t. 4, pp. 167-8.

John of St. Thomas, Log II, P., Q., 21-22, *Cursus Philosophicus Thomisticus* (Taurini: Marietti, 1930). This is a standard and classical analysis of the nature and divisions of the sign.

Maritain, J., *Les Degrés du Savoir* (Paris: Desclee de Brouwer, 1946), pp. 217-230. On the metaphysics of knowledge.

Parker, Francis H., "Realistic Epistemology," *The Return to Reason*, ed. by John Wild (Chicago: H. Regnery Co., 1953), pp. 152-176. This essay is particularly good on the relational character of the act of knowledge.

Sertillanges, A. D., *The Foundations of Thomistic Philosophy*, trans. by G. Anstruther (St. Louis: Herder, 1931), pp. 1-44.

Simon, Yves, *Introduction à l'ontologie du connaître* (Paris: Desclee de Brouwer, 1934).

‹ 9 ›

A Review of the Psychology of Knowledge

This chapter deals with matter largely proper to the philosophy of man, but which is indispensable background for the full theory of knowledge; that is, the causal process leading to, and terminating in, judgment.

Things cause human knowledge.

The single epistemological issue in this context can be phrased quite simply: What is the ultimate cause of my knowledge? The sole answer compatible with realism can be worded equally as tersely: The things I know cause me to know them. The answer is evident, but—as the reader now knows—the evident is often missed by philosophers who needlessly complicate the problem of knowledge.

(1) OCCASIONALISM

Occasion-alism: God causes me to know; there-fore, if noth-ing existed but God and me, God could cause me to know that which is not.

In late medieval and early modern times, there flourished a number of schools maintaining that God was the cause of human knowledge.[1] God was thought to cause man to know the things he knew, not in the broad metaphysical sense in which God is the author of all being and operation, but in the narrower sense that things were not capable of making themselves known. God made up this lack by directly infusing into the human mind its

---

[1] For example, Malebranche; see Gilson, *The Unity of Philosophical Experience* (New York: Scribner's Sons, 1937), pp. 185-196, 210-218; A. A. Luce, *Berkeley and Malebranche: A Study in the Origins of Berkeley's Thought* (New York: Oxford University Press, 1934).

knowledge of existing reality. The theory was a *realism* in that man was thought to know existing reality; it was an *irrelevant* realism in that the existence of the thing known was irrelevant to the knowledge man had of it. If I look out the window and see a tree, although I really do know the tree, the tree does not cause me to know it. God—said the occasionalists—uses the existence of the tree as an occasion or as a pretext for planting in my mind the knowledge I have of the tree. On this hypothesis, what would happen if the tree ceased to exist? Would I still go on knowing it? Since the existence of the tree did not cause me to know it in the first place, the nonexistence of the tree could not affect my knowledge of the tree unless God decreed that it should. And if God did not so decree? Then it would follow that I would continue to know the tree, even though there were no tree to know. This is an exceedingly curious epistemology! I might be the only person in the world, and God—for reasons of His own—might be causing me to know a universe that does not exist. The theory is absurd simply because the existence of things is evident to sensation. God could not make me know the nonexistent, not because He could not do whatever can be done, but because this is something that cannot be done. Knowledge is *of* being, and to make me know nonbeing is to turn knowledge into not-knowledge; in short, to violate the principle of contradiction.

(2) INTENTIONALITY AND RELATION

If the occasionalist position even looks plausible to the reader, it is because he has somehow identified intentional existence with mere intra-mental existence. This is a common misunderstanding of St. Thomas' doctrine. Once a student has seen the absurdity of the "copy theory of knowledge," he is led to the truth that the same essence existing physically has intentional existence in the mind. At this point the student tends to relax, imagining that he has mastered the issue. But if he stops here, if he is not fully aware that knowledge is not merely intra-mental

Knowledge not merely the intra-mental existence of an essence. Such a position is exposed to attacks by both occasionalism and idealism.

existence, he is open not only to the occasionalist position sketched above, but also to a last ditch attack by idealism and positivism, an attack revealing his own failure to understand the position he espouses.

Granting that essences exist in the mind as objects of knowledge, does it follow that they also exist in reality as subjects of existence?

An idealist might propose the following: Granting that knowledge is an act whereby an essence comes to exist within the mind, how do we know that the thing existing in knowledge is the same thing existing in reality? Granting that knowledge somehow reiterates a world of essences by giving it existence in the mind, how do we know that the world reiterated is *real?* Put it this way: The thing existing in knowledge is an *object* placed before the intelligence; the thing existing for itself is a *subject* of existence. How do you know that the object of knowledge is also a subject of existence?

The act of being-known is related to, and terminates in, the act of being: To know a being is to know it to be.

The objection, although admittedly clever, indicates that the objector has missed the point about knowledge. We might add that a realist who cannot answer the objection has missed the point as well. Knowledge is not simply the intra-mental existence of an essence; knowledge is not simply a mighty "super-life" a reality lives in the mind: If knowledge were exclusively immanence, then how could knowledge be an attainment of the real —of that which *is not immanent* to the mind? From one point of view, the act of knowing and the thing known are identical, but from another point of view they are diverse. They are identical because to know is to become the other; they are diverse because the other I become is not the act of becoming it. Knowledge, in short, intends a reality which *is not itself.* Knowledge is *of* the other. Knowledge is thoroughly relational. But all relations involve their terms, that to which a thing is related by the relation itself. The relational act of being which is knowledge renders present to the knower a thing itself in its very existence as a subject of being.[2] The object of knowl-

---

[2] Parker, Francis H., "Realistic Epistomology," *The Return to Reason,* ed. by John Wild (Chicago: H. Regnery Co., 1953), pp. 163-164. The whole essay by Dr. Parker is a valuable contribution to the metaphysics of knowledge. (The relational character of knowledge is detailed in Chapters IX and X in our analysis of judgment as an act terminating in being as it is.)

edge (the thing *known*) is known as a subject of existence (known *to be*) because the act of existing of the subject *as an object* (its act of being *known*) is an act of existing issuing from, related to, and terminating in the act of existing that the subject exercises *as a subject* (its act of *being*). This is the precise meaning of *esse-ad* as applied to knowledge: *esse-ad* terminates in *esse*.

If I know that things are, then it follows that these very things cause me to know them in such a fashion that my knowledge—since it is *of* them—is related to them in their very being.

Knowledge of being is caused by the being known.

The whole causal process of knowledge must move from the existence of the thing to the mind and from the mind back to the existence of the thing. Before reviewing the opening phases of this causal process in their psychological aspects, it might be well to note that two principles are presupposed in this discussion: (a) A thing acts as it is; (b) A thing is formally and existentially present in its action to the thing on which it acts.

Causation of knowledge is from the thing to man, and then back to the thing. Two principles involved: (a) A thing acts as it is; (b) A thing is present, formally and existentially to the thing acted on.

(3) A THING ACTS AS IT IS

(a) *A thing acts as it is.* Action is proportionate to being; that which in no sense exists, in no sense acts. He who is infinite—God—acts infinitely; that which is finite, acts finitely. Finite action results from two factors within being: existence and form.[3] Existence is the act of being, and things act only in proportion to their participation in that act. Form limits the act of existing to this kind of being rather than to that; therefore, things operate in proportion to their forms. Existence renders things *being;* form determines the *ways* of being. Thus dogs act like dogs, men like men, trees like trees, and so on.

Esse is act of being; form determines esse. Hence things act in proportion to their determined acts of existing.

[3] Matter is not an *active* cause of action. Material causality is receptive and limiting. However, the action of material things—since they *are* material—is completely dependent on, and one with, the material principle which is part of their very nature.

(4) THE PRESENCE OF A THING IN ITS ACTION

A thing present existentially in its action; this is a re-presence of the thing to the reality acted on. A thing is formally present because its action is determined by its form.

(b) *A thing is present, existentially and formally, to the thing on which it acts through the very exercise of its action.* This presence is not simply the presence of the thing to itself in its own existence. It is a second presence, a re-presence of the agent to the thing receiving its action. Therefore, the thing that acts is present existentially—in a new or second existence as a result of its action—and it is present formally, because its action is determined by the form it possesses.

The action spoken of is transitive, not immanent: (a) immanent action remains in agent acting; (b) Transitive action passes into thing acted on.

The kind of action spoken of is called *transitive* as opposed to *immanent* or living activity. The perfection of an immanent act remains in the agent acting; it does not flow into another being and thus perfect that other. For example, the total perfection of the act of love, an immanent act, remains in the lover. A man can love a woman all the days of his life, but if he does not manifest this love in some external sign his love will have absolutely no effect on the person loved. The full immanent actuality of love, as of all immanent acts, remains in the agent acting. It is otherwise with transitive activity: A transitive act is an act whose perfection passes into the being acted on; the transitive act fulfills some capacity inherent in a reality having existence separate from the agent. For example, the act of building results in a house built; the act of operating surgically results in a patient's being operated on. Should the perfection of the act of building remain in the builder, the house will never be built; should the perfection of the act of operating remain in the surgeon, the patient will die. Thus transitive activity involves giving perfection or actuality of some kind to the thing acted on. When we say that a thing is present, existentially and formally, to the thing acted on, we refer to transitive activity. In such action, to repeat the proposition, the agent acting presents itself to the thing acted on; since its action depends on its being and flows out of its being, it presents itself as being; since its action is the kind of action it is because the being is the kind of being it is, the agent presents itself formally. Thus the dog which is first being in a canine fashion to himself is now being in a canine fashion to the ankle of the pedestrian he bites.

How do these principles function in the process leading up to human knowledge? Since this discussion belongs properly to the science of psychology, as said above, we shall simply give a report of the process without treating it in the full detail it would receive were this an essay in psychology.[4]

What follows is a brief review of the steps leading up to cognition.

(5) A REVIEW OF THE PSYCHOLOGY OF INTELLECTION

The thing acts first on our sense organs, which, in receiving the action, are thereby altered. The thing is then present to the sense organ both existentially and formally (and—in this case—materially as well, because the thing acts materially on a material organ); the sense organs are altered only so long as the thing acts, and the thing can continue to act only so long as it exists. The sense organs are altered the *way* in which they are altered, because the thing acts the *way* in which it is.

The thing acts on the sense organs and alters them; the thing is thus present to the sense organs in its action.

The modification in the sense organs produces a sensible and formal likeness of the thing acting (formal, because things act in proportion to their forms; sensible, because the thing acts in a material way on the sense organs). This likeness is impressed on the sense power, thus informing it with a likeness of the thing to be sensed. This likeness is called an impressed species. This formal sensible likeness carries with it all the material conditions proper to the material thing in its action.

Modification of sense organs produces a sensible likeness on the sense power; this is called the sensible species.

Once informed by the impressed sensible species, the sense power senses the object; it is actually united with its object and thus becomes it intentionally on the level of sensation. This whole process is simultaneous and existen-

Once informed by sensible species, the sense power senses.

[4] It is the author's practice to refrain from reporting or simply systematizing Thomistic doctrine. Philosophical writing must follow the very reasoning establishing the proposition in question. However, an exception is made of the following matter in this chapter, because it is presupposed that the student has studied philosophical psychology. If he has not, the reasoning is sufficiently indicated for him to grasp its general strength. For more, see: G. Klubertanz, *The Philosophy of Human Nature* (New York: Appleton-Century-Crofts, 1953), pp. 103-155.

tial. The thing is sensed only so long as the species is impressed on the sense power, and the species is impressed on the power only so long as it is produced as a result of the modification of the sense organ, and the sense organ is modified only so long as it receives action from the thing, and the thing acts only so long as it exists. Suppress any step along the way and the act of sensation ceases.

External sensation sets off perception. Thing is perceived as a unified and sensed whole.

The act of external sensation sets off the act of internal sensation or perception. External sensations are synthesized, worked over, refined, stored in memory, referred to other sensations, grasped instinctually as harmful or beneficial, and so on. Perhaps the most central function of perception is the synthesizing of external sensations so that man perceives a sensible object *as a whole.*

Perceptual process terminates in a phantasm expressing the thing as sensed and perceived.

The act of perception terminates in a highly refined sensorial image which is the expression of the whole sensorial-perceptive process. This image is technically called a phantasm. It can be audial, visual, tactual, kinesthetic, and the like. The phantasm captures, as it were, the riches contained in the sensorial life of a man. The phantasm expresses the thing as perceived. (The full significance of the phantasm for epistemology will emerge in later chapters.)

Since the phantasm represents the thing sensed, it specifies the act of the intellect.

The phantasm presents the thing to the intellect in the sense that the phantasm specifies the intellect to know this thing rather than that thing. The phantasm is, therefore, the link between intellectual and sensible knowledge. But the thing as re-presented in the phantasm (by way of the sensible species caused initially by the action of the thing on the sense organs) cannot put the intellect into act, because:

But the phantasm cannot activate the intellect, because: (a) Intellect, being spiritual, can only be actualized by a spiritual species.

(a) The intellect is a spiritual potency and can be put into act only by a principle which is itself spiritual. (Reason: things can be acted on only in proportion to their natures. The potency of the table for color is actualized only by putting on a coat of paint, not by jumping up and down on top of the table; the potency a man has for learning metaphysics is not actualized by his learning to play the piano; so, too, a spiritual potency can be actualized only by a principle itself spiritual.)

(b) The thing present in the phantasm is bound up with the restrictions proper to materiality; that is, the thing is presented in the image as an individual, quantified, extended reality. (This last is easily verified by concentrating on your own phantasms: The things presented are not *there* in their physical materiality, but they are there as re-presented with all the conditions proper to their physical materiality.) The form of the thing is present in the phantasm, but present in a material manner. It must be disengaged from these material conditions before it can activate the intellect, a nonmaterial potency.

(b) Thing, as present in the phantasm, is present with the conditions proper to its material existence.

The active intellect, a power constantly in act, produces the impressed intelligible (that is, spiritual) species by disengaging the form of the thing from the material conditions in which it exists within the phantasm.

Active intellect is needed to disengage the intelligible species from the material conditions surrounding it in the phantasm.

As a result, the intellect is both activated by the intelligible species and informed by the likeness of the thing it will know. The intellect is now in the position of a radio actor who has been handed a script; before being given his fifteen-minute part, the radio actor is undetermined and without activity. Once handed the script, he can act, and, when he does, he plays the part he plays because his action has been determined by the script before him. Analogous to this situation (which limps, as must all examples in such discussions) is that of the intellect when impressed by the species: It is in act in order to operate.

The intelligible species puts the intellect into act, so that it can operate, and it specifies this act by presenting the thing to the intellect.

The intellect operates and thus knows the thing, becomes the thing intentionally. Once actualized by the species, the intellect cannot refrain from acting. It is in a position comparable to that of a diver who has left the board, who is hanging in mid-air, who has not yet dived, but who must and will dive.

The intellect operates and thus knows the thing.

(6) THE NATURE OF THE INTELLIGIBLE SPECIES

So much for our review of the psychological process leading up to the act of knowledge. But before moving to our next and most important investigation—the epistemology of judgment—let us be absolutely certain that we *really* understand the psychological principles involved.

Species is not a little "thing," not a small picture.

The species is not a small thing that flies up and hits the knowing power square in the center of its being: it is not a little arrow. Nor is the species a miniature cameo representing the thing in minuscule fashion. It is in this direction that the "copy theory" lies with all its tangled mass of contradictions. The species is not the thing known —if it were, two absurdities would follow: (a) I would know before I knew; the species precedes intellection and is a condition for it; (b) I would know the effect of a thing's action on me, not the thing itself. Nor is the species the act of knowledge—if it were, the act of knowledge would be a transitive act exercised on me by the thing I am supposed to know, and knowledge would be reduced to the physical reception of a formal likeness. The species is nothing but a prolongation of the action of the thing on the knowing power; the species is the impact of the thing acting on the power. Therefore the species bears within itself a relation to the existence of the thing as well as presenting the formal nature of the thing acting. The species, briefly, is the vehicle whereby the thing is presented to the faculty so that the faculty might know it.

Species is not the thing known, nor is the species the act of knowing.

Species is a prolongation of the action of the thing on the intellect.

The form of the intellect is the form of the thing to which it is in act through the species. Intellect's act is the very act of the thing known on the intentional order.

The intellect is a spiritual potency. Before it is impressed by the species, the intellect is neither in act nor is it determined to any act. When put into act, it will act in so far as it is in act, and it will be determined or specified to its act by the form it possesses. This is simply a reapplication of the principle discussed earlier in this chapter: Things act so far as they exist and their acts of existing are limited and determined by their forms. When impressed with the species, the intellect is informed by a formal and existential "prolongation" of the form and being of the thing. As so informed, the intellect is in act to the very form of the thing whose species it receives. *The intellect's act will be the act of the thing itself.* The intellect, impressed with the species of a horse, is totally informed by that nature, totally in act on the intentional level to the act exercised by the horse on the physical level. In its operation, the intellect can do nothing but *do* the act of the horse—become the horse intentionally.

(7) THE ABSTRACTIVE CHARACTER OF THE SPECIES

But the intellect is a *spiritual* power. The species impressing the intellect presents the form of the thing, not the individuating characteristics of the thing which have been abstracted in the phantasm by the agent intellect. But individuated matter is a condition for the physical existence of a material thing. For example, if a triangle is to exist, it must exist in white chalk on a blackboard, in three sticks of woods, in cigarette smoke, or in some other kind of matter; if the form of a horse, to take another instance, is to have existence, it must have that existence in flesh and bones. Therefore, the intelligible species lacks something necessary for the understanding of existence: that is, individuated matter. To abstract from a condition for existence in the order of representation is thereby to abstract from existence in the same order. Before man can understand that the form to which his intellect is in act has existence in a thing, his intellect must "restore" the form to the thing—must recapture individuality and, through and in it, existence (otherwise he could only know "horseness," never *this* horse). In order that the intellect might know *being,* it must bring the form actualizing it back to the thing. It does this by reflecting to the phantasm and through the phantasm to the whole sensorial process wherein man grasps the thing concretely sensed in its physical existence.

What causes the intellect to reflect? Clearly, the thing itself causes the intellect to reflect by producing the

Species lacks individuated matter; therefore, it lacks existence. Intellect can grasp existence of the thing whose species activates it only by reflecting to the phantasm and to sensation where the thing is grasped concretely as it is.

Thing causes the intellect to reflect by producing the species.

species by way of sensation and thus causing within the intellect its act of being known, its second presence, its "being-before-a-knower," and thereby moving the intellect to operate, moving the intellect to know itself as it really is.

This reflexive act terminates in judgment.

The act in which the intellect knows the thing—as indicated throughout—is the act of judgment: the crown of human knowledge. To that very act we must now turn because the philosophy of judgment is also the crown of the theory of knowledge.

Bibliography

St. Thomas Aquinas; *S.T.*, I, 78, 3, on external sensation; I, 78, 4, on internal sensation; I, 84-88, on intellection.

Holloway, M., "Abstraction from Matter in Human Cognition," *The Modern Schoolman*, Vol. XXIII (1946), pp. 120-130.

Klubertanz, G. P., S.J., "The Unity of Human Operation," *The Modern Schoolman*, Vol. XXVII (1950), pp. 75-108.

—— *The Philosophy of Human Nature* (New York: Appleton-Century-Crofts, 1953), pp. 103-155.

Muller-Thym, Bernard J., "The Common Sense, Perfection of the Order of Pure Sensibility," *The Thomist*, Vol. II (1940), pp. 336-361.

Parker, Francis H., "Realistic Epistemology," *The Return to Reason*, ed. by John Wild (Chicago: H. Regnery Co., 1953), pp. 152-176.

Ryan, Edmund J., C.PP.S., *The Role of the Sensus Communis in the Philosophy of St. Thomas Aquinas* (Carthagena, Ohio: Messenger Press, 1951).

Simon, Yves, *Introduction à l'ontologie du connaître* (Paris: Desclee de Brouwever, 1934).

‹ 10 ›

Judgment: Its Structure
and Meaning

Our subject in this book is human knowledge, its nature and being; and this nature and being are not alone
conclusions to a process of reasoning—they are facts, and
with facts one does not argue but accepts them as they
are. It may be otherwise in another world, but in this
one we can do nothing but take things as they are and
make the best of them as they come forth from the Hands
of the Creator. And if this is true of the natural world,
it is even truer of that world which is part of ourselves,
the world of knowledge. Knowledge is not a fact given
our experience as something other and foreign to our
being. Knowledge is given us as an activity open and
conscious of itself in act.

(1) THE CONSCIOUS EXPERIENCE OF JUDGMENT

We are aware that we know; we are conscious of our
own understanding. This awareness and consciousness we
possess of ourselves knowing is one with the openness of
spirit to itself. But here we are not concerned with the
reasons for the fact, but with the fact itself and all it
might imply.

Our subject is knowledge; our immediate subject is
judgment. Of what are we aware in judgment? The firm-
est answer we can give to that question is that we are
aware something exists. True enough! But not only are

*Knowledge
is given us
as a fact
open to
itself; we
are aware
of our own
knowing.*

*Awareness
is directly
of the
thing, im-
plicitly of
the act of
knowing.*

101

we aware that something exists; we are also aware of our own knowing. Knowledge is an act revealing both the object known and the act of knowledge. The object, of course, is in the forefront of the mind; it is directly revealed in the act of knowledge because this act is the object's act of being known. But the knower is also aware of his own knowing in an implicit fashion. Perhaps an analogy can be drawn by asking ourselves what a man knows when he takes a hike through the woods. In all probability he is directly conscious of his surroundings, of the trees above and the brush about; but he is also conscious, in an indirect way, of the fact of his own walking. Although he does not advert to this fact, he certainly knows it. Should the hiker come to a steep hill and begin to puff and wheeze as he climbs it, his attention will be turned from his surroundings to the action of his own walking. He will place in the forefront of his consciousness what had hitherto been in the background. And this is even truer with the fact of knowledge itself: We can turn our attention from the object and concentrate on our own knowing. This is what we shall be largely doing in the following pages of this chapter.

We shall look at judgment as it is given in our own self-consciousness.

Whatever we might find concerning the meaning and structure of judgment as it is given us in experience, no matter how startling it may appear to the theoretical mind, is a *fact* and all our theories must be brought in line with this fact if we would be faithful in our profession of realism.

(2) INDIVIDUALITY AND THE SUBJECT OF JUDGMENT

Individual is sensed and perceived, but not thought nor understood as such.

When I first point at a thing and then afterwards say something about it, I have gained and I have lost in my knowledge of that thing. I can see, hear, savor, imagine, remember, take hold of with my hands, and with my finger point out—the existing, individual, material thing. I perceive it as concrete, one with its being, structured in place, carved in space, enduring in this single, irreducibly distinct moment of time. Be the thing magnificent or trivial, captivating or commonplace, it imposes itself upon my senses, makes an impact on my body, and commands my emotions. But when I say something about it, not necessarily in words but in the dialogue the mind carries on with itself, something is lost. And that is concrete material individuality.

I understand the thing before me *as paper;* I am aware that the mesa, rising in the desert, is what scientists call *a geological formation;* I become conscious that the child whose hand I take in the garden is *heiress to a fortune of some millions.* I have advanced in knowledge, if not in wisdom. To know that the thing is "such and such"— paper, geological formation, heiress—is to possess information about the things I have sensed. But "paper" is not unique to *this* thing crumpled in my hand; "geological formation" is not an exclusive attribute of *this* mesa; "heiress to millions" is not restricted to this child I befriend in the garden. These attributes (or "formalities," to use the somewhat chilling technical term) exist truly in the things I know, but they are not one with their stubborn, factual individuality. The information I possess has been distilled from the things by my mind, but their individuality has been left behind; it escapes the filtering of the intelligence. *It is sensed and perceived, but not thought or understood.* The individual assumes a posture in space that cannot be reiterated in the human intelligence; in time, it flits through a moment hovering between two hypothetical eternities—destined never to be repeated, never to be caught in intelligible formulation, never to be expressed by the mind to itself.

The unintelligibility of the individual to the human mind,[1] paradoxically enough, is itself intelligible. We

---

[1] The statement in the text must be read formally. The existing, individual, singular thing is *not* unintelligible to *man* on the level of judgment, because *man* grasps the singular with his senses and affirms its being with his intellect. But the human intellect, *in abstraction from sensation,* cannot know the individual as such. This is attested to by the fact, a fact of consciousness, that we cannot *think* or *conceive* the individual as individual. We can only think or conceive the universal: that is, that which is formally applicable to many. The fact that the human mind cannot come to grips with the existing singular in its concrete individuality is accounted for in the light of the *abstractive* character of human intellection. Matter, being a principle for the actual

Unintelligibility of individual for the human mind is rooted in the unintelligibility of matter for that mind. Individual is known to man through sensation, not through conception.

know why we cannot grasp the individual as such. The reader will recall that matter is the principle in material essence individuating and restricting form to this rather than that thing. Matter was seen, therefore, to be the antithesis of knowledge. Knowledge was seen to be an act freeing things from the restrictions imposed by matter. Things were understood to participate in knowledge just so far as they were freed from the limitations of sheer materiality. Because matter restricts the knower in the exercise of knowledge, and because the knower is united to the thing known so that they become one in the intentional order, it follows thereby that matter also restricts the knowability of the thing.

A thing is know*able* in so far as it is actual, in so far as it exists; this is axiomatic: The more there *is* to know, the more there *can be known*. Form determines and limits the act of existing to this given grade of being, and form itself, in turn, is limited by matter which receives and individuates form to this, rather than that, qualified substance. Matter, therefore, is the root principle of potency in the real order. Matter is furthest removed from the act of existing and matter receives that act only through limiting and individuating form.[2] Hence matter is the

existence of a material thing, must be defaulted in the order of intentional representation before the intellect can be actualized by an intelligible species. (The intellect—as indicated—being spiritual, can only be actualized by the spiritual.) Therefore, although *man* has a properly intellectual knowledge of the singular, the *human intellect* has no such properly intellectual understanding. (See *Q. de Anima*, a. 20, ad. 1; *S.T.*, I, 86, 1 c.)

2 The descending order of perfection within the principles existing within a material being is described carefully by St. Thomas in his *De Natura Accidentis* (the author accepts the authenticity of this work): "Et hoc esse formalius se habet ad rem constituendam in genere entis, quam ipsa forma rei quae hoc esse dat vel materia cui datur, ex quibus compositum resultat cujus est hoc esse ut entis. Intimius ergo ad rem ipsam, quae est ens inter omnia, est ipsum esse ejus, et post ipsum ipsa forma rei qua res habet ipsum esse, et ultimo ipsa materia quae, licet sit fundamentum in re inter omnia, ab ipso esse rei magis distat. Cui propinquissimum est ipsa res, ut cujus est, cum per rem sit et formae et materia, nisi in homine; si esse formae communicatur toti, et illud esse est formae ut a qua est, quia ipsa est principium ipsius esse, et ultimo est ipsius materiae, ut ejus in qua recipitur. Materia igitur rei cujus est esse plus a re distat quam ipsa forma qua est esse; et ideo materia non est ens de sua natura, sed per ipsum compositum vel per ipsam formam." *(De Natura Accidentis,* in *Opuscula Omnia,* ed. R. P. Joannes Perrier, O.P. (Paris: P. Lethielleux, 1949), pp. 490-491.

precise "point" within the thing that defies human understanding. The human intellect, being spiritual, can assimilate to itself a *formal* likeness of the thing it will know; the intellect will grasp the material individual—as indicated in the last chapter—only by reverting to the phantasm and thus to sensation. Therefore, the fact that the individual as sensed and perceived cannot be understood as such by the human intellect is intelligible in the light of the role matter plays within the metaphysical structure of finite being.

But it is the very *this* of a thing, encased in all its concreteness, that is the primitive *subject of judgment.* The most fundamental judgments are those dealing with existing material things. From these judgments arise all human knowledge, and all other judgments get their strength ultimately from those that meet existing singular things as they impinge themselves upon the senses.[3] From this it follows, not only theoretically but as a matter of direct experience, that the *subject is never understood as such in any judgment.*

Because the concrete "this" is the ultimate subject of judgment, it follows that the subject is not understood as such.

(3) INTELLIGIBILITY OF THE SUBJECT IS THE
PREDICATE

What then is the intelligibility of the subject and from whence does it come? The subject must in some sense mean something to the understanding. We do not merely point at things; we do not merely sense reality. We understand what we sense. *The intelligibility of the subject is the predicate.* The predicate makes known the subject or is the light under which the subject is understood. In fact, the subject has no other meaning in any one judg-

The predicate is the "meaning" or intelligibility of the subject. In the judgment, the subject "means" what the predicate says it means.

[3] The reader will remember that judgments dealing with *possible* being are rooted in judgments dealing with *actual* being, and the only actual beings contacted directly by man are material singulars. Therefore, the subject of every judgment—even if it be an accident of a substance or some "meaning" or intelligibility not immediately identifiable with a thing—is *ultimately some thing itself,* existing in extra-mental reality or existing as a "thing" within the human psyche. See B. J. Muller-Thym, "The 'To Be' Which Signifies the Truth of Propositions," *Proceedings of the Sixteenth Annual Meeting of the American Catholic Philosophical Association,* XVI, 1940, pp. 234-245.

ment than that given it by the predicate. Man can "walk" around the self-same thing, make it a subject of many judgments, and see it under a host of differing predicates; in each instance, the subject means what the predicate says formally and nothing more than what the predicate says formally. In every judgment bearing on an existing singular, we are aware consciously: (a) of a *thing* sensed —the subject; and (b) of some *way* in which this thing is known to exist—the predicate.[4]

The above contradicted by many adherents of classical logic; they maintain that both subject and predicate are distinct conceptual meanings.

The facts advanced above have been challenged occasionally, ignored usually, by those philosophers who tend to confuse logic with epistemology. In classical logic, judgment is often defined as an act of the intellect uniting or separating two "ideas" or concepts by way of some form of the verb "to be." Under this hypothesis of the classical logicians, I hold before my intellect two fully articulated concepts, meanings, intelligibilities—call them what you will—and then, understanding both concepts in one single act of knowledge, I pronounce an identity (or separation) between them. For example, I take the concept "man"; in some fashion I link it with this singular man. I take the concept "American citizen," and, moved by the evidence, I judge: "This man is an American citizen."

I can understand subject and predicate as distinct in meaning only by defining them in separate acts. It is impossible to think them both formally in one act and at same time.

Now it is certainly true that I know what "man" means; it is also true that I know what "American citizenship" means. If asked to define my terms, I can do so. But— and this is crucial—my definitions are given one after the other, not merely in the sense that one definition follows the other in time, but in the deeper sense that the first act of defining *is not* the second act of defining. First, I shall hold the meaning of "man" before my mind while I mark off mentally all the constituent elements making up the nature of man; then I shall stop thinking about the nature of man and take up the meaning of "American citizenship." Having scrutinized both meanings, pondered each in turn, I might well declare in some judgment that,

---

[4] In the so-called "existential judgment," the subject is presented *as existing reality*. The subject is formally grasped *as existing intelligibility*. In short, the subject is formally intended, but it is intended *as existing* because it is grasped as such through the instrumentality of sensation.

let us say, "Humanity is no obstacle to American citizenship." But in one act of judging, I do not hold before my mind the meaning of "man" and the meaning of "American citizenship." I do not do this because I could not do it even if I tried. I cannot be *rationally* conscious of both meanings simultaneously in one act of understanding. God can, but my experience is that I cannot. No man can hold two formally distinct meanings before his mind and simultaneously think both of them in one act of knowledge. There are philosophical reasons for this truth; they shall be advanced in time; here we simply appeal to the facts, to the experience of the reader.

What am I conscious of when I judge that the watch before me is worth fifty dollars? I am certainly not conscious of all that I am capable of packing into two concepts—watch and fifty dollars—if they were held before my mind separately, one after the other. I am conscious of something else. I am aware of a *thing* given to my senses, which thing I understand as being worth fifty dollars. Although I call the thing "a watch," I do not understand it at this time and in this act in those characteristics which make it a watch. A watch is a mechanism with a spring-driven movement for telling the time. But I am not thinking of all that when I judge: "The watch is worth fifty dollars." The watch invades my consciousness as an object of economic value, not as a mechanism with springs and wheels and so forth.

In judgment, I am conscious of: (a) a thing: subject; (b) the way in which the thing exists: predicate.

If you want to pawn your watch, and if you lay it on the pawnbroker's counter, it becomes an object of two different judgments: yours and the pawnbroker's. "*It* is worth a good deal to me." "*It* is worth very little to me." Both of you are looking at a mechanism with a spring-driven movement for telling the time: neither of you is directly conscious of this particular bit of technical information at the moment. You *intend* the watch as an object of economic value, not as a watch. If you would understand the watch formally as a watch, you must make watch the predicate of your judgment: *you must think the thing formally as a watch.* The point becomes clearer when we reflect on a series of judgments made about the same watch: "The watch is my property"; "It is about thirty years old"; "It is a *Hamilton*"; and so forth. A man holding the same thing before his intellect by way of sensation can circle around it and understand it under many distinct intelligible aspects, each one differing from the last.

The subject is the "finger" of the intellect. The predicate is the "voice" of the intellect.

The subject of judgment is, as it were, the finger of the intelligence pointing at a thing; and the predicate is the voice of the intelligence declaring that the thing exists in this or that way.

Therefore, there is but one meaning of which man is rationally conscious in any single judgment: the predicate. The meaning of the predicate presents again to the mind some aspect of the thing which is designated by the subject. No one writing in English has expressed this better than John Henry Newman:

> . . . I apprehend a proposition when I apprehend its predicate. The subject itself need not be apprehended *per se* in order to give a genuine assent: for it is the very thing which the predicate has to elucidate, and therefore by its formal place in the proposition, so far as it is the subject, it is something unknown, something which the predicate makes known.[5]

When subjects are not simply material things designated by "this," but are things named by man in judgment, does it not seem as though such subjects have some kind of meaning of their own in the judgments at issue?

Nonetheless, even though the predicate makes known the subject and is its meaning, it is still true that some subjects are not simply things designated by "this," are not given simply as material singulars to sensation. How do we explain the fact that we can *name* the subject if the subject has no meaning except that of the predicate? Does not "man" mean something other than "American," and do I not know what I am talking about when I say that, "This thing—*a man*—is an American citizen"? Granted that I here and now think "man" *as American citizen*. Do I not —in some sense—think *man* as well? And if I do not, how is it possible for me to call the subject a man?

[5] John Henry Newman, *An Essay in Aid of A Grammar of Assent* (London: Longmans, Green and Co., 1887), p. 14.

(4) THE UNICITY OF SPECIES AND THE SYMBOLIZATION
OF THE SUBJECT

The question is well-taken and deserves an answer, but the answer can be understood fully only in the light of certain truths concerning the psychology of knowledge.

The act of intellection, it will be remembered, is a unitary operation. The intellect is a potency which must be determined to its act by an intelligible species. The intellect, like all potencies, can be actualized only by one act in any one operation. For example, the potency the table possesses for color cannot be actualized simultaneously by red and green; the potency the piano possesses for music cannot be actualized simultaneously by both a Bach fugue and boogie-woogie; so, too, the intellect can be actualized by but one actual principle in any single act of understanding. The principle of the act of intellection is the intelligible species, that prolongation of the action of the thing, which, of itself, is an impression of the form of the thing to be known on the faculty of understanding. Once the intellect is put into act, it is informed completely by the form presented in the species. When the intellect understands the thing in judgment, the intellect understands the thing in the light of the form to which it is in act. In terms of self-consciousness, a man is aware of the subject of judgment under one given aspect or "meaning"—the meaning of the predicate. The subject of judgment could, of course, be many distinct things glimpsed in sensation (for example, ten figures marching down the road), but they will be unified under the formality of one species presenting them to the mind (that is, they will be known as "ten," or as "ten policemen"). We can and do know many things at once in judgment, but we know them only as unified in a common species. Thus the fact that the judgment has but one formal meaning is rooted in the impossibility of the intellect's being in act to more than one species in any one operation.

But the intelligible species which actualizes the intellect and sets off the process of understanding is itself pre-

Answer to this question can be given only after reviewing certain truths concerning the psychology of knowledge.

Intellect can be actualized by only one species in any one act of understanding. This is the reason why only one meaning is formally present in any one judgment.

The species actualizing the intellect is presented in a phantasm which re-presents the thing as sensed and perceived.

sented to the intellect by both the phantasm and the agent intellect. The agent intellect illuminates some formal structure belonging to the thing by disengaging it from the individuating characteristics of the phantasm. The phantasm itself presents the thing to the intellect. Remember that the phantasm is the peak of sensation, a sensible image expressing and presenting the thing as sensed and perceived. It is in this phantasm that the intelligible species is illuminated by the agent intellect and it is to this phantasm that the intellect, once actualized by the species, must revert if it would grasp the concretely existing thing. The phantasm, therefore, is the vehicle by which meaning or intelligibility is presented to the intellect and the phantasm is the instrument used by the intellect to "see" that this meaning or intelligibility actually has being in an existing thing.

We can now answer our earlier question: what, if any, is the "meaning" of the subject when the subject is named in judgment?

We are now in a position to answer the question posed above: If the predicate is the formal meaning given the subject in any judgment, how is it possible to name the subject, to talk about it at all, when the name designates a meaning which is formally other than the meaning of the predicate? To repeat our earlier example: If the meaning of the judgment "This man is an American" is reduced to the predicate—"American"—is the word "man" then meaningless?

Phantasms carry intelligible species previously used by the intellect formally. These species or "meanings" are present within the phantasm and are present in the judgment on the memorative and habitual order, even though they are not adverted to formally.

Man possesses a memory and he associates a "meaning" or intelligibility with phantasms that once presented this phantasm formally to the intellect. In psychological terms, the intelligible species exists habitually within the intellect and potentially within the memory when it is not here and now informing the intellect. This latent, semiconscious existence is lived within the phantasm that previously presented this given species to the intellect. To revert to our example once again: In past acts of understanding, I used *this* phantasm to present the meaning of man; in the new judgment, I use the *same* phantasm to present a man but I do not understand the thing formally as a man—formally, I understand him as an American citizen. I can, however, call the thing a "man" because the meaning of man is present within the phantasm habitually, it is present in memory to the man who judges; but this meaning is not adverted to formally, nor is it thought formally in the judgment at hand. In short, I am aware of the meaning of "man," the subject, not on the level of intellectual consciousness but on the level of symbolization.

To see this is to see that the meaning of the subject is *symbolized* meaning, as opposed to the meaning of the predicate which is *formal* or *rational* meaning.[6] A symbol, the reader will remember, is a material thing or action standing for meaning or intelligibility. The phantasm presenting the subject—the thing—to the intellect also symbolizes or stands for meaning, for all the meaning which previous acts of understanding have disengaged from, or associated with, this particular phantasm. The intellect, actualized by one of these "meanings" through an intelligible species, understands the thing in the light of this "meaning," which is expressed formally by the predicate.[7]

Meaning of subject is symbolized meaning; meaning of predicate is formal, rational.

When pushed to their ultimate epistemological significance, symbols are seen to function within judgment itself, as well as being realities existing in the extra-mental world. There are three broad ways in which the phantasm can symbolize in judgment:

Symbols function within judgment in a three-fold way.

(a) When the phantasm carries directly to the mind an existing thing here and now sensed by the body, the phantasm does not represent or symbolize the subject: the phantasm presents (re-presents) it. But even here the phantasm can, and often does, act symbolically by representing previously acquired species which are not adverted to formally by the intellect in this judgment. Thus I am able to hold before my intellect a thing presented in a phantasm and understand it formally under the light of this given predicate. When I do this I can *call* the thing by a name designating an intelligibility or mean-

(a) Phantasms can present the subject directly and symbolize previously acquired information about the subject, and this information is not adverted to formally in this given judgment.

---

[6] This contribution to epistemology, a major triumph in the opinion of the author, was first made by the Rev. George V. Kennard, S.J., after an exhaustive study of the Thomistic texts on judgments: See *The Intellect Composing and Dividing According to St. Thomas Aquinas,* Unpublished Dissertation, St. Louis University, 1948, pp. 166-168.

[7] Therefore the phantasm also symbolically re-presents the predicate, because the predicate has been abstracted by the agent intellect *in* this very phantasm.

ing distinct from the predicate while not formally adverting to that meaning in the judgment at hand. Am I conscious of this meaning? I am not *rationally* conscious of
it because I am not thinking about it, but I am aware of
the meaning on the symbolic level. It is present to my
memory; it is known by me, but I do not look to this
knowledge in this specific act.

(b) Phantasms can: (i) symbolize the subject and (ii) present it intentionally to the intellect. Same phantasm can also (iii) symbolize previously acquired species not formally adverted to in this one judgment.

(b) When the phantasm presents a thing known in the
past and now recalled by memory, the phantasm symbolizes the subject of judgment. When the Scot sings "my
bonnie lies over the ocean," he cannot be presented with
the subject of his judgment—"his bonnie"—in direct sensation. He recalls his bonnie in judgment by conjuring up
an image symbolizing her, and this image places her intentionally before his intellect (thus presents her again).
Note carefully the two uses of representation in this context: on the sensorial level, the level of phantasm, the
bonnie is represented symbolically by an image (ambassadorial or substitutive use of the term), which symbolic
representation presents again (re-presents—intentional,
cognitive use of the term) the bonnie herself in an intentional way. The same phantasm can also symbolize an
army of previously acquired species which are not adverted to formally in this judgment. The phantasm of the
bonnie undoubtedly symbolizes the Scot's affection for
his beloved, their former life together, and so on, but *here*
"bonnie" is not understood formally in the light of these
meanings, but in the light of the predicate "lies over the
ocean."

(c) Where the subject is a complex of meaning, it is held before the intellect (in symbolic phantasms) which now predicates of it the meaning formally contained in the predicate.

(c) In judgments wherein the subject is not a sensible
reality, it is held before the intellect in a phantasm construct which symbolizes it—in an image or group of images
(visual, audial, kinesthetic, perhaps even tactual) which
act as a vehicle through which the mind comes to grips
with the issue at hand. For example, "the spirit of rationalism" is a force that an historian of ideas, let us say, has
spent his career in mastering. In this one judgment, he
lets a sensorial image stand for the complicated meaning
of "rationalism" built up through years of reasoning and
meditating upon the subject. He then predicates of this

subject—symbolized by the phantasm—the intelligible content, "grew out of the old Catholic culture it repudiated eventually." He sees the subject, "rationalism," symbolized by the phantasm construct in the light of this particular predicate—"having grown out of the old Catholic culture it repudiated eventually."

Thus we see, not only how such judgments are possible, but also how they safeguard the formal unity of meaning intrinsic to all judgments. The man judging does not formally grasp two conceptual essences held before his intellect. This is impossible, both in fact and theory, as shown earlier in this chapter. The only meaning understood formally, the only meaning *thought by the intellect,* is the meaning of the predicate; but the phantasm not only presents the subject, the phantasm symbolizes the subject, as well as symbolizing meaning or intelligibility previously understood about it.

Thus the unity of meaning of judgment is safeguarded: Only one meaning is formally present—that of the predicate; the other meanings are held symbolically in the phantasm.

> In previous acts of knowing the phantasm could, and probably did, mean something else. This prior meaning is latent within the phantasm; it pervades it, and, lying low, it hovers beneath conscious intelligibility. . . . Hence, in the judgment, the explicit rationality of the predicate plays over and works through a large body of unarticulated knowledge.[8]

This truth, perhaps oversubtle in the telling, comes home to us when we concentrate on the fact that many judgments do not bear on things immediately sensed. Many judgments, as said above, deal with complex intellectual issues, highly refined and abstracted from material singulars. I can only present these subjects to the mind by symbolizing them in phantasms and then predicating of them some intelligibility to which my intellect is in act at the moment. And this is precisely the way in which we build up our understanding of any "subject" whatever. Our phantasms are increasingly enriched with meaning, so that the scholar who brings a new meaning to "rationalism" sees more deeply into the subject than does the school boy who hears of it for the first time.

Our knowledge of any "subject" is built up by enriching phantasms which present the subject with more and more meaning as time moves on.

[8] Frederick D. Wilhelmsen, "The Philosopher and the Myth," *The Modern Schoolman,* Vol. XXXII, November, 1954, p. 46.

Misunder-standing is often rooted in the diverse symbolic meanings attached to subjects about which men are in formal (predicated) agreement.

Judgment is a subtle act, rich and dense with latent intelligibility.[9] There are men who can take a whole block of matter, packed with insights hewn from a lifetime of learning; they can hold all this before their minds, symbolize it with a scant word symbol, and then see it rationally and consciously under some new (or old) intelligibility. Many misunderstandings are rooted precisely in this very symbolic function of the phantasm. Two men make the same judgment, formally intend the same predicate of the same subject, but the subject itself *means* something more to the one than it does to the other. The difference is not one of formal content but of symbolic undertones. Formal and explicit rational agreement may well conceal an underworld of conflict. How often the man of learning, the man of high imagination, is irked beyond all patience because people, he says, do not know *what* he is talking about! He says something about a reality and gets excited or alarmed. Others say the same thing and remain sunk in indifference and lethargy. They really do see what he sees, but the thing means much more to him than it does to them, and this meaning is masked in the unarticulated intelligibility of the phantasm. His irritation grows the more because nobody contradicts him; everyone agrees monotonously that this predicate belongs to this subject. There is no formal argument at

---

[9] Our explanation of judgment, while epistemological in character, throws light on the role of the pre-conscious and the symbolic in man's emotional and cognoscitive life. Since Freud and Jung, philosophers can no longer ignore the vast ocean of the unarticulated, the hinted, the "personal and collective unconscious" in Jungian language, that lies just barely submerged from the light of reason and that accounts for a large part of human action and motivation. Following Freud, we restrict the term "unconscious" for the elements in psychic life which are non-conscious in a permanent manner, which the person does not recognize as his own, and which he cannot call up at will. We restrict the term "pre-conscious" for the "virtual field of consciousness" in Freudian language; the "pre-conscious" takes in psychic elements which are only non-conscious rationally at a given moment and which the person can call into full consciousness at will. The symbolic function of the phantasm, as described in the text, refers, therefore, to the Freudian pre-conscious, not the unconscious. See Sigmund Freud, *Introductory Lectures on Psychoanalysis*, trans. by Joan Rivière (London: Allen and Unwin, 1931), pp. 124, 192 ff.; Roland Dalbiez, *Psychoanalytical Method and the Doctrine of Freud* (London: Longmans, Green and Co., 1948), pp. 10-12.

all—the field of battle is symbolic, sub-rational, pre-conscious.

The issue is worthy of far more meditation than it is given nowadays. It lies at the root of alienation and it drags in its wake more than one broken friendship. Debating manuals, for example, quite rightly insist that debators define their terms in order that everyone concerned know exactly what is meant by each term. But wise and sophisticated people smile at this device as a mark of naïveté and as a sign of adolescent optimism and academic rationalism. A term defined in any one act will later become a subject of judgment and a swarm of symbolized meanings will underlie the formal content of the predicate. The agreement reached at the end of the debate—assuming an agreement is reached—will extend only to that portion of intelligibility formally predicated and communicated of the subject. To look for more in this life is to seek after an illusion. Only the rationalist and idealist mentality, demanding absolute clarity in a world where there is none, is shocked by the above confession of human weakness. But such are the facts; they cannot be undone. After all, the life of a man stretches through decades and often nears the century mark. Such a man, at the end of his days and in the fullness of his wisdom, can rationally hold before his intellect, at one time and in one act, only a minute fragment of what he *really* knows in the depths of his being about any given subject. Complete communication between any two men on any one subject would demand the impossible. It would entail an actual physical exchange of phantasms, an exchange of experience—it would entail one man's becoming the other. The closest mankind can ever come to mastering the symbolic is to live in a common culture, worship at the same altar, and face a like destiny.

Let us take one more instance of the power of the phantasm to symbolize meaning. Few men would disagree with the great British statesman, Edmund Burke, that "without a natural aristocracy there can be no nation." Almost everyone has sufficient common sense to know that a people must have leaders, that all cannot follow, that some must rise to preeminence and guide the corporate activity of the nation. Everyone is aware that a natural aristocracy—an aristocracy of talent and ability, service and breeding—is a necessity for any sane polity. With few exceptions, we would agree to the proposition: We would see this subject, "natural aristocracy," under the light of this predicate, "is necessary to all nations." We are in agreement with Burke. But wait! Listen to what *he* means by a natural aristocracy:

> To be bred in a place of estimation; to see nothing low and sordid from one's infancy; to be taught to respect one's self; to be habituated to the censorial inspection of the public eye; to look early to public opinion; to stand upon such elevated ground as to be enabled to take a large view of the wide-spread and infinitely diversified combinations of men and affairs in a large society; to have leisure to read, to reflect, to converse; to be enabled to draw the court and attention of the wise and learned wherever they are to be found; to be habituated in the pursuit of honour and duty; to be formed to the greatest degree of vigilance, foresight, and circumspection, in a state of things in which no fault is committed with impunity, and the slightest mistakes draw on the most ruinous consequences; to be led to a guarded and regulated conduct, from a sense that you are considered as an instructor of your fellow-citizens in their highest concerns, and that you act as a reconciler between God and man; to be employed as an administrator of law and justice, and to be thereby amongst the first benefactors of mankind; to be a professor of high science, or of liberal and ingenuous art; to be amongst rich traders, who from their success are presumed to have a sharp and vigorous understanding, and to possess the virtues of diligence, order, constancy, and regularity, and to have cultivated an habitual regard to commutative justice—these are the circumstances of men, that form what I should call a *natural* aristocracy, without which there is no nation.[10]

The theory of natural aristocracy which is unfolded in twelve separate judgments (marked off by semicolons),

[10] Edmund Burke, "Appeal from the New Whigs," *Works,* III, 85, Bohn Ed. (London: Longmans, 1854), p. 57.

several of which contain subordinate judgments, is swept into the unity of one subject and is seen there under the light of one predicate: "without which there is no nation." This rich and complex texture of meaning and affirmation is gathered together and symbolized as a unity, and this unity is formally bathed in the light of one predicate.

There is no formal distinction between our judgment and Burke's. But his is the fruit of decades of meditation. His is richer than ours, not because he sees the need for a natural aristocracy and we do not. We agree with Burke. But he sees much more deeply into the issue than we do, and, if called upon, he could give an account of his convictions at far greater length and with more than a show of profundity.

Such is judgment in its meaning and structure. What is known is a thing designated by a subject; what is intended of the subject is the formal meaning designated by the predicate. All judgments reach existence in some order. To this consideration we must now turn, first treating the matter psychologically and then, seeing the issue in the light of truth, complete the theory by lifting it to the level of being itself.

Suggested Texts for Discussion

I answer that, as unity of term is required for unity of movement, so unity of object is required for unity of operation. Now it is possible that several things may be taken as several or as one, like the parts of a continuous whole. For if each of the parts be considered by itself, the parts are many and consequently neither by sense nor by intellect are they grasped by one operation, nor all at once. In another way they are taken as forming one in the whole, and thus they are grasped both by sensation and intellection all at once and by one operation; and this obtains as long as the entire continuous whole is understood, as is stated in *De Anima III*. In this way our intellect understands together both the subject and the predicate, as being parts of one proposition; and also two things compared together, according as they agree in one point of comparison. From this it is evident that many things, in so far as they are distinct, cannot be understood at once; but in so far as they are comprised together under some intelligible unity, they can be understood together. Now everything is actually intelligible according as its likeness is in the intellect. All things, then, which can be known by one intelligible species, are known as one intelligible object, and therefore are understood simultaneously. But things known by various intelligible species are apprehended as different intelligible objects. (St. Thomas, *Summa Theologiae*, I, Q. 58, a. 3, *corpus.*)

All that an intellect understands it understands by means of some form. Consequently, keeping in mind the kinds of forms by which an angel understands, we must now consider whether or not he can understand many things at one time.

It should be observed, therefore, that some forms belong to one genus, others to different genera, and the forms belonging to different genera are related to different potencies. Now, as the Philosopher says, the unity of a genus is determined by the unity of matter or of potency. Consequently, it is possible for the same subject to be perfected simultaneously by forms belonging to different genera, because then the one potency would not be terminating in different acts but differently. For example, if a body is both white and sweet at the same time, it has whiteness in it in so far as it shares the nature of the transparent medium, and sweetness in so far as it shares the nature of the moist. But forms belonging to one genus are related to one potency, whether they be contraries (as blackness and whiteness) or not contraries (as triangle and square).

Now, these forms are said to be in a subject in three ways. In the first, they exist only potentially and, consequently, simultaneously, because one potency has for its object different forms of one genus and their contraries. In the second, they exist in imperfect act, so that they are coming into being. In this manner, they can also exist simultaneously. This is evident in the case of one who becomes white; for, during the whole period of alteration, whiteness inheres in him as something coming into being, and blackness as something going out of being. In the third, they exist in perfect act, as whiteness does when the whitening process is finished. In this manner, it is impossible for two forms belonging to the same genus to be present simultaneously in the same subject, because the same potency would have to terminate in different acts; and this is just as impossible as it is for one line, beginning from one point, to be terminated at different points.

We should understand, therefore, that all intelligible forms belong to one genus, even if the things whose forms they are belong to different genera, because all intelligible forms are related to an intellectual potency. Consequently, in the intellect they can all simultaneously exist in potency, as well as in incomplete act—a mean between potency and perfect act. This latter condition is that had by a species which is present habitually, for habit is a mean between potency and act.

But many species cannot exist simultaneously in perfect act in an intellect, because, in order to understand actually, an intellect must be in perfect act with respect to that species by which it understands. Hence, it is impossible for the intellect to understand actually according to different forms taken together at one time. Therefore, all the different things which it understands by different things cannot be understood at one time, but all that is understood by the same form will be understood at one time . . .

Similarly, when our intellect considers a proposition, it considers many things as one. Hence, in so far as the things are one, many things are understood at one time when the one proposition made up of them is understood; but, in so far as they are many, they cannot be understood at one time, because this would mean that the intellect can simultaneously turn itself to understanding the intelligible characters of each one taken in itself. Consequently, the Philosopher says: "I mean, however, by understanding things 'together' or 'apart' in an affirmation or negation that they are not understood in succession but as one thing." For they cannot be understood simultaneously in so far as a relation of distinctness exists between them, but they can be understood simultaneously in so far as they are united in one proposition. (*On Truth*, Q. 8, a. 14, trans. by Robert W. Mulligan, S.J. [Chicago: H. Regnery Co., 1952], Vol. I, pp. 386-388).

Now just as God knows material things immaterially, and composite things simply, so likewise He knows what can be enunciated, not after its own manner, as if in His intellect there were composition or division of enunciations, but He knows each thing by simple intelligence, by understanding the essence of each thing; as if we, by the very fact that we understand what man is, were to understand all that can be predicated of man. This, however, does not happen in the case of our intellect, which proceeds from one thing to another, since the intelligible species represents one thing in such a way as not to represent anything else. Therefore, when we understand what man is, we do not thereby understand other things which belong to him, but we understand them one by one, according to a certain succession. On this account, the things we understand as separated we must reduce to one by way of composition or division, by forming an enunciation. (*Summa Theologiae*, I, Q. 14, a. 14, *corpus*).

Bibliography

St. Thomas Aquinas:

Unity of species in judgment: S. T., I, 16, 2; I, 34, 3, 1; I, 58, 2; *In I Sent.*, d. 19, 5, 1; *In III Sent.*, d. 14, 1, 2, ad. 4; Q. *Quodlibet.*, 7, 2; *De Ver.*, 1, 9; 8, 14 c. and ad. 6; *In I Periher.*, 1, 8; *S. C. Gent.*, I, 59; IV, 14; *In VI Met.*, 1, 4; *In IX Met.*, 1, 11.

Nature of the components in judgment: S. T., I, 14, 14; I, 16, 2; I, 58, 2; I, 85, 4, c. and ad. 4; I, 85, 5, ad. 1; *S. C. Gentes.*, I, 48; I, 55; I, 57; IV, 108; Q. *Quodlibet.*, VII, 2; *De Pot. Dei*, 9, 5; *In I Periher.*, 1, 3; *In III de Anima*, 1, 11; *In VI Meta.*, 1, 4; *De Ver.*, 8, 14, c. and ad. 6; 26, 10, ad. 10; *De Malo*, XVI, 4.

Power of the intellect to symbolize: S. C. Gent., II, 73; S.T., III, 60, 4, ad. 1; *De Ver.*, 9, 4, ad. 4.

Man's knowledge of the singular: S.T., I, 84, 1-5; I, 86; Q. de *Anima*, 20, ad. 1.

Brooks, Cleanth, "The Language of Paradox," *Critiques and Essays in Criticism*, ed. by Robert W. Stallman (New York: Ronald Press Co., 1949), pp. 66-80. Illustrative of the complexity of meaning on the symbolic level as it functions within the judgment of poetry.

Dalbiez, Roland, *Psychoanalytical Method and the Doctrine of Freud* (London: Longmans, Green and Co., 1948), *passim* and esp. pp. 10-12. On the reality and significance of the preconscious in psychic life.

Freud, Sigmund, *Introductory Lectures on Psycho-Analysis*, trans. by Joan Rivière (London: Allen and Unwin, 1931), *passim.* Important for an understanding of the role of the pre-conscious. Freud tends, however, to reduce the symbol to a mere natural and physical sign; in short, he reduces intentionality to the order of *efficient* causality.

Gilson, E., *Réalisme Thomiste et Critique de la Connaissance* (Paris: J. Vrin, 1939), esp. Chapter 8. For man's knowledge of the singular.

Hoenen, Peter, S.J., *Reality and Judgment According to St. Thomas Aquinas* (Chicago: H. Regnery Co., 1952). A valuable study, although the author tends to minimize the relational character of judgment and to destroy its unity by making judgment the juxtaposition of two acts of simple understanding.

Jung, C. G., *Archetypes and the Collective Unconscious, The Collected Works, Vol. 9* (London: Routledge and Kegan Paul, 1953). Indispensable for an understanding of the symbolic background to conscious, rational discourse. (However, the reader should be on his guard against certain gnostic tendencies in Jung's thought.)

Kennard, George V., *The Intellect Composing and Dividing According to St. Thomas Aquinas,* Unpublished Dissertation, St. Louis University, 1948. The most thorough study known to the author. Invaluable for: (a) the unicity of species in judgment; (b) the role of the phantasm; (c) the nature of the subject-predicate components.

Klubertanz, George, *The Philosophy of Human Nature* (New York: Appleton-Century-Crofts, 1953), pp. 143, 187, 192. On the symbolic phantasm.

Muller-Thym, Bernard J., "The 'To Be' Which Signifies the Truth of Propositions," *Proceedings of the Sixteenth Annual Meeting of the American Catholic Philosophical Association,* Vol. XVI, 1940, esp. pp. 234-245. Brilliant study of judgment; especially valuable for its discussion of the kinds of judgments and their dependence on judgments bearing on singular existents.

Tate, Allen, "Tension in Poetry," *Critiques and Essays in Criticism,* ed. by R. W. Stallman (New York: Ronald Press Co., 1949), pp. 55-66. Illustrative of the "tension" between rational, predicted meaning and sub-rational, symbolic meaning, particularly as it functions in poetry.

Wilhelmsen, Frederick D., "The Philosopher and the Myth," *The Modern Schoolman,* Vol. XXXII, November, 1954, pp. 39-55. An analysis of the meanings of the term "myth" and their relations to the symbol as it functions within judgment.

‹ 11 ›

Judgment: The Process

---

(1) THE DIFFERENCE BETWEEN UNDERSTANDING AND THINKING THAT YOU UNDERSTAND

What is the difference between a master sergeant reading the Articles of War to a company of recruits and a lawyer citing the same in a court-martial? What is the difference between a memorized recitation of the causes of the American Civil War and the tempered judgment of a sound historian? And this difference, whatever it might be, is it not the same that exists between reporting the conclusions of a philosopher, and thinking them through for yourself?

The knowledge of those who somehow succeed in making judgments that are reasonable facsimiles of the genuine article cannot be condemned as simply false. These people "say" the truth, but do they really see it? They are not in the position of those who really do see the "point" but who do not see it as deeply as someone who may have given much time and great pains to the subject in question. The difference between penetrating the truth that "man's soul is spiritual" and penetrating it profoundly is a difference of degree, not of kind. The intelligible species informing the intellect of a man who sees profoundly is richer than the species possessed by a man who sees to a lesser degree: nonetheless, both see the same truth. But the difference between seeing the truth and simply thinking you see it is a difference of kind, not of degree.

This difference in kind is due to the fact that the agent

122

intellect is not restricted to illuminating intelligibilities in phantasms which present things directly to the intellect; the agent intellect can also illuminate species existing in phantasms which symbolize other phantasms. In such instances, the intellect is actualized by a species presenting a phantasm, rather than by a species presenting a thing. When the intellect predicates, it predicates a symbol of meaning rather than meaning itself. Thus the word-symbol "rectangularity" can be associated with an image of a rectangle. Without penetrating the *meaning* of rectangle, I can still know that this meaning (whatever it might be), is somehow contained in the picture of the rectangle held in my imagination. I really know *that* some attribute which I can designate sensibly exists in a given subject, but I do not know the essence of the attribute itself.

This is the way in which a man can dupe himself into thinking he knows when he does not. Should he become aware some day that he has been predicating symbols of things, he will be in the enviable position of knowing that he does not know. He will cease passing judgments on Democracy, Cambodian Art, or whatever it was that he had imagined himself to understand.

Clearly, this class of pseudo-judgments is not the archetype of judgment. The theory of judgment must be built around those terminating in genuine insights into being as it is. In the following pages, judgment is to be taken in this sense unless otherwise noted.

(2) INSIGHT INTO THE PHANTASM

Imagine, for an instant, that you are a youngster sitting in a first-grade classroom on a warm spring day. Your attention has lagged. Your intellect has stopped working. As you sit there in your chair dreamily looking out the window but not really looking at anything in particular, you are in that condition of half-sleep known as "day dreaming." A cinema of images rolls through your imagination with never a care for the why or the wherefore. You are in a state of not-knowing and not-seeking-to-know.

The teacher attempts to capture your attention by holding up a pie for you and your classmates to see. She has a motive: She wants to teach you the meaning of "whole" and "part" and their relationship. She uses the pie as bait. She balances it in her right hand and points with her left, thus getting your attention. Holding up the pie for all to see, she says: "This pie is a whole. If I cut a piece out of the pie and give it to one of you to eat, I have given you a part of the pie." She makes an imaginary cut. "Do you see now what I mean by a 'part'? Now the 'piece' of the pie is not as large as the 'whole' pie. The 'whole' pie is greater than one part of it. Now every 'whole' thing—be it pie or cake or anything else—is greater than any of its 'parts'. Do you all understand?"

By now, you understand that a whole is greater than any of its parts.

What happened to you from the time you lounged in your seat, daydreaming, to the point where you realized the whole-part relationship? In the first place, your attention was alerted by the teacher, who, using symbols (words and gestures), caused you to look at the pie so that you might know something about it that you did not know before. At that point you were in the state of not-knowing, but seeking to know. Your attention was gained; your powers of knowledge were stiffened to a point of concentration: to the thing you were trying to penetrate rationally. Gradually you came to realize the meaning of the whole-part relation as it existed in the pie in front of you. The relation, first grasped in the pie itself, was seen subsequently to be an intelligible relation existing between whole and part as such.

Not-knowing, not-seeking-to-know: pre-rational.

Let us translate the situation into philosophical terms:

(a) As not-knowing and not-seeking-to-know, your knowing powers were not working together in any truly human unity. You were functioning, for the moment, on hardly more than a vegetative level.

Not-knowing, but seeking to know: sensibility attempting to fashion phantasms containing the desired meaning.

(b) As not-knowing but seeking to know, your external sense of sight and hearing were coördinated by your inner senses and all were brought to bear on the object here and now sensed. Your intellect was in the state of seeking to understand. Your sensibility, commanded by your will and under the "impetus" of your agent intellect, was attempting to fashion an appropriate phantasm, one containing a species of the as yet unknown meaning of "whole" and "part."

(c) By grasping the gestures and words of the teacher, comprehending the fact that she wanted you to understand something, you fashioned a phantasm—under her direction—that potentially contained an intelligible species representing the "whole-part" relationship. Once this phantasm was fashioned by the body and placed before the mind, the agent intellect illuminated the species. Your intellect was put into act and, because the species was illuminated in *this* phantasm which adequately presented *this* meaning as well as *this* thing, your intellect grasped spontaneously the "whole-part" relationship in the thing itself. The form actualizing your intellect through the species was seen to have being in the thing grasped in sensation.

Moved by words and gestures, you were caused to make a phantasm containing the meaning (in potency) desired.

Once made, the agent intellect illuminated the species and understanding followed.

(d) Through a reflection, you grasped the truth that the "whole-part" relation held true wherever the conditions given in the example were reiterated. You saw the intelligible relation as universally necessary.

First seen in the thing, the truth is then seen as an intelligible relation universally necessary.

The example may seem disarmingly simple, even naïve, but it presents, nonetheless, the process typical to judgment. Man understands nothing in this life without the use of phantasms because only phantasms are connected vitally with sensation and thus with things as they exist. It follows that the proper phantasms must be presented to the intellect if the intellect would understand anything properly. Not only do phantasms initiate the process of understanding, but the phantasms used must be appropriate to the understanding man seeks to have. The phantasm of a rock is without any *direct* value for an understanding of the nature of man; to know something about man, the intellect must be presented with a phantasm representing man. To say this is merely to repeat what was said earlier: Things themselves cause us to know them by acting on our intellects by way of species which are both illuminated in the phantasm by the agent intellect and which carry the action and being of these things to the intellect.

This truth throws light on the essence of teaching. The whole process of teaching consists merely in causing the proper phantasms to exist within the sensibility of the student. The teacher can be a book, nature, history, personal experience, a human being. When the teacher is a person, he or she fashions a series of symbols which are capable of causing the student to fashion within himself a phantasm potentially containing the meaning that the teacher knows and that the student wants to know.

By the repeated use of symbolic examples the proper phantasms are actualized, and once actualized, the process of understanding is automatic. To take one more example: If I want to teach a friend how to play chess, I do not call down to earth a heaven of universal rules and laws. I place a chessboard in front of him and I keep repeating the moves of the different chessmen again and again until he gets "the point," until my symbolic gestures (words of explanation linked with my moving of the pieces: my "examples") have done their job of bringing to birth within his psyche a phantasm or group of phantasms capable of presenting the complex rationality of the game. We are all conscious of this phase of knowledge. The hunt for meaning is what we call "studying" in the English language. Once the proper symbolic matrix has been constructed, the intellect understands, and, although understanding is essentially trans-temporal, the process leading up to it takes time because it involves matter and motion.[1]

Phantasms needed: (a) to initiate, (b) to complete, (c) to recall, and (d) to deepen understanding.

Therefore phantasms are needed to initiate the process of understanding. They are also needed to complete, to recall, and to deepen understanding.

[1] A basic flaw in contemporary American educational philosophy, inasmuch as it is under the influence of the late John Dewey, is its failure to grasp the essentially *artistic* character of teaching. Due to an inflated opinion of "science" and all things supposedly "scientific," educators have been loathe to admit that teaching is an art, not a science. The art of teaching is a mingling of the liberal and the dramatic arts. Above and beyond the subject matter, the teacher actually needs but two assets: (a) a grasp of the liberal arts of grammar, rhetoric, and logic; (b) a mastery of the dramatic art of presentation.

Phantasms are needed to complete the process of understanding. Phantasms are the link between the material world and a spiritual intelligence. The reader is asked to remember that a spiritual power can only be actualized by a species that has been disengaged from the conditions of materiality. The agent intellect is the power exercising this activity of abstractive illumination. Therefore, the species presenting the form of the thing lacks something necessary for the complete representation of the object as it is: The species lacks individuated matter. Because individuated matter is a condition for the actual existence of a material thing, the defaulting of individuated matter in the order of representation entails the defaulting of actual existence. The intellect must reflect to the phantasm and—through the phantasm—to sensation in order to grasp its object, the thing whose intelligibility is informing the intellect.[2] This reflection is natural because there is no break between the intellect and the phantasm. The species is not illuminated by being cut away from the phantasm: The species is illuminated *in* the phantasm which presents it potentially. The intellect grasps this by a simple reflection in which it becomes aware of itself as being in act to a form which is related to a thing presented in the phantasm in unison with external sensation. Therefore, in order that the intellect know its object, the phantasm must be present in act. This is verifiable in common experience because when we first grasp some new meaning, no matter how abstract it might be, we grasp it in a thing, in a reality exemplifying the meaning itself.

Intelligible species do not contain individuated matter nor existence. Intellect reflecting to phantasm grasps its "meaning" as being in a concrete thing sensed.

Phantasms are needed to recall the process of understanding. If I once understood that man is spiritual and if I now wish to recall that understanding, not simply verbally but in the sense of going back over my reasoning, I bring out of my memory the phantasm or phantasms that previously presented the intelligibility to my mind. Once brought out of memory and placed before the mind,

To recall past understanding, I must recall old phantasms potentially containing the old species.

---

[2] The intellect reflects *upon* itself, but it reflects *to* the phantasm. Although current English usage frowns on "reflect *to*," I have retained the phrase because it emphasizes the *relational* character of intentionality.

the agent intellect illuminates the old species present there potentially. This phase of understanding is also a direct object of personal experience. We are aware that "we search our memories" when we wish to understand anew.

Phantasms are needed to deepen the process of understanding. Phantasms are the result of a thing's action on our sensibilities. The stronger and more powerful the action, the more is the thing present in the phantasm in its nature and being, and the more capable is the phantasm of presenting the nature of the thing to the intellect. If a man's phantasms are trivial, his understanding is trivial. If his phantasms are thin, his understanding is thin. If a man wishes to deepen his understanding, he must deepen his phantasms. This can be done in two overlapping ways: (a) by directly exposing ourselves more fully to the action of the thing we would understand, our phantasms of the thing will be deepened and our understanding thus enriched; (b) by relating a number of phantasms that are the result—direct or indirect—of the action of the thing we can build within ourselves new phantasms that present the nature of the thing in a fuller and more complex fashion than could be accomplished in a number of less sophisticated phantasms. This ability to orchestrate phantasms varies from man to man. It depends on the strength and suppleness of the sensibility. It is the work of the cogitative sense functioning as an instrument of the intelligence.[3] It is not a process of reasoning although it often exists for the sake of reasoning. Although the result of experience, it is not experience itself but rather its refinement within the sensibility. In this fashion, indirect experience can occasionally compensate for a lack of direct experience. For example, there are men who have a deeper insight into the spirit of a country they have never visited than many who have lived there all their lives. Raw experience without the ability to set it in order and build it into a full symbolic

Because things are presented to the intellect in phantasms, understanding of things is enriched by deepening our phantasms through: (a) direct experience; (b) indirect experience.

---

[3] See Klubertanz, G.P., S.J., *The Discursive Power* (St. Louis: The Modern Schoolman, 1952), esp. Chapters V to IX; B. J. Muller-Thym, "Of History as a Calculus Whose Term is Science," *The Modern Schoolman*, Vol. XIX, Note 3, pp. 45-46.

matrix can never produce understanding of any profundity.

(3) REFLECTION TO THE PHANTASM AND TO THE
THING

Having discussed judgment as a fact of experience and
having pointed out the role of the phantasm, we are
now in a position to set forth the psychological "moments"
found in the total process terminating in judgment:

(a) Once in act to a form through the species, the
intellect . . .

(b) Reflects to the principle of its specification (that
is, the species). Continuing the reflection, the intellect . . .

(c) Reflects to the principle of the species, which is
the phantasm. Continuing the reflection, the intellect . . .

(d) Reflects, through the phantasm, to external sensation wherein the intellect—grasping the thing—

(e) Begins to see that the form to which it is in act is
related to the thing existing in the extra-mental world.

This reflection is spontaneous. It is not thought out
deliberately, nor is it undergone consciously. *Consciously,*
man is aware of the thing he knows (and, implicitly, of
his own knowing), but this conscious awareness is the
result of the causation sketched above.

The reflection to the phantasm is intellect's bringing
an intelligibility (some aspect of the essence of the thing,
be it substantial or accidental) back to the thing which
is grasped consciously in and through the phantasm-
sensation process. The intellect sees that *its* form (remember always that the form actualizing the intellect *is
the form of the intellect in act*) is related to the thing,
has being in the thing. The intellect judges, declares that
"A *is* B," that "the form of circle," for instance, actualizing the intellect exists in a thing, a "ball," presented in
sensation.

The "application of a form to a thing" (in the words
of St. Thomas) must be identified with the act of predication, with the composing of predicate with subject. The

*Reflection
to phantasm
is the ap-
plication of
form to
thing.*

Reflection to phantasm is the application of form to thing. It is to be identified with predicating formality of subject.

subject is the very thing itself, held before the intellect in the phantasm-sensation relationship.[4] The predicate is the formal content, the "meaning" or intelligibility initially abstracted in the phantasm by the agent intellect and thus caused to actualize the intellect, now restored to the thing by the intellect, "said of the thing," predicated of the subject. Once again, we see that there is only one formal content in any judgment; that is, the predicate. The subject, *as such,* is not understood—it is sensed as a thing.[5] The predicate, in the words of Newman, "makes known" the subject. As body and soul coöperate in the act of judgment, so too does the act of judgment partake of the matter-form relationship in an intentional way. For example:

(a) The subject stands to the predicate as matter stands to form.

(b) As matter gets its whole determination from form, so does the subject get its whole determination from the predicate.

(c) As matter is intelligible only in the light of form, so is the predicate the very intelligibility of the subject.

(d) As matter of itself is unintelligible, so is the subject of itself unintelligible.

(e) As matter individuates in space and time, so is the

---

[4] In negative judgments, the intellect "divides the form" actualizing it from the thing presented in sensation. Negative judgments always involve the use of species acquired in the past. I hold a thing before my intellect in sensation and I bring out of memory (by way of a phantasm) a species which then actualizes the intellect. Reflecting to the thing, I see that the form actualizing the intellect does not exist in the thing itself. For instance, somebody hands me a pipe and asks me if it is a meerschaum; I take the pipe in hand, search my memory for the criteria of a genuine meerschaum. Once the proper phantasm is disengaged from memory and presented to the intellect, my intellect is actualized by the proper species.

In negative judgments we usually employ symbolic phantasms which somehow unite symbolically both the attribute denied and the thing of which it is denied. This symbolic phantasm is the result of linking the direct phantasm of the thing with the phantasm containing the intelligibility to be denied of the thing. In this manner, *one species* presents the "meaning" denied of the thing, and, because of its association with the direct phantasm, moves the intellect to grasp the thing of which it is denied.

[5] When the subject is not a thing sensed, it is presented—as shown in detail in the last chapter—by a phantasm symbolizing the subject and thereby causing it to be present intentionally to the intellect.

subject the same material thing individuated in space and time and presented intentionally to the intellect by way of sensation.

(f) As a material essence can exist only in individuated matter—matter capable of being sensed—so, too, man knows that the form actualizing his intellect has physical existence in a thing only by grasping the subject of judgment in sensation.

The above analysis does not complete the theory of judgment: Judgment, as has been emphasized through all these pages, is the act in which man understands something to exist. The theory of judgment must terminate in the existentiality of judgment, in its very being.

When a man "applies a form to a thing," when he reflects to the phantasm, he understands that an intelligibility informing his intellect has actual *existence* in a thing. He sees that something existing in his mind *is related to* an existing reality. When he knows this, he is said "to know the truth." Why? Because *it is true* for him to say (not necessarily in words, but in the sense that his intellect says the truth to itself) that this thing exists in this given way. What is this truth that he speaks? What is this truth that man knows? What is truth?

Suggested Texts for Discussion

The image is the principle of our knowledge, as that from which the operation of the intellect begins, not as something fleeting, but enduring as a sort of foundation of intellectual activity, just as principles of demonstration must remain in every procedure of science; for images are related to the intellect as objects in which the intellect sees whatever it does see either through a perfect representation or through a negation. So when knowledge of images is impeded, the intellect's knowledge must be completely obstructed even in divine science. (St. Thomas, *In Boetii. de Trin.*, Q. 6, a. 2, ad. 5, ed. Paul Wyser, O.P. [Louvain: E. Nauwelaerts, 1948], p. 65).

In the state of the present life, in which the soul is united to a corruptible body, it is impossible for our intellect to understand actually, except by turning to phantasms. And of this there are two indications. First of all because the intellect, being a power that does not make use of a corporeal organ, would in no way be hindered in its act through the lesion of a corporeal organ, if there were not required for its act the act of some power that does make use of a corporeal organ. Now sense, imagination, and the other powers belonging to the sensitive order make use of a corporeal organ. Therefore it is clear that for the intellect to understand actually, not only when it acquires new knowledge, but also when it uses knowledge already acquired, there is need for the act of the imagination and of the other sense powers. For when the act of imagination is blocked by a lesion of the corporeal organ, for example, in a case of apoplexy, or when the act of the memory is hindered, as in the case of lethargy, we see that a man is hindered from understanding actually even those things of which he had a previous knowledge. Secondly, everyone can experience this of himself, that when he tried to understand something, he forms certain phantasms to serve him by way of examples, in which as it were he examines what he wants to understand. For this reason when we wish to help someone to understand something, we lay examples before him, from which he can form phantasms for the purpose of understanding. (*Summa Theologiae*, I, Q. 84, a. 7).

Bibliography

St. Thomas Aquinas:

 Reflection upon the phantasm: S.T., I, 16, 2; I, 84, 7; I, 84, 8; I, 85, 5, ad. 2; I, 86, 1 and ad. 4; II-II, 51, 3; S. C. Gent., II, 73; II, 96; *De Ver.*, 12, 3 and ad. 2 & 5; 28, 3, ad. 6; 1, 9; 2, 6; 19, 5; 19, 1; *In Lib. de Mem. Et. Remin.*, 1, 2; *In II Sent.*, d. 20, 2, 2, ad. 2; *In III de An.*, 1, 8; *In Boethii de Trin.*, 6, 2; Q. *de An.*, 20, ad. 1 (in contra); *De Malo*, XVI, 7, ad. 5.

 Role of the phantasm in intellection: S.T., I, 84, 7; I, 85, 1, ad. 5; III, 11, 2, ad. 1; S. C. Gent., II, 73; *In I Post Analyt.*, 1. XXX, n. 5; *De Ver.*, 12, a 3; *In Boethii de Trin.*, 6, 2, ad. 6.

 Subject-Predicate relationships: S.T., I, 14, 14; I, 85, 4 c. and ad. 4; I, 85, 2; I, 85, 5, ad. 1; III, 60, 4, ad. 1; S.C. Gent., I, 18; I, 65; *De Pot. Dei.*, 9, 5; *In I Periherm.*, 1, 3; *In III de Anima*, 1, 11; *In VI Meta.*, 1, 4; *De Ver.*, 8, 14 c. and ad. 6; 26, 10, ad. 10; *De Malo*, XVI, 4.

Henle, Robert J., S.J., *Method in Metaphysics,* The Aquinas Lecture of the Aristotelian Society (Marquette: Marquette University Press, 1951). Every student should buy a copy and read it once a year.

Klubertanz, G. P., S.J., *The Discursive Power* (St. Louis: The Modern Schoolman, 1952), esp. Chapters V to IX.

Lonergan, Bernard, S.J., "The Concept of *Verbum* in the Writings of St. Thomas Aquinas," *Theological Studies,* Vol. VII (1946), pp. 372-380. Brilliant, but difficult reading. A close analysis of the role of the phantasm in understanding.

Muller-Thym, B. J., "Of History as a Calculus Whose Term is Science," *The Modern Schoolman,* Vol. XIX, No. 3, pp. 45-46. A discussion of the "experimentum."

‹ 12 ›

Truth

---

(1) TRUTH AS THE CONFORMITY TO AN IDEAL OR STANDARD

When a race horse measures up to expectations, his owner says: "She ran *true* to form." Conversely, when a music pupil fails, his teacher groans: "He cannot tell a *true* note from a false one."

Truth: conformity of a thing with a standard of excellence understood by the mind.

Both use the word "truth": what do they mean by it? The owner means that his horse ran as a race horse should run; the teacher means that his pupil failed to respond to music as he should. The term "truth" is used in relation to some standard understood by the intellect and applied by the intellect to reality. A thing or an action is considered true if it conforms to the standard; false, if it does not conform. In this sense of the word, truth refers to the way things or actions measure up to some ideal of excellence. That which meets the ideal is true; that which fails, just so far as it falls short of the standard, is false.

While valid, the above is incomplete. The fullness of truth is not restricted to a narrow conformity of a being with an abstract essential ideal.

Sound as far as it goes, this consideration is nonetheless radically incomplete. The examples given refer to the extent to which a thing measures up to the perfection of the essence it carries. For example, the horse comes up to the standard engraved in the nature it possesses. This kind of conformity exists; it has its legitimate place in the order of being, it is a film floating on the ocean of truth.

134

(2) TRUTH AS THE CONFORMITY OF A THING TO THE MIND AND WILL OF GOD

Essence is for the sake of existence, not existence for the sake of essence: *potentia dicitur ad actum.* The essence of a thing must be judged by whether or not it fits for that thing to take its place in the economy of being and in the rise and fall of the tides of history. This deeper standard by which a thing conforms to the rhythm of existence itself, relates it—not only to its own essence— but to all being and, finally, to the Being and Will of God.

Essence is for the sake of existence. Truth, ontologically understood, measures an essence by its conformity to the actual existence of a thing faced to all being and to God.

It is God who governs all things by His Providence. Although it is possible, now and again, to get a glimpse of this Divine Standard, its fullness is hidden in the Will of God. For example, we can understand that it is necessary for big fish to eat small fish in order that the physical harmony of the world be maintained. On the other hand, we find it impossible to understand why one man should be marked out for glory and ease, another for obscurity and pain. Yet the pain of the one as well as the ease of the other fulfill the Divine Will and stand related and conformed to the Divine Mind, and, within the Divine Vision, both are known to be true.

Metaphysicians teach us that God's knowledge is His Being.[1] In God there is no distinction between *to be* and *to know.* That which He is, is His Knowledge of Himself; that which He knows, is Himself. In knowing and being Himself in all eternity, God knows all the ways in which His Being can be imitated. These ways in which God can be imitated are not imposed on Him from without—the way in which our knowledge is imposed on us from without. If God were determined by the objects of His knowledge, He would be actualized by the finite: He would be finite. God, being infinite, is His own Act: He is Himself, solitary and alone in the infinity of His perfection. But His Being is imitable in an infinite number of ways. This imitability is one with God. *In God,* creatures are nothing other than God as capable of being imitated; *in God,* Peter

Creatures are ways of imitating God's Being; in God, creatures are God as imitable.

[1] See Gerard Smith, S.J., *Natural Theology* (New York: Macmillan, 1951), pp. 193-201.

is nothing other than God as capable of being imitated in this particular way. God, in His Eternity, joins His love with His Intellect and wills into existence some of the ways in which He is imitable.[2] This act of love is God's act of creation: Through and in His Love, things are.

The creature does not pre-exist its own existence; before its existence, the creature is nothing other than God knowing Himself to be imitable in this given way.

This is a mystery, but mystery is intelligible: God's Will causes me to exist, and, when I am willed into existence, not only am I a way of being-like-God, a way in which God is imitable: *I am.* I exist with an act of existing given me by Existence Himself. But even this is an improper way of speaking: God does not give me existence in the sense that, before I exist, I am a being capable of existence. Before I exist, I am absolutely nothing whatsoever. Before I exist, I am not a shadowy object hovering before the mind of God, waiting for a push into existence. Before I exist, I am nothing, which is to say—paradoxically enough—that before I exist, the being that I shall be is God Himself knowing Himself as being imitable by me.

The creature's essence is a potency for existence; hence Existence Himself—God—is the ultimate ground of the possibility of the creature.

This is an awesome mystery. No man comprehends it fully. Creatures are ways of being. To say "being" is to say that some subject participates in its own manner in an act of existing (for example, the angel is a way of existing; the man is a way of existing). The existing thing, therefore, is a way or mode of existing, and the Divine Imitability is the ground or possibility of its very being. God is Being Himself, *Ipsum Esse Subsistens:* "I Am Who Am." [3] Thus God in the burning bush to Moses; thus God through reason to the philosopher. The possibility of any existing thing, since it is a possibility *for existence, is Existence:* God as imitable.

Every analogy fails, but perhaps that which fails the least is the analogy taken from art: When the artist paints on canvas, he projects his personality into his painting. Before the artist paints, his personality exists in his soul and in his emotions; after he paints, his personality—while continuing to exist in himself—exists in a new order as well: in the painting itself. The painting is not the

---

[2] For the philosophy of creation, see James Anderson, *The Cause of Being* (St. Louis: Herder, 1952).
[3] *Book of Exodus,* III, 14.

painter, yet everything in the painting is the painter's; [4] the creature is not God, yet everything in the creature is God's. Everything in the painting is the painter's, not only in the sense that the painting belongs to him and was made by him, but in the deeper sense that the very being of the painting in the fullness of its artistic intelligibility *is*—in a new order—the being and personality of the painter himself. Everything in the creature is God's, not only in the sense that everything in the creature belongs to God and depends on Him for its existence, but in the deeper sense that the existence of the creature is nothing but a way of imitating God, a way of being God-like. Because a way of imitating God is a way of being rather than simply Being, because it participates in an act of existing rather than being identified with an act of existing, because it is finite rather than infinite, it is not God Himself. It is irreducibly distinct from Him, cut away from the Terrible Majesty of His Being with a "sundering sword," as Chesterton once put it: yet its whole reason for being is God Himself. My being is God's being, but not the Being of God.

In the light of the above, intelligence moves us to declare that the ultimate standard of truth is the Intellect and Will of God. This conformity, as insisted upon earlier in this chapter, is not the relation of a creature to an abstract norm existing in a human or Divine Mind: There are no abstractions in God. A man broken in body, living his life on a bed of pain, is a failure when measured by the standards of a physiotherapist. An illiterate peasant is a slave when looked at from the standpoint of a pedant who makes education his god. But if the sick man accepts his cross, he buys back his wealth; if the unlettered peasant shelters his family and worships before

A thing is true if it conforms to the Divine Intellect and the Divine Will.

[4] The statement in the text is not strictly true. The analogy breaks down at this point. Everything intrinsic to the artistic intention incarnated in the painting is the painter's, but the artist is dependent on matter which exists independently of his intention; that is, his paints, his canvas, the public symbolic structure he uses to incarnate his poetic vision, and so on. Finally, his intention, although belonging to him and revealing his soul, arises as a result of his confronting existing reality which is other than himself. See Jacques Maritain, *Creative Intuition in Art and Poetry*, Bollingen Series XXXV.1 (New York: Pantheon Books, 1953), pp. 3-44.

whatever altar he knows, he gains a wisdom before which letters are folly. Both are supremely true in the sight of God; both play their appointed roles in the scheme of Divine Providence.

Truth is grounded in existence because things imitate God in existing. Existence is the act of acts; essences specify existence from within.

Existence, not essence, grounds the truth of being. Because creatures are ways of existing, because they are ways of imitating the Divine Being, they are true when their acts of existing (in all their many relations) are conformed to God. It is only the creature endowed with freedom who can refuse to be conformed to the Divine Will. It is only freedom, turned from the destiny God inscribes in the being of each thing He makes, that can render the creature false in the sight of God.

(3) TRUTH AND THE ACT OF EXISTING

Therefore it follows that the touchstone of truth in the metaphysical order is the act of existing. The reader will recall that the act of existing is the act of all acts, and as a result is the perfection of all perfections. No man, says St. Thomas, can be said to possess wisdom unless he *be* wise. The act of existing is the act without which they are no other acts. But—let us insist upon it once again— we must not imagine that existence adds to formal or "essential" acts the way in which a frosting adds to a cake. Nor must we imagine existence to be a common substratum underlying everything else the way in which a foundation supports a house.

The former conception was that of the Mohammedan philosopher and theologian Avicenna, who imagined existence to be an accident that "happened" to a fully constituted essence.[5] If this were true, then existence would "happen" to the non-existent; existence would actualize that which is not.

The latter conception was that of Hegel and it partially accounts for his curious identification of being and nonbeing. For Hegel, the most universal of attributes was being or existence. To this most universal of attributes were added all other perfections: thus substance added

[5] See Gerald Smith, S.J., "Avicenna and the Possibles," *The New Scholasticism,* Vol. XVII (1943), esp. pp. 347-9.

to being; living substance to substance; animal substance to living substance; human to animal; and John to human.[6] Hegel, of course, was perfectly correct if the question be put in terms of the logical distinctions between concepts. In the mind, substance does add to being (considered as a least minimal residuum of content—that is, "the concept with the greatest extension and the least comprehension"). But *in being*, nothing adds to being. If substantiality, life, and so forth, really add to being, they are attributes separate from, and above and beyond, being. To say this is to say that they are something other than being. If they are other than being, they are nonbeing: nothing at all. If they are nothing, they do not add to being, because nothing adds nothing. *In being*, essences are ways of being; they contract or specify an act of existing: They do not add to it. They do not come to existence from without; they determine it internally. An essence is the intrinsic limit of an act of being.[7] To see this (and to see it, a man must think about things, not thoughts) is to see that the act of existing is truly the act of acts, the perfection of perfections, the heart and spring of being.

Existence, therefore, is the ultimate principle of truth. But this principle must not be frozen and thus debased to the mere fact of a thing's existing with a certain kind of substantial nature. The act of being, according to St. Thomas (and reason bears him out), is not merely the act through which being exists as a substance; but it is also the act through which being tends to its end and it is the act through which being rests in its end once it has found it.[8] *Esse* is that by which being subsists, exists

The conformity of a thing's existence to God englobes the full sweep of being: subsisting, tending, resting in its end.

[6] For an analysis of the general Hegelian position, see James Collins, *A History of Modern European Philosophy* (Milwaukee: Bruce Publishing Co., 1954), pp. 600-662.

[7] E. Gilson, *Le Thomisme*, Fifth Ed. (Paris: J. Vrin, 1944), esp. pp. 51-55.

[8] See the remarkable test in the *De Veritate*, Q. XXI, a. 2, where St. Thomas discusses the convertibility of "being" and "the good." The intelligibility of the *end* belongs to the good. This intelligibility contains two elements, the seeking of the end by those who have it not and the resting in the end (peace) by those who have it. Both, he says, belong to the act of existing itself ("Haec duo inveniuntur competere ipsi esse"). In this manner he links the dynamism of the good with the supreme perfection, existence itself.

as a certain kind of thing; *esse* is that by which being tends towards its end; *esse* is that by which being rests in its end, reposes in that peace which is its fulfillment, makes—in the case of man—"that harbour which is not of this world."

To sum up: Things are true in so far as they participate in the act of existing, because their very existence is conformed to the Mind and Will of God.

Transcendental truth —the truth of things; relational truth—the truth of knowledge.

But the truth of things, transcendental truth as it is called, is only one kind of truth. It founds a second kind of truth, one most proper to epistemology: the truth of knowledge.

(4) RELATIONAL TRUTH

Truth of knowledge totally dependent on being. Man knows the truth when he knows that his judgments are conformed to things as they are. This is relational truth: knowledge terminating in being, and known as so terminating.

This latter truth is totally dependent on being. Common usage attests to this dependence. "It is true to say that the thing exists; it is true to say that the thing does not exist." Man is aware that he knows the truth when he knows that the propositions he forms about reality are conformed to things as they are. Falsity, on the contrary, is known by all men to consist precisely in a lack of conformity between the propositions men form and things as they are. In this sense of the term, truth is something which the intellect knows. This kind of truth is frequently called "logical" truth, but a better name for it is "relational" truth. Knowledge is an act which intends its object relationally; knowledge terminates in the thing known in the sense that the act of knowledge is caused by, and is related to, the thing's physical act of existing. Relational truth is found only in judgment, because only judgment lays hold of existence, lays hold of things as they are. Relational truth must be denied sensation, reasoning, and simple understanding.

Relational truth must be denied sensation, reasoning, simple understanding.

The senses are true in the transcendental sense of truth. Like everything else in being, the senses exist; they also operate. In both instances—in simply being and in operating—the senses possess the truth of being. But the senses are not aware of their own conformity to reality; the senses, even though they *are* conformed intentionally to material reality, are not able to *know* this conformity, are not able to measure their own relationship with the real. Therefore they do not know the truth.

Reasoning is not a terminal act of understanding: it is a process of searching for new knowledge in the light of knowledge already possessed. Reasoning, therefore, exists for the sake of a new judgment which will put man in touch with a new truth. But when this judgment is reached, when man knows the truth, he has ceased to reason: he understands. Therefore, reasoning does not have relational truth. No man need reason about the truth if he already knows it.

Truth is related to simple understanding in a more complex manner than to sensation and reasoning. Simple understanding (or "apprehension," as it is often called) is the act wherein the intellect merely understands an essence or nature without understanding whether or not the essence exists in any order. The act is *simple* because the intellect does not compose the form actualizing it with a thing grasped in a phantasm; the intellect does not "apply a form to a thing." The act is a genuine *understanding* because the intellect understands some nature, even though it does not understand the nature existentially. The act of simple understanding is nonexistential because, as demonstrated in Chapters VIII and IX, the intelligible species presenting the object to the intellect abstracts from individuated matter. Individuated matter, to repeat the argument, is a condition for the actual existence of any material thing. To abstract from a condition for existence in the order of representation is to abstract from existence in the same order. Therefore, the intellect also abstracts from the actual existing of the thing. In order to grasp the object whose species informs the mind, the intellect must reflect to the phantasm and to the thing. The nature of a horse, for instance, cannot be known as it is until it is known as existing in some singular; reflecting back to the phantasm, the intellect beholds the nature of the horse existing in the concrete thing. The intellect applies the form to the material singular

The senses are true in being as they are; but the senses do not know the truth; they do not measure their own conformity to the real.

Reasoning is for the sake of judgment. As such, reasoning is not conformed to being as it is. It does not possess relational truth.

Simple understanding considers an essence in abstraction from existence: it is not conformed to being as it is; relational truth is not found here, except accidentally.

existent. In so reflecting, as we have seen, the intellect judges.

However, should the intellect lack sufficient evidence to understand that the form actualizing it has being in a subject, the intellect cannot judge truly. In act to the nature of a "sea monster," I lack an existing singular within which this nature has singular being; I lack a subject of judgment.[9] I can only apprehend the essence in question. Or, should I desire—for reasons of my own, reasons probably scientific in character—to ignore the evidence of existing singulars in order to simply contemplate the essence in question, my will can block my intellect from reflecting; my will can move my intellect simply to understand an essence in abstraction from the things in which it has being. In either situation, I merely understand a "meaning." My intellect is not conformed to things as they exist. Truth, being grounded in existence rather than essence; truth, being a known conformity of the mind with things as they exist, must be excluded, strictly speaking, from the act of simple understanding.[10]

(5) REFLECTION AND KNOWING THE TRUTH

Truth as known is the intellect's knowing itself to be related to things.

How does the intellect know that what it is intentionally within itself is also physically "outside" itself?

Truth is not known until the intellect is aware that it is actually related to things by being conformed to them. The truth as known is the truth as said by the mind.

How is it possible for the intellect *to know that it is true,* as well as simply being true? What enables the intellect not alone to absorb the object immaterially, but to know that what it has absorbed is related to what exists physically? Put it in slightly different terms: The thing exer-

[9] I abstract from the possibility that the intellect might fashion a fictional subject within itself, to which subject it could then apply an intelligible form. When this occurs, the intellect judges and such judgments follow the pattern proper to all judgment.

[10] Truth, as well as falsity, can *accidentally* enter simple understanding. Definitions are both the results of judgments and can be predicated in judgments. In this sense, a definition "truly" or "falsely" represents an essence or nature. Nonetheless, the definition is only accidentally true or false in the epistemological sense, because I *truly* understand ("truly" taken transcendentally) whatever meaning is presented in the definition, even though the definition might not truly ("truly" taken relationally) represent the thing in question.

cising existence in itself also exercises existence in knowledge. This last is its act of being-known. How can the intellect know that what it confronts intentionally as an object of knowledge is also a subject of existence in its own right?

Once again we are faced with the ultimate meaning of intentionality: knowledge is not simply the intra-mental existence of an object. As seen before, the act of being-known is an act of intentional existing caused by, measured by, related to, and thus terminating in the act of physical existing the thing exercises as a subject of being. In knowing the thing as an object of my knowledge, I also know it as a subject of existence because the object's act of being-known terminates in its act of being as a subject.[11] *And I am aware of all this because I am aware of my own knowing.* I am conscious that I am conformed to things as they exist. We must now turn to the explanation of this awareness, of this knowing the truth, knowing my own conformity to the real.

Man is aware that what exists intentionally also exists in itself; the intellect is aware of its own conformity to the object as it is.

The key unlocking this mystery is the experienced fact of intellectual reflection. We have appealed to this fact before. At that time we saw that intellectual reflection, our awareness of our own knowing, was a fact experienced by all men, not only in highly scientific judgments wherein intellectual consciousness may be found at a peculiarly high pitch of refinement, but in every single judgment exercised by the race. To anticipate our full answer to the question posed, let us say that in judgment not only do I know an object but I also know my own knowing. My understanding possesses itself and it possesses the thing understood: in this fashion, my intellect is not only true, is not only conformed to things, but my intellect knows its own conformity, its own relatedness to being, its own truth.

In intellectual reflection, the intellect grasps its own knowing, its own relatedness with the object, its own truth.

The ability to reflect totally upon oneself is a privilege that is one with the nature of spirit. By spirit we mean that which has an act of existing intrinsically transcending the order of matter and all that order implies. Noth-

Complete reflection is spiritual, not material.

11 See Chapter IX, pp. 133-135 and Note 2 quoting Dr. Parker on knowledge as a relation.

ing material can reflect completely upon itself; therefore, sense knowledge, which partakes of the conditions of matter, cannot know its own knowing, cannot be aware of its own conformity to the thing sensed. So much for the thesis; now to the proof.

It is of the essence of matter that it possess quantified parts occupying space. Each of these parts is outside every other part. Each part, filling such and such a place in space, excludes every other part. For this reason a material thing is extended; it deploys its parts, as it were, over an area which it occupies; it takes its stance in space in such a fashion that the whole material thing is not present to the whole. This follows from the above: The material thing, being composed of self-excluding parts, cannot be physically present to the whole of itself. To put the issue in less technical and more visual terms, let us say that a material thing scatters its being through space: part of it is here, part there. This part is not that part, and yet both are integral to the being of the whole. Hence the whole is not concentrated together in any manner permitting us to say that the whole being is present to itself. This nonpresence of the whole to itself is a natural condition for material existence.

Therefore a material thing cannot reflect completely upon itself. In a certain sense, the part can reflect upon the part, but never the whole upon the whole. For example, a flat piece of paper can be folded in half, so that one half of the paper has been bent back—"reflected"—upon the other half; one half is physically present to the other half. The paper, now folded in half, can be folded again and again; no matter how often it is folded, only part of the paper will be "present" to the rest of the paper—the whole will never be present to the whole. This truth is evident to anyone who meditates a moment upon the necessities intrinsic to materiality. Matter simply cannot effect a complete conversion upon itself. It cannot return upon its nature and stand revealed to itself in its fullness.

But what matter cannot do, spirit can. By nature the spiritual is that which excludes those conditions intrinsic to material existence. Spirit is not composed of quantified parts deployed through space. It follows, therefore, that it is possible for spirit to reflect completely upon itself, to return to its own essence, or, to speak metaphorically, to be all that it is in the center of its being.

Spirit lacks material parts. Hence, it can reflect completely upon itself.

All that is said above about spirit may sound highly abstract and even unreal; nonetheless, each one of us experiences directly this power of the spiritual to return to itself in reflection. We experience this in the act of judging: Not only do we know an object confronting the intellect but we are aware of our own knowing of that object. Immediately, directly, we are conscious of the thing known, but we are also aware, although we do not usually advert to the fact, that it is we who know the object. This openness of knowledge to itself is what is usually called, in English, "concomitant consciousness," the consciousness *that I am knowing* the thing I know.

Complete reflection of the intellect is possessed by man in judgment. I know my own knowing. This is concomitant consciousness.

At first glance it might appear as though there were no relation between our discussion of the inability of the material whole to reflect upon itself and of the ability of the intellect to understand its own knowing. Paradox though it may be, this is the precise point we are making. There *is no* parallel in the material world for the reflexive activity found in intellectual knowledge. There is no parallel because matter and spirit are not distinct in degree, they are distinct in kind.

Experientially, it is a fact that we do know both the thing and our own knowing. This knowing of my own knowing is not a second act. If it were, I would never know that I am knowing: I would only know that I *did* know in the past. I would only possess a retrospective awareness of my knowledge. But I did not first judge a thing to exist and, in a second judgment, judge my first judgment. If I went through this procedure, I would never really know that I knew things: I could only know my own knowing. One act of understanding would be judged by a second act, and this second act by a third, and thus into infinity. I would be trapped in an idealist universe wherein knowledge would bear on knowledge, never on things. Each act of understanding would re-

My awareness of my own knowing is not a second act of knowledge. If it were, knowledge would have to be checked by further knowledge, and so on.

move me, just so far, from things as they really exist. The
history of human understanding would be the history of
a progressive alienation from things as they are. The relational character of knowledge would be destroyed. The
evident fact that we know our own knowing would be
unintelligible.

*In knowing:
(a) the
object is
known; (b)
the act of
knowing
is known
in and by
itself. The
intellect
grasps
something
in itself
which is
related to
something
outside
itself.*

Let us translate this evident fact into metaphysical and
psychological terms. Once the intellect has been actualized by an intelligible species, it is in act so that it
can now operate. Then the intellect proceeds to its act
of judgment. This understanding is reflexive in character.
The intellect, *in knowing the object,* knows its own act
and knows something within itself *to be related* to something outside of itself. The intellect can be said to have
understood twice in one and the same act. The intellect
has understood: (a) the object; (b) its own knowing of
the object, which is a knowing related of itself to the
thing, an act of being "to or toward" an object, an act
of being-known, an *esse-ad* rather than an *esse.* This self-
understanding, this reflection, reveals to the intellect its
conformity to being: *The intellect knows its own conformity to the object because, in knowing its own knowing, it knows its own relatedness to the object.*

*The
intellect
does not:
(a) first
know a
thing and
then its
own know-
ing—this
leads to
idealism;
or (b)
know a
likeness in
itself and
then the
thing rep-
resented
by the
likeness—
this is the
copy
theory.*

This doctrine, while evident as a fact of psychological
experience, must be interpreted in all its metaphysical
subtlety lest it be radically misunderstood. The intellect
does not first go outside of itself and take a look around
and then crawl back into its shell like a snail. The intellect does not first know something and, through a sub-
sequent reflection, distinct from its act of knowing the
thing, come to know its own knowing and thus its own
conformity to the thing. Such an explanation, once again,
would throw us back into the idealist prison we discussed
above. Nor does the intellect, once it is in act through
the species, turn in upon itself (like a man turning his
pockets inside out) until it discovers within itself a form
which, like a thread, would lead it out to an existing
thing. This way of looking at the situation would force
us into some version of the copy theory. The intellect,
reflecting on itself, would find a likeness of an object im-

pressed on its nature; this likeness would lead the intellect out to the thing represented by the likeness. But how could the intellect compare the likeness to the real thing since the intellect—under this hypothesis—would be in act to the likeness, not to the thing? Both these explanations are the Scylla and Charybdis upon which countless epistemologies have been wrecked beyond rescue.

The intellect directly knows the existing thing; but the intellect can know the thing directly because the thing's act of being-known is caused by, related to, and thus terminates completely in the object's act of being as a subject of existence. Conversely, the intellect knows *that* it knows the thing because the intellect is thoroughly related to the thing in knowing it, compelled by its very nature to know the object through the relation its act bears to the object. Therefore, in reflecting, the intellect knows its relation to the thing because the act of the intellect *stands revealed to itself*. In one vital act, the intellect grasps the object and, *in* grasping the object, grasps its own relation to the object.

The intellect directly knows the object, but its very knowing of the object is open to itself. In knowing the object, the intellect knows its own relation to the object.

To say all this is simply to state in new terms what was said before: The intellect knows the truth when it knows that something existing within itself, something proper and intrinsic to its act—namely, the form actualizing it, that is, *its* own form—is related to something existing beyond itself. The intellect directly and consciously knows the object. This is knowledge *in actu signato:* The thing known presented to the intellect in its second act of existing, its act of being-known. But the intellect also knows its own knowing because it sees its own relatedness to the thing, its own conformity to the object, its own act of being "to or toward" the thing. This is knowledge and truth *in actu exercito,* in the language of Cardinal Cajetan.[12] It is knowledge as exercised by the intellect, knowledge done as an act rather than the thing which is "done" intentionally in the act. This intentional "doing" which is the act of knowing is, once again, self-conscious, open to its own being. *This openness of knowledge to it-*

---

[12] Thomas de Vio Caietani, *In S.T.,* I, Q. 16, a. 2, ed. Leonina n. VI, t. IV, p. 209.

self, this awareness man's intellect possesses in judgment of its own being-related-to-a-thing, is intellectual reflection.

Intellectual reflection is the result of reflecting to the phantasm. Only then does the intellect know that it is conformed to being. The application of predicate to subject, of form to thing, reveals to the intellect the "to be" of the relation it bears the thing. This act of being "to or toward" the thing is the act of being-true, the act of intellect's knowing its own conformity to reality.

How does the intellect reflect on its act and thus discover that it is conformed to a thing? It does so only by reflecting to the phantasm, because only through such a reflection can the intellect discover that the form actualizing it through the species is related to an existing thing. In this reflection to the phantasm, the intellect applies a form (signified by the predicate) to a thing (signified by the subject). The intellect grasps the relational act of existing exercised by the predicate in the subject when, having applied its intelligible form to the thing, it completes the reflection by bending back on itself so as to reveal the *relation* inhering in its intelligible form, the term of which relation is the thing itself. It is the reality of this existential relation that constitutes the act of existing exercised by the predicate in the subject. This act of existing is *not*—as insisted upon throughout this essay—merely the intra-mental existence of an object; it is an act of existing related and referred to extra-mental existence. *This act of relational existing is the thing's act of being known to exist. It is the act of being-true which is also the intellect's act of knowing the truth, because it is the act in which the intellect is both conformed to being as it is and the act in which the intellect knows this conformity of itself to being. It is the act in which the intellect knows its own knowing.*[13]

We have answered our question: how can the intellect both be true and know the truth? "Truth is in the intellect as known by the intellect" says St. Thomas. Truth

[13] The intellect not only knows its own act (and therefore its own conformity to the real), but the intellect—in completing the reflection—knows both the power exercising the act and the soul in which the power exists. Thus it follows that the knowledge man has of the "ego" is dependent on the knowledge he has of the "other." In short, we come to know ourselves only in knowing the non-self. This teaches us, once again, the impossibility of beginning philosophy with the "ego," as though the "ego" were the first thing known. The "ego" is only known in and through the knowledge man has of the "non-ego." This is vividly verified in the growth of the infant who becomes aware of himself as something other than his environment only in and through that very environment.

as known is the intellect's knowing its own relation to the object.

We are now in a position to summarize everything we have discovered about the intentional act of existing—knowledge—as it functions within judgment. The act of being of the judgment is:

(a) A living act exercised in and by the intellect.

(b) An act of being exercised by the predicate in the subject, and, because this act is caused by an extra-mental physical act of existing, the act is . . .

(c) Totally relational, totally "to or toward" the object, completely dependent on, and completely terminating in, extra-mental being which is the very term of the relation of knowledge.

(d) It is the thing's act of being-known to exist.

(e) It is the intellect's act of being-true.

(f) It is the intellect's act of knowing the truth, its act of being conformed to being as it is.

Let us apply this metaphysical analysis to an example:

I am introduced to a man called John. I am told by a number of reputable citizens that John is the soul of honesty. But I am unimpressed because I have heard similar stories before, believed them, and in time found myself duped by more than one supposedly honest fellow. I suspend judgment: I wait and see. But John does something proving to me that he really *is* honest. He performs some action impressing me with his honesty. Let us say that he sells a used automobile to a friend of mine, charges him a fair price, and the automobile does not collapse shortly thereafter as do most automobiles purchased under such circumstances. Honest John makes an impact on my intelligence. Now I judge, now I assent to the proposition—"John is honest."

In physical existence, John *is being-honest*. As a result of his honest action (action follows being), he impressed my intellect with his honesty. My intellect, in act to the species presenting John's honesty, reflects to the phantasm and to sensation where I sense John himself as subject of my incipient judgment. I apply the form "honest"

to the subject "John." John's honesty now exercises two
acts of existing: its act of being and its act of being-
known. What are the relations between them? Clearly,
John's honesty in my mind is not a *simple* duplication of
John's honesty in himself: if it were, we would have
(among other monstrosities) two acts of physical being,
rather than an act of being and an act of being-known.
Rather, the intentional act is derived from and is dependent on the physical act John exercises in himself: John's
being honest caused John's *known to be honest*. As a result of reflection to the phantasm, I have become aware
that the intentional existence of honesty in me is related
to the physical existence of honesty in John. My judgment
is conformed to the thing itself. I know the truth about
John's honesty.

(6) THE TRUTH OF NEGATIONS AND PRIVATIONS

*To what
being are
true
negative
judgments
and
privations
conformed?*

The absolute dependence of truth on being extends to
negative judgments, whether they be judgments of mere
negations or judgments of privations. A negation simply
denies that a given attribute exists in a subject: "Man is
not the moon." A judgment of privation denies the existence of an attribute in a subject, even though the subject in question ought to have the attribute: "This man
does not have sight." If truth is the conformity of the
intellect to being, it follows that every true judgment
must be conformed to some being. But to what being am
I conformed when I judge that "John is blind"? What
form do I assert to be in John? Do I assert, that, in reality,
John exercises an act of being-blind? That some positive
formality designated by "blindness" has actual existence
in John? That this positive reality causes the intentional
existence of blindness in my judgment? These are obvious absurdities. To say that John is exercising an act of
being-blind is to say that John is exercising an act of nonbeing; it is to affirm that a non-act—blindness—is an act.
This is a clear contradiction. The point about John's blindness is that John lacks a perfection due to his nature,

namely, the sense of sight. He fails to exercise an act he ought to exercise. But if blindness is a lack in John, does it follow that my judgment is conformed to a lack, to nothing at all? And if my judgment is conformed to nothing, then it is simply not conformed! Would not the whole theory of truth, as we have developed it, collapse if this were so? Plato, unable to surmount this difficulty, thought it necessary to assert the *positive* reality of nonbeing: to judge that "John is not-flying" is to assert—according to Plato—that "not-flying" exists positively in John. But to resolve the problem in this way is to place nonbeing on the same level as being; it is to assert the positive existence of the non-existent! [14]

St. Thomas, in this most crucial test of his theory of truth, insisted that the intellect is conformed to being in *every* true judgment. In true judgments bearing on negations and privations, the intellect fashions a quasi-form (with the aid of phantasms) which signifies or symbolizes a lack of perfection; this quasi-form is then predicated of the subject which lacks the perfection. The predicate thus exercises an intentional and relational act of existing in the subject. Completing its reflection, the intellect sees that the predicate *truly is in the subject:* The act of being exercised by predicate in subject *is true*, and the intellect is thus both conformed to being (intentional being) and knows its own conformity. For example, the

The intellect fashions a quasi-form and predicates it of a subject. The being of predicate in subject is the being to which the intellect is conformed. The predicate is truly in the subject.

[14] For Plato (who is more interested in the real inherence of forms in one another than in the problem of singular predication), "is not" means either: (a) different from; or (b) does not exist. Both share in the form of "otherness." "Otherness," in turn, is just as real as "sameness." Fundamentally, however, the crucial problem in this connection in Platonism is not the possibility of negative predication; it is the very possibility of *affirmative* predication itself! "A is B" does not *really* mean what it says. Because "A" is formally other than "B," "A is B" really means "A is *not* B." A participates in B; but to participate is not to be what is participated; the principle or form participated in is the nonbeing of the form participating. This, of course, is rooted in the Platonic participation theory, a theory of participation in diverse formalities, rather than a participation in existence (which last is Thomistic). See *The Sophist*, ed. by Francis M. Cornford (London: Rutledge, Keegan Paul, Ltd., 1951), 251 cd 255 e, pp. 255-292; esp. 255 c 255 3, pp. 281-282; *The Parmenides*, in *The Dialogues of Plato*, ed. by B. Jowett (New York: Random House, 1937), 142, p. 106. For St. Thomas' theory of participation, see L.-B. Geiger, *La Participation dans la Philosophie de S. Thomas d'Aquin* (Paris: J. Vrin, 1942).

intellect fashions a form signifying "blindness" and predicates it of John who lacks sight. This is a true judgment because "blindness," as a predicate, is in the subject "John." The situation affirmed in the judgment is so. The lack of sight in John does not *efficiently* cause the act of being-true, because nonbeing cannot efficiently cause anything. The lack of sight "exemplarily" (says St. Thomas) causes the being of the predicate in the subject.[15] Knowing what man is, I know that man should have sight; this understanding moves me to signify the lack of sight in *this* man—"John"—by fashioning the form "blindness" and predicating it of him. Take the strongest of all negations: "Nonbeing is nonbeing." This is a true judgment, but to what being is the intellect conformed? Certainly not to any extra-mental being, because the judgment is about nonbeing itself! The intellect symbolizes "nonbeing" by constructing a phantasm presenting this symbolized meaning to itself; once presented to the intellect (as a result of the illumination of the agent intellect and the action of the intelligible species), it is predicated *back* to the subject "nonbeing" symbolized in the same phantasm: the subject symbolically represents what the predicate represents formally. Thus the predicate exercises existence in the subject. The intellect is conformed to the act of existing which of itself it has given its subject, and the "being" of the predicate, "nonbeing," in the subject, "nonbeing," is an *esse-ad* and hence an *esse verum*.

Therefore our original proposition holds true absolutely: In every true judgment the intellect is related to some being, be it extra-mental or be it merely a being within the reason fashioned by the intelligence itself.

There is only one absolute Nothing and existentialist philosophy has rendered a service by exploring it.[16] The nonbeing of the true negative judgment is not an absolute nothing: nonbeing, as indicated, exercises an intelligible act of existing, an act of being-true, in every true negative judgment, even to the extreme of all negations: "nonbeing

15 *De Veritate*, Q. 1, a. 8, ad. 7.
16 Frederick D. Wilhelmsen, "Meditation on Nothing," *The Downside Review*, Spring, 1954, pp. 135-146.

is nonbeing." The only pure Nothing is the Nothingness
of the simultaneous affirmation that being is and is not:

> This simultaneous affirmation and negation can have
> no relation at all to the intelligibility of being, not even
> that of non-being; for its being destroys its non-being,
> and its non-being destroys its being.[17]

To assert being both to be and not to be is to say nothing whatever. To deny the principle of contradiction is
to put forth a desire; it is not to intend a reality. As seen
very early in this study, men can *want* to deny the principle of being, but they cannot *exercise* this denial, they
cannot carry out their wish, because even nonbeing exercises intentional existence in the judgment. The denial of
being, therefore, is fundamentally not an intellectual position, but a moral crisis. At bottom it is a resentment of
existence; less a failure in metaphysical speculation, it is
an inability to rise like a man to the challenge of being.
It is a refusal to affirm that which is. Ultimately, it is the
"I shall not serve" of the Prince of this World.

Suggested Texts for Discussion

Truth is both in intellect and in sense, but not in the same
way. It is in intellect as a consequence of the act of the intellect and as known by the intellect. Truth follows the operation of the intellect inasmuch as it belongs to the intellect to
judge about a thing as it is. And truth is known by the intellect in view of the fact that the intellect reflects upon its
own act—not merely in knowing its own act, but as knowing
the proportion of its act to the thing. Now, this proportion
cannot be known without knowing the nature of the act; and
the nature of the act cannot be known without knowing the
nature of the active principle, that is, the intellect itself, to
whose nature it belongs to be conformed to things. Consequently, it is because the intellect reflects upon itself that it
knows truth.

Truth is in sense also as a consequence of its act, for sense
judges of things as they are. Truth is not in sense, however,
as something known by sense; for, although sense judges

[17] *De Potentia Dei*, Q. 1, a. 3, c.

truly about things, it does not know the truth by which it judges truly. Although sense knows that it senses, it does not know its own nature; consequently, it knows neither the nature of its act nor the proportion of its act to things. As a result it does not know its truth.

The reason for this is that the most perfect beings, such as, for example, intellectual substances, return to their essence with a complete return: knowing something external to themselves, in a certain sense they go outside of themselves; but by knowing that they know, they are already beginning to return to themselves, because the act of cognition mediates between the knower and the thing known. That return is completed inasmuch as they know their own essences. (*De Veritate*, Q. I, a. 9, c., tr. by Robert W. Mulligan, S.J. [Chicago: H. Regnery Co., 1952] pp. 41-42.

I answer that, as was stated before, truth resides, in its primary aspect, in the intellect. Now since everything is true according as it has the form proper to its nature, the intellect, in so far as it is knowing, must be true according as it has the likeness of the thing known, which is its form as a knowing power. For this reason truth is defined by the conformity of the intellect to the thing; and therefore to know this conformity is to know the truth. But in no way does sense know this. For although sight has the likeness of a visible thing, yet it does not know the comparison which exists between the thing seen and that which it itself is apprehending concerning it. But the intellect can know its own conformity to the intelligible thing; yet it does not apprehend it by knowing *what the thing is*. When, however, it judges that a thing corresponds to the form which it apprehends about that thing then it first knows and expresses truth. This it does by composing and dividing: for in every proposition the intellect either applies to, or removes from, the thing signified by the subject some form signified by the predicate. This clearly shows that the sense is true in regard to a given thing, as is also the intellect, in knowing *what the thing is;* but it does not thereby know or affirm the truth. This is, in like manner, the case with propositions or terms. Truth, therefore, may be in the sense, or in the intellect knowing *what a thing is,* as in something that is true; yet not as the thing known is in the knower, which is implied by the word *truth;* for the perfection of the intellect is truth *as known.* Therefore, properly

speaking, truth resides in the intellect composing and dividing; and not in the sense, nor in the intellect knowing *what a
thing is.* (*Summa Theologiae,* I, Q. 16, a. 2).

Since there are in a thing both its quiddity and its act of
existing, it must be said that truth is founded in the act of
existing of a thing more than in its quiddity, just as the name
being is taken from the act of existing, and in that operation
of the intellect in which it takes the act of existing of a thing
to itself by a certain assimilation is completed the relation of
conformity in which the intelligibility of truth consists. Therefore I say that the very act of existing of a thing is the cause
of truth inasmuch as truth is known by the intellect. (*In I
Sent.,* d. 19, Q. 1, a. 1 resp. ed. Mandonnet p. 486).

Bibliography

St. Thomas Aquinas:
   Truth and the judgment: S.T., I, 16, 2 c.; I, 17, 3 c; I, 85, 6
   c; *In I Sent.,* d. 19, 5, 1 c; *De Ver.,* 1, 3 c; i, 9 c; 1, 11 c; *In
   VI Meta.,* 1. 4; *In IX Meta.,* 1. 11; *In I Periherm.,* 1. 3; *S. C.
   Gent.,* I, 59; IV, 108; *De Pot. Dei,* VII, 7.
   On the being of privations: In VII Meta., 1. 4; *S. T.,* I, 48, 2,
   ad. 2; *In I Sent.,* d. 38, 1, 4 c. and ad 3 & 4; *De Pot. Dei,* I, a.
   3, c.; VII, a. 2, ad. 1.
   *On the real "to be" of the truth attained in judgment: In I
   Sent.,* d. 19, q. 5, a. 1, ad. 1; d. 38, q. 1, a. 4, c. and ad. 4; d.
   33, q. 1, a. 1, ad. 1; *In II Sent.,* d. 34, q. 1, a. 1 c; d. 37, 2. 1,
   a. 2, ad. 3; *In I Periherm.,* 1, 5.
   On truth as a relation of conformity: In I Sent., d. 19, q. 5,
   a. 1, c. and ad. 7; *S. T.,* I, 58, 6 c; I, 58, 7 c; *De Malo,* XVI,
   6, ad. 19; *S. T.,* I, 16, 2, c.; *S. C. Gent.,* I, 59.

Anderson, James, *The Cause of Being* (St. Louis: Herder, 1952).
   On the metaphysics of creation.
Collins, James, *A History of Modern European Philosophy* (Mil-
   waukee: Bruce Publishing Co., 1954), pp. 600-662. On Hegel.
Caietani, Thomas de Vio, *In S.T.,* I, Q. 16, a, 2, ed. Leonina XIII,
   P.M., t. IV, n. VI, p. 209. On truth as exercised and truth as
   signified. Should be read by all students.
Gilson, E., *Le Thomisme,* Fifth Ed. (Paris: J. Vrin, 1944), pp. 43-
   68; *Being and Some Philosophers* (Toronto: Pontifical Insti-
   tute of Medieval Studies, 1949), pp. 190-217.

Hoenen, Peter, S.J., *Reality and Judgment According to St. Thomas,* (Chicago: H. Regnery Co., 1952), pp. 36-70.

Muller-Thym, B., "The 'To Be' Which Signifies the Truth of Propositions," *Proceedings of the American Catholic Philosophical Association,* Vol. XVI, 1940, pp. 231-254. Perhaps the most thorough analysis in English. Difficult to read but worth the trouble needed to master it—a truly brilliant study.

Phelan, Gerald B., "Verum sequitur esse rerum," *Medieval Studies,* Vol. I, No. 1; "The Existentialism of St. Thomas," *Proceedings of the American Catholic Philosophical Association,* Vol. XXI, 1946, pp. 25-40.

Plato, *The Sophist,* ed. by Francis M. Cornford (London: Rutledge & Keegan, Ltd., 1951), pp. 255-292. On Plato's doctrine of the actual existence of privations; also, see Plato's *The Parmenides,* in *The Dialogues of Plato,* ed. by B. Jowett, M. A. (New York: Random House, 1937), p. 106.

Smith, Gerard, J. S., "Avicenna and the Possibles," *The New Scholasticism,* Vol. XVII, No. 4, October, 1943, pp. 340-355; *Natural Theology* (New York: The Macmillan Co., 1950), pp. 193-201. The first cited work deals with the essentialism of Avicenna; the second, with the knowledge of God.

Wilhelmsen, Frederick D., "Meditation on Nothing," *The Downside Review,* Spring, 1954, pp. 135-146. On the meaning and significance of the concept of "Nothing" in the philosophy of Martin Heidegger as contrasted with the meaning of "Nothing" in St. Thomas' metaphysics.

Zedler, Beatrice, "St. Thomas and Avicenna in the 'De Potentia Dei'," *Traditio,* Vol. VI, 1948, pp. 105-159.

‹ 13 ›

Assent to Truth and
the Verbum

(1) ASSENT

When a man composes a predicate with a subject, he only *begins* to judge. He judges when he gives assent to the composition.

The distinction between these two phases of judgment is usually missed by consciousness when the object judged is present to external sensation. But when a pause exists between intellectual composition and assent to that composition, man is aware of the difference between beginning to judge and judging. Abstract scientific propositions, historical questions, the courtroom drama of guilt and innocence, the reflective pause preceding practical decision and action—all such propositions are sufficiently difficult and complex that assent cannot be given them without first searching consciously for evidence to move the mind to the assent. All unanswered questions, in short, are instances of intellectual compositions which are not followed by assent.

Assent is a conscious discernment and commitment to the truth. The intellect makes its own one side of an issue; the intellect excludes the possibility of the truth of the opposite. A final adherence to the truth possessed, assent is the mind's ratification of the proposition it has formed. Although intellectual, assent is the closest that the intellect comes to the volitional order. When I assent to a truth, I take a stand. I no longer balance possibilities; I come

To compose predicate with subject is to begin to judge; to assent to the composition is to judge. The distinction is present to consciousness in all judgments except those dealing with things immediately sensed.

Assent is conscious commitment to the truth; a ratification of the proposition already formed. Assent is the mind's positive response to being.

157

down on one side or the other. I commit myself to the real. Assent is intellect's response to being. In the words of Martin Heidegger, assent is a positive "letting being be." By no means something merely passive, assent is a spiritual saying of the truth by the mind.

Assent is not to things, but to the truth about things. Completing its reflection to the thing (by way of sensation), the intellect sees its own truth, its own relation to the real: this is assent.

Strictly speaking, we do not assent to things: we assent to the *truth* about the things we know. We assent to *our own* intentional possession of reality. Assent states that the intellect in its order is what things are in their order. Therefore it follows that the truth must be present in the composition the intellect makes before the intellect can assent to it. To assent is to judge about the truth of the composition. Completing intellectual reflection, assent seals the act of judging by stamping it with the mind's commitment to its own possession of the truth. From one point of view, assent is exactly the same thing as intellectual self-consciousness in completed act. Following upon its reflection to the phantasm and to sensation, the intellect sees that it is related to an object. Not only is the predicate in the subject, not only is the act of existing exercised by predicate-in-subject an act of being-true, but the intellect *knows that it is true.* This is the intellect's ratification of its own act, its awareness of its own relation of conformity to things as they exist.

(2) THE CAUSALITY OF ASSENT

The thing's existence causes assent by causing the act of intentional existing, which is the intellect's act of being related to things, intellect's act of possessing its own truth.

What causes the act of assent? Why does the intellect at one time refrain from assenting and at another time assent? In a general manner we have already answered the question: If assent is consciousness of the truth possessed, and if the truth is the act of being-known that the thing exercises in the intellect, and if the act of being-known is caused by and is related to the thing's act of existing, then it follows that the thing itself, in its very physical existence as a subject of being, causes the mind to assent to the truth about it. Things cause my knowledge of them, and this knowledge—self-possessed and conscious of its own relation to being—is my knowledge of the truth. When being presents itself to the intellect, the intellect assents. When being is not present to the intellect, the intellect—left to itself—cannot assent.

An epistemology which said no more would have explained man's assent to the truth. Nonetheless, by probing deeper into the issue it is possible to bring out in fuller detail and in greater strength the absolute supremacy of being in the process terminating in assent.

Being stands as both origin and destiny of judgment. The thing both wakens the intellect so that the intellect might know and presents itself to the intellect as the object to be known. Thus the thing initiates the process of judicative understanding and furnishes the mind with an adequate motive for completing the process of understanding; even more, the thing is the moving cause holding the act of knowing in its very being, because the act of knowing is nothing other than the thing's act of being-known.

Being initiates and terminates the process of judgment. Being puts the intellect into act and presents itself as the thing in which the act finds its completion, its term. Also, the thing keeps the act of judgment in being because intentional being is caused by physical being.

The intellect is the faculty of being and, like all faculties, is a potency which must be moved into operation by an active principle. The thing to be known begins the process of understanding by acting on the faculty, initially by way of sensation. The action exercised by the thing on the intellect produces the intelligible species which is the thing present to the intellect in its action, in so far as this action is impressed on the faculty. The intelligible species is the immediate active principle of judgment; it is also the specifying principle. It moves the intellect from potency into act so that the intellect can operate, and it informs the intellect with the nature of the object to be understood. Since the species is a formal and existential prolongation of the action of the thing, since the action of the thing is determined by, and is in proportion to, the act of existing the thing exercises in itself, it follows that the thing in its very being is the cause of judgment in the sense that judgment is the fulfillment of the act begun by the intellect's reception of the intelligible species.

Thing produces the species which: (a) moves the intellect into act; (b) specifies the intellect to its object.

But the intelligible species is not related to its cause the way in which an egg is related to a hen. Once the farmer has collected his eggs in the morning, their destiny

The species is related to the thing; this relation is grasped when the intellect reflects to the thing as a result of the action of the species on itself.

is unconnected with the destiny of the hens that hatched them. The egg can continue to be an egg, even though the hen is killed that afternoon and thus ceases to be a hen. In philosophical terms, the hen is not the cause of the egg's here and now existence. But the actual existence of the intelligible species germinating the intellect depends, in some manner, on the causal action of the thing here and now producing the species. The species is presented to the intellect in a phantasm illuminated by the agent intellect. The phantasm is the result of the thing's immediate action on the senses, or, in the case of judgments in the past tense, of the past action of the thing as now present intentionally in memory. Therefore, the intellect is activated by the species only so long as it is produced through the action of the thing, be that action immediate or the result of past experience preserved intentionally in memory. The species, activating the intellect and in living contact with the phantasm and with

The thing also causes assent by presenting itself to the intellect as the term of the relation of knowledge. This presentation of the thing is effected by the relation the species bears the thing, by the act of being-true. Evidence is the thing present before the mind, moving the mind to assent to the truth about it.

sensation, bears an existential relation to the thing it presents. This existential relation—which terminates, of course, in the thing known—is the effect of the efficient causality of the thing on the knower. This is revealed to the intellect, as treated in detail in the preceding chapter, when the intellect reflects and thus discovers that it is related to a thing. Thus the thing is the moving cause only through the species it produces. The species is really the pivot upon which the act of intellection swings: The species puts the intellect into act; the species causes the intellect to reflect; the species, linked with the phantasm and sensation, relates the intellect to the existing thing.

Left to itself the intellect cannot assent to the truth unless the intellect is fully aware of its own relation to the real. The thing is the *term* of the relational act of being, which is knowledge. Knowledge is *terminated* when the intellect, applying a form to a thing through reflection to the phantasm and to sensation, becomes aware that the form actualizing it has existence in the thing. Unless the intellect is aware of the term of its own reflection, the intellect cannot judge of itself. The perfection of judgment, as insisted upon throughout the last chapter, demands that the intellect complete its reflection and stand revealed to itself in its act. The intellect must take itself in hand, look itself full in the face, and thus see its own conformity to the real. As indicated, the thing itself moves the intellect to grasp its own being "to or toward" reality. But this is not all: The thing also furnishes an adequate motive for terminating the process by presenting itself to the intellect. The thing present to the intellect in its very existence moves the intellect to assent to the truth about it. Through causing the species and thus causing the intellect to reflect and discover its own relation (its "being to or toward") to a physically existing thing, the thing moves the intellect to assent to the truth about it. Evidence is not something which steps between the intellect and being, nor is evidence a logical "property" belonging to a proposition. Evidence ("objective evidence" it is often called) is nothing other than the thing itself confronting the intelligence and calling forth assent to the proposition the intellect has formed about it.

To begin and sustain the process of judgment the thing must act on the intelligence; it must *do* something. But to cause assent the thing does not have to do anything but *be*—that is, simply exist before the intellect whose act terminates in that very existence.

(3) THE VERBUM

Assent to the truth is one with intellectual self-consciousnses. But to be aware of my own understanding of reality is to "say" or "utter" the truth. The intellect thus speaks to itself and tells itself that it does possess the truth. The self-expression of the intelligence is called the *verbum*—the "word of the mind"—an interior and spiritual conception by the mind of the truth it possesses. Man is conscious of the existence of the *verbum* because the *verbum* is consciousness itself: We do not really know any truth whatsoever until we can express it to ourselves, and our expression is our consciousness that we do know the truth. The *verbum*, therefore, is a pure formal sign, a sign of pure meaning or intelligibility given birth by the

When man assents, he says the truth. This spiritual saying of the truth is intellect's consciousness of the truth possessed: This is the verbum of judgment— the truth consciously expressed.

intelligence expressing to itself the object it has understood.

The *verbum* is necessary to all human intellection because the intellect can only grasp an object not present to it physically by expressing it intentionally in knowledge; and, even when the object is physically present to the sensibility, man is conscious of the object intellectually only by giving it intentional existence within itself.

Thus the *verbum* is not the intelligible species; the latter stands at the beginning of intellection and underlies the whole process as its moving cause, whereas the *verbum* terminates intellection and is its result. The *verbum* is not the act of knowing *as such,* because the *verbum* is the truth about the thing which is revealed in the act of knowing. The *verbum* is not the thing in its physical existence as a subject of being. The *verbum* is the thing in its intentional existence—the thing *as known.*

Although produced by the mind, the *verbum* must not be thought of as though it were some reality or "thing" separate from the mind conceiving it. The *verbum* does not stand to the act of understanding the way in which a chair stands to the act of carpentry as exercised by a craftsman. The chair is really separate from the act of building it; once the carpenter has stopped acting on matter, once he has completed the job of making the chair, the chair is capable of existing in its own right. A product of the act of building, the chair stands separate and apart as a reality produced. Although made *by* the act of carpentry, the chair is not made *in* the act of carpentry: It is made in matter which is other than the act of carpentry. Therefore, the chair can exist apart from the exercise of the act which produced it. The *verbum*, however, is not only produced *by* the act of understanding, but it is produced *in* the act of understanding. The very act of existing of the *verbum* is the thing's act of being-known, which is the intellect's act of knowing the thing. Thus the *verbum* exists by the intentionality of the act of understanding. For this reason the *verbum* is nothing other than a pure sign. It is intelligibility consciously expressed: the being of the *verbum* is a "being-known."

Marginal notes:

Verbum *necessary:* (a) to grasp an object not *physically present;* (b) to lift the object to the level of the *intellect.*

Verbum *is not:* (a) *species;* (b) act of knowing; (c) thing as existing *physically.* Verbum *is* the thing *as known.*

The verbum *does not exist apart from the act of knowing. The* esse *of the* verbum *is the* esse *of the act of under-standing.*

When the intellect assents, it says the *verbum*. Since assent is one with the intellect's consciousness of its own relation to the real, the act of uttering the *verbum* is one with the act of assenting to the truth. The *verbum* is nothing other than the known object *as known:* the object thought or judged under this particular intelligible light or meaning. To look at the act of understanding from the standpoint of the knower possessing the thing it knows is to concentrate on the intellect's awareness of what it knows and of its own relation to this object: This is the *verbum*. It is that *by which* the object is known because the object is known only when we are conscious of knowing it. It is that *in which* the object is known because it is the object as intentionally present to the knower.

Assenting and uttering the verbum *are one with self-consciousness. The* verbum *is not the object which is known, but it is the object as consciously known.*

The *verbum* is a product only in the profound ontological sense that the intellect, fecundated by the seed of being, conceives within itself intentionally the object to which it is in act. To say the truth is to give birth to the intentional existence of the object. To say the truth (to change the figure) is to ratify being, let stand intentionally that which stands physically. The *verbum*, in very truth, is the intellect's laying hands on being and consecrating intentionally the existence of the things that are.

The verbum *is the child of the understanding, the intellect's response to its marriage with being.*

Suggested Texts for Discussion

It is clear from what has just been said that assent is not to be found in that operation of the intellect by which it forms the simple quiddities of things, for there is no truth or falsity there. For we are not said to assent to anything unless we hold it as true. Likewise, one who doubts does not have assent, because he does not hold to one side rather than the other. Thus, also, one who has an opinion does not give assent, because his acceptance of the one side is not firm. The Latin word *sententia* (judgment), as Isaac and Avicenna say, is a clear or very certain comprehension of one member of a contradictory proposition. And *assentire* (assent) is derived from *sententia*. Now, one who understands gives assent, because he holds with great certainty to one member of a contradictory proposition. Such a one, however, does not em-

ploy discursive thought, because he fixes one side without any
process of comparison. For by the very act of relating the
principles to the conclusions he assents to the conclusions by
reducing them to the principles. There, the movement of the
one who is thinking is halted and brought to rest. (*De Veritate*, Q. 14, a. 1, tr. by James V. McGlynn, S.J. (Chicago: H.
Regnery Co., 1953), Vol. II, pp. 210-211.

Therefore this reality expressed, i.e. formed in the soul, is
called the interior word: and it is related to the thing understood not alone as that by which it is understood, but as that
in which it is understood; because, in this expressed and
formed *verbum,* the intellect sees the nature of the thing understood. (*Comm. in Joann.*, c. I, 1.)

Bibliography

St. Thomas Aquinas:
    On the verbum: S.T., I, 34, 1; I, 85, 2; S. C. Gent., I, 53; IV,
    11; Q. Quodlibet., V, 9; VII, 2; In Evangelium Joannis, c. 1;
    In V Meta., 1. 17; De Pot., 7, 9 & 10; In I Sent. d. 19, 5, 1;
    De Ver., 4, 2 & ad. 5; Compend. Theol., c. 85; In III de An.,
    1. 8; De Pot. Dei, 9, 5; 8, 1;
    On assent to the truth: In III Sent., d. 23, 2, 2, s. 1; De Ver., 14,
    1; De Malo, VI ad. 14; S.T., I-II, 17, 6; I-II, 1, 2, ad. 2; S.T.,
    II-II, 9, 1; S. C. Gent., II, 48;
    On the identification of assenting and uttering the verbum:
    De Ver., 1, 3; 14, 1; S.T., I, 3, 4; I, 107, 1; I, 85, 2, ad. 3;
    I, 16, 2;

Lonergan, B., S.J., "The Concept of *Verbum* in the Writings of
    St. Thomas Aquinas," *Theological Studies,* Vol. VII, 1946.
Maritain, J., *Les Degrés du Savoir,* nouvelle éd. (Paris: Desclée de
    Brouwer), pp. 770-819. A classic discussion of the *verbum*
    of simple understanding—concept and definition—most of what
    Maritain says applies to the judgment as well. Particularly
    valuable for its close reasoning of the key texts of St. Thomas,
    which are all marshalled in the lengthy appendix.
Simonin, R. P., "La notion d'intentio," *Revue des Sciences Philo-
    sophiques et Théologiques,* July, 1930, pp. 450-471.

Certitude, Opinion, Falsity

---

(1) MOTIVE FOR ASSENTING IS BEING ITSELF

When reality is present to the intellect and known by the intellect to be present, the intellect assents to the truth in such a fashion that the intellect knows there is no possibility that the opposite of its judgment could be true. This understanding that there is no possibility of the truth of the opposite is what is usually called intellectual certitude. We shall return to it in a moment. Here we are concerned with the fact that the motive for an assent given with certitude is the evidence of being: being present to an intellect fully conscious of its own possession of the truth.

Adequate motive for assent with certitude is the presence of the object to the faculty conscious of that presence.

(2) INTELLECTUAL CERTITUDE AND THE FIRST PRINCIPLES

A judgment must be assented to with full consciousness that the opposite could not be true when the first principles of being and human knowledge enter the structure of the judgment in question. As pointed out in the earlier chapters of our study, the first principle of being is simply being itself. Because the intellect is the faculty of being, the first principle of intellection is being. Because being, in the exercise of its proper act—existence— is contacted by man only in sensation, sensation is also a first principle of human knowledge. Sensation, therefore, is the sensorium of existence. Assent with full knowl-

The intellect is necessitated to assent with certitude when the first principles enter judgment. These principles are: (a) being; (b) sensation.

165

edge that the opposite could not be true is given: (a) judgments confronting the intellect with being in the present exercise of existence, here and now sensed; (b) judgments reducible to past sensation of the existent; (c) judgments which, although transcending sensation in their objects, conclude a process of reasoning whose point of departure was the sensation of a material existent. If the first principles of being and knowledge do not play an intrinsic role within a judgment or if the judgment is not reducible to the first principles, assent with full knowledge of the absolute character of the truth cannot be given. The intellect can judge, in such instances, only if it is moved to the judgment by the will and the emotions. Speculative judgments made under the influence of the will yield probability at the very most, unless the will moves the intellect under the influence of Supernatural Grace, which is a consideration beyond the scope of this essay.

Intellectual certitude is possessed when the first principles enter judgment. But the term certitude is a highly ambiguous word which can signify more than one thing: Certitude can be either *intellectual* and *objective,* or *emotional* and *subjective* (to use the current terminology).[1]

Intellectual certitude is: (a) metaphysical; (b) physical; (c) moral.

As stated, intellectual certitude is possessed when the first principles enter judgment or when judgment is resolvable to them. In such judgments the intellect is compelled by the evidence of being to assent. *Intellectual certitude* is usually divided into *metaphysical, physical,* and *moral.*

---

[1] "Subjective" and "objective" in current speech have exactly the opposite meaning they had in the lexicon of St. Thomas. Today "subjective" means—at best—"existing within the mind of the individual knower," and—at worst—"arbitrary." "Objective" means "grounded in reality," "knowledge impersonally held," and so on.

For St. Thomas, an "object" was a thing *as known;* it was that which "is thrown up" before the intelligence. "Subject" was that which exists in its own right as an ultimate subject of predication.

The change in usage reflects the tremendous influence idealism has had in the Western world. An "object," in classical idealism, is that which is "objectified" by the spirit and only what is objectified by spirit itself is genuinely real.

(3) METAPHYSICAL CERTITUDE

Metaphysical certitude is possessed when the matter for judgment bears on the act of existing. This statement must be interpreted cautiously: All judgments bear on existence in some order; all judgments declare that something is or is not in some manner, but certain judgments do so by affirming truths rooted in the ontological structure of being or reducible to it, while others affirm truths that either are not reducible to the necessities of being or cannot be reduced to them by us because of the weakness of the human intelligence. For an example of a truth rooted in the necessities of being, consider the judgment: "The typewriter on which I am now typing exists." It is not absolutely necessary that the typewriter exist. Once it did not exist; very soon it will exist no longer. But it is necessary that the typewriter exist so long as it does exist, because it is necessary that being be so long as it is. This necessity of being-with-itself is nothing other than the first principle of being itself. The first principle enters the judgment because this principle is one with being; the first principle of sensation enters the judgment because the typewriter is here and now sensed by a man in full consciousness of that sensation. These two factors are themselves sufficient (indeed, overwhelmingly sufficient) for a perfect judgment yielding absolute or metaphysical certitude. The only factor needed above and beyond the first principles is the consciousness the intellect possesses of itself in act to these principles and thus to the thing presented in and by them.

> *Meta-physical certitude is reducible to the impossibility of being's not-being while it is.*

Let us take two more examples and compare and contrast them. "This thing before my senses exists, and, since it does not explain its own existence, there must be a First Cause of its existence who is Existence Himself—that is, if God does not exist, this thing does not exist; but it does exist, therefore God exists." Second example: "Mr. Roosevelt was President of the United States in 1936." Note that the first judgment is metaphysical; the second, what we usually call "historical." Both have in common that they deal with the existent: the first as an act, the second as a fact. Although metaphysics begins with the fact of existence, it goes on to penetrate the intelligible relations intrinsic to existence as the act of being. History does not explore existence as an act, but history affirms it as a fact of some subject. We can possess metaphysical certitude in both judgments; there is not the least hint of weakness in either affirmation. They both affirm being; they are both linked with sensation. To deny either judgment would be to deny the first principles. The fact that it is difficult to grasp the truth of the first judgment and easy to grasp the second does not affect the kind of certitude possessed by the mind which has worked its way through to a vision of either. Once confronted with being, no matter how tortuous the road traversed, the mind must assent and it cannot possibly be in error because being cannot not-be so long as it is, nor can being fail to have been if it actually was. Being is being: This grounds the certitude of metaphysics. What once was, need not have been; but once it has been, it remains eternally true that it was: "What is written, is written." This grounds the certitude of history.[2] Metaphysical certitude must not be restricted to the *disciplines* of metaphysics and history formally understood. The other philosophical sciences and, perhaps, a handful of affirmations from the physical and mathematical sciences are reducible to first principles and therefore possess metaphysical certainty. Finally, metaphysical certainty is had by man in a large area of his day to day living.

Physical certitude bears on a proposition belonging to a class whose members are almost always true. This class of propositions concerns the physical, material universe.

(4) PHYSICAL CERTITUDE

Physical certitude bears on a judgment belonging to a class of propositions whose members are almost always true; these propositions concern the physical world and the uniform way in which it carries out the business of being. There is a constancy and rhythm to the world in which we exist: The ever recurring coming and going of

[2] "History" is used in the text in the broad, nontechnical sense of any information possessed about the past.

the seasons, the proper time for the planting and harvest-
ing of the crop, the ebb and flood of tides and of all things
belonging to the sea, the perennial cycle of birth, life,
and death—all these things and many more besides teach
the race that nature is guided in its coming and going and
that this world moves through time, seasonably, according to laws which are one with things themselves. To
the natural philosopher, physical laws are tendencies toward a steadiness and constancy of operation, tendencies
inherent to material essence and one with its natural bent
toward being and becoming.

We have very little certain knowledge about the intrinsic structure of most of these physical laws. Our scientists symbolize them mathematically and our scientists
possess certitude about their own symbolizations. But the
laws, as they are in themselves, remain largely unpenetrated in their essential being. Nonetheless, man does know
that there are laws governing the rhythmically repetitive
operations of the things existing round and about him in
the material world. We know the world is not made up
of chance events.[3] We know laws exist because we know
that steadily determined action results from steadily determined nature. By an induction we can formulate propositions about the way in which things act and will act.[4]
These propositions, according to St. Thomas, are "probably certain."[5] The mind can assent to their truth without any *reasonable* fear of the contrary. When I go to bed
in the evening, I can conclude with reasonable certainty
that, should I arise in the morning, I shall see the sun
come up from the east. It is theoretically possible that
God, who made the physical world and its laws, might
cause the sun to come up from the north or from the
south; it is even possible that He might let the sun vanish

---

[3] See Yves Simon, *Travaux d'approche pour une Théorie du Déterminisme*, in *Etudes philosophiques, Ecole des Hautes Etudes* (Belgium:
1939); *Prévoir et savoir* (Montreal: Editions d'Arbre, 1944). Gerard
Smith, S.J., *Natural Theology* (New York: Macmillan, 1951), pp. 148-
151, 251-252.

[4] For the structure of induction from the logical point of view, see
Maritain, J., *Formal Logic* (New York: Sheed & Ward, 1946), pp. 258-
283.

[5] *Summa Theologiae*, II-II, Q. 70, a. 2 and 3.

from the cosmos by the simple fact of ceasing to will its existence. These cosmic considerations are theoretical possibilities, but I have no solid reason for thinking that He will act in this way. Therefore, it would be irrational for me to withhold assent to the proposition: "The sun will rise in the morning from the east."

To take a more mundane example, consider the proposition a captain of a sea-going vessel makes when he charts his course: He says to himself—at least implicitly—"*If* I am to follow this course, I shall eventually make *this* landfall." He gives an assent to the proposition yielding physical certitude. It is theoretically possible that the land mass which is his destination—Australia, let us say —might sink to the bottom of the ocean, and that he might find nothing but water covering the vast area where once stood Australia. This is possible, but the captain has *no reason* to think this remote possibility will be actualized. It would be unreasonable to withhold assent to the proposition, unreasonable to think the statement false or even merely probable in itself. A skipper who actually feared that Australia would not be there waiting for him at the end of his voyage would be a candidate for a rest home; there would be reason to doubt his sanity. To conclude: Propositions about the physical world grounded in a steadiness of being and action observed over a long period of time yield physical certitude.

(5) MORAL CERTITUDE

Moral certitude is similar to physical, except that it bears on the usual way men act.

Moral certitude bears on a class of propositions looking to the *moral* world. The members of this class of propositions are almost always true. Man has a nature and he tends to act in certain ways which are co-natural to him. It is natural for *most* men to marry and rear a family; it is natural for mothers to feel affection for their children; it is natural for man to eat when hungry and warm himself when cold. It is natural for man to tell the truth unless there be a sufficient motive—vanity, gain, pathological viciousness, and so on—constraining him to lie. Man acts naturally unless the particular circumstances in which he finds himself move him to the contrary. These motives might be religious, and thus a man will fast when hungry for the good of his soul. The motives might be worldly, and thus a man will give up marriage and even wealth in order to devote himself to the scholarly life. The motives might be pathological, and thus a mother will hate her children. The motives bending a man away from the usual course of action taken by men in the large may be high or low, good or evil, rooted in him or in the circumstances of his own life, but unless they be present he will follow the customary bent of human nature.

Thus the usual way men act, linked with an insight into the qualifying circumstances in which men are found, are evidence sufficient for moral certitude. For instance, we judge that the mailman will not murder us. We *must* make this judgment unless we possess particular information inclining us to think the contrary, or unless we act in such a manner that we might well bring on our own murder. But where there is no adequate reason to think men will act other than they always act, we possess moral certitude when we assent to the kind of proposition in question.[6]

To sum up, assent with intellectual certitude is threefold: (a) metaphysical, wherein there is absolutely no possibility for the truth of the opposite; (b) physical; and (c) moral, wherein there is a remote possibility for the truth of the contrary, but we have no sufficient reason to think this possibility will be fulfilled in the situation at hand.

(6) EMOTION AND CERTITUDE

Subjective or *emotional certitude* is something else altogether: It is a feeling of conviction that sweeps over a man and grips him powerfully when he assents to what may or may not be the truth. Subjective certitude may be brief and intense; it may be enduring and unobtrusive.

Subjective or emotional certitude is a "feeling" of conviction. Although psychologically important, it has no epistemological value as such.

[6] In this context human nature means nature *as now constituted after the Fall*—man with all his weaknesses.

Philosophers in the scholastic tradition have usually defined intellectual certitude as a proposition in which we have no reasonable *fear* of the opposite proposition turning out to be the truth. But this "fear" of which the medieval scholastics spoke does not convey their teaching to a mind trained in the proper formalities of the English language. A lack of fear, in this context, means that we cannot *judge* the opposite to be possible and that we are fully conscious of the reasons why we cannot. We have no reason permitting us to withhold assent to the proposition at hand. "Lack of fear," in this context, is something intellectual; it is not really a "lack of fear" in the emotional sense at all, and "fear"—in English—connotes the emotional. A man can possess intellectual certitude about a proposition and still fail to possess *subjective* or *emotional* certitude. He can emotionally fear the opposite, even though he cannot think the opposite to be a possibility. A man can be absolutely certain that a God exists and still feel His absence. Many of our propositions bear on objects which transcend and even contradict the exigencies of our emotional life. For example, a man can affirm the immortality of the human soul after a searching analysis of the evidence—intellectually he is certain that the soul is immortal—yet he might fear annihilation in the sense of shuddering at the thought of death. To the emotions, belonging as they do to the sensitive part of man (and, thereby, to the whole composite), life is material and nothing else; the body does not live on; the body dies, corrupts, and ceases to be even a reasonable facsimile of what it was. But man is both body and soul: He can know immortality and mortality at one and the same time, but he does not know them in the same way and therefore they often seem in conflict, even in contradiction. Very often the emotions are not brought into harmony with what the mind knows. In such a man there is a conflict between higher and lower. This is often a tragedy, always a burden. But it is the common lot of human nature after the Fall. *If* the emotions are brought into harmony with the truth as penetrated by the intellect, so much the happier will be the life of the man. If the emotions are not brought into harmony with the truth affirmed by the intellect and the good adhered to by the will, then we have what Mr. T. S. Eliot calls a "disassociation of the sensibility," a cutting away of the sensibility from those truths to which the intellect and will give a formal allegiance. (It might be well to note in passing that, although some disassociation of the sensibility seems intrinsic to the human condition, a profound tearing of the intellect and will away from the sensibility can result in a personal and cultural schizophrenia, a Platonic neurosis in which a man spontaneously reacts and feels one way about life, while affirming consciously and intellectually something else.)

Subjective certitude often works in the opposite direction as well. A feeling of conviction can so invade the rational powers that the will moves the intellect to assent where there is no sufficient evidence or where there is no real evidence at all. Here the intellectual life of a man is drowned in the power of his temperament and personality. Subjective certitude is intellectually irrelevant. Practically, however, it is very relevant: a tonic desired by all men, it is a balm to the sores of the spirit.

(7) COMMON AND SCIENTIFIC CERTITUDES

There is one final division of certitude: that is, into *common* and *scientific*. The former is certitude of the fact; the latter, certitude of the reasons for the fact. The certitudes of the untrained mind are of the former kind; the certitudes of philosophy and the other sciences are of the latter.

Common certitude: of the fact; scientific certitude: of the reason for the fact.

(8) PROBABILITY AND CERTITUDE

Below certitude, we rank *opinion* or *probability*. A judgment yielding opinion is a judgment in which one assents to the truth of a proposition as a result of evidence which is not sufficient to compel the assent. The judgment is probably true and we are conscious that it is only prob-

Probability: a proposition with evidence to incline us to assent to its truth, but not sufficient to compel assent.

ably true; we do not assent to its absolute truth, but to its probability. Newman defines opinion very neatly as "an assent to a proposition, not as true, but as probably true, that is, to the probability of that which the proposition enunciates; and, as that probability may vary in strength without limit, so may the cogency and moment of the opinion." [7]

Certitude resulting from the convergence of probabilities: Newman.

Newman thought a series of probabilities could generate assent. If I am confronted with an impressive number of probable arguments pointing to one conclusion and if there are no solid arguments which could account for the opposite conclusion, then the mind must assent to the conclusion with certitude. Newman's position seems to be a definite advance beyond the older tradition on the subject of certitude, an advance issuing—in all likelihood—from Newman's wide reading in history, his vivid awareness of the meaning of tradition, and his felicitous mingling of common sense and intellectual vision.

Each argument, says Newman, taken in isolation from the rest, would lead to the conclusion that the proposition is probably true. There are no solid arguments leading me to think that the conclusion is probably false. I must, he concludes, assent to its truth with certitude. The motive moving my assent, according to Newman, has nothing to do with the influence of the will. The motive inducing assent is the *convergence* of probabilities. The convergence can be explained reasonably only by the truth of the proposition. There is, therefore, no reason to withhold assent, and when there is no reason to withhold assent we possess, as seen above, either physical or moral certitude depending on the matter of judgment.

The motive for assent is the convergence of probabilities; the convergence is intelligible only in the light of the truth to which the propositions converge.

Newman's position has been attacked on the ground that probability can yield only probability, never certitude. But if we put the issue negatively, it is difficult to see how Newman can be contradicted. If assent is withheld, how do we explain the convergence of probabilities? The only alternative explanation for the convergence other than the truth of the propositions would be to write off the

[7] John Henry Newman, *Grammar of Assent* (London: Longmans, Green, and Co., 1887), p. 72.

convergence as a chance event. But a chance event is an event without any ascertainable cause. Although known and willed by God, a chance event has no natural cause for its existence; it is the result of the collision of two or more causal sequences, essentially unrelated.[8] So far as man is concerned, a chance event is unintelligible. But a convergence of probabilities is a convergence of reasons, of intelligibilities. To declare the convergence a chance event is to declare that an intelligible meeting of intelligibilities is itself unintelligible: this is untenable! But if the convergence is intelligible, the only ascertainable reason for its being intelligible is the truth itself, and, although man—absolutely speaking—could be wrong, he has no reason for supposing that he is. Therefore he must assent to the truth of the proposition. The certitude possessed is moral or physical, depending on the matter of judgment.[9]

(9) ERROR AND ITS CAUSALITY

What is the motive moving the intellect to assent to a false proposition? The fact that the intellect is in error bespeaks an assent of the intellect to the erroneous proposition. In order to explore the question, we must look to the meaning of error.

What motivates assent to the false?

Error is a defect or privation. As truth is grounded in being, so is error the opposite of truth and being. Because error is spoken of in opposition to the truth, error—formally understood—is found only in the judgment. Error is, in fact, the privation of being proper to judgment. The acts of simple understanding and sensation do not possess relational truth, the truth as known. Therefore they are free from error. This last statement must be taken formally: Simple understanding *is true* (transcendentally) in being what it is. A faulty definition, for example, must result from a false judgment, but the act of simple un-

Error a defect of relational truth; therefore error is found formally only in judgment.

8 Ives Simon, *Prévoir et savoir* (Montreal: Editions d'Arbre, 1944).
9 An epistemologist cannot determine *a priori* when a convergence of probabilities has been reached. This issue is intrinsic to the matter of judgment and must be settled by those competent in the field in question.

derstanding will always be an act wherein the intellect knows *what* is presented to it, even though what is presented does not accurately report things as they are in themselves. Sensation *is true* (transcendentally) in being what it is; a sense power working through a diseased sense organ will not function as it should, but inasmuch as it does function, in so far as it does possess being, it is true. It is *what it is.*

Thus a man who is color-blind is a man whose sense of color is as it is: that is, color-blind. Red is sensed by him as though it were green. The sense power becomes the object as it is presented by the sense organ. This is a source of error, as shall be pointed out shortly, but it is not error strictly speaking. For instance, the man who is color-blind may be aware of his defect; he will then judge that "Red seems to be green to me." This is a true judgment: It bears truly on the way red strikes him. His sense of sight is diseased and he knows that it is. His judgment is as true as any other judgment. So, too, with perceptions: A man who dreams that he is flying through the air with the wings of a bird experiences a series of perceptions linked together in a reasonably coherent whole; these perceptions are *in him* as perceived *by him;* they are the result of a host of experiences stored in the memory, now brought together in the unity of the dream. He perceives them in his dreaming as they are. The sensible in act and the sense in act are one and the same. There is no error here; error would result only if the man judged that things existed in reality the way they did in the dream. This often occurs and is a source of error.

Sensation and perception can be *called* false only in the analogical sense [10] that a diseased organ or a perception isolated from external sensation do not report things as they actually exist. Thus we commonly speak of false perceptions, meaning thereby perceptions which do not intentionally reiterate things as they exist outside of our psychic life. Although we can call them false, they are not really false in the proper sense of the term, for the reasons advanced above.

[10] That is, analogy of attribution.

When the intellect is unable to reflect to the first principles, the intellect runs the risk of judging falsely. Only external sensation confronts being as it is. In so far as the external sense organs are diseased, the intellect is blocked from reflecting to being. A man whose entire sensorial equipment failed him would be unable to judge at all. This occurs in shock and coma. A man whose external senses gave way gradually through disease or old age or through some other cause, would be able to judge accurately about the *past* (except when he related it to the present), but not about the *present*. Thus very old people are more often accurate in observations they make about the past than in observations made about present experience.

Impossibility to reflect to sensation is a source of error.

Diseased or atrophied sense organs are not the only causes of error. Lack of complete self-consciousness is a second cause of error. If the intellect cannot reflect completely upon itself, the intellect cannot judge infallibly about that to which it is in act. When dreaming, when drunk, when diverted by something more interesting, when bored with the object confronting one, man's intellect is unable to effect that complete reflection upon itself, which perfect judgment demands.

Incomplete consciousness is a source of error. This results from: (a) dreaming; (b) drunkenness; (c) illness; (d) lack of attention.

Finally, the will (in conjunction with the emotions in most instances) can move the intellect to judge. All being abhors a vacuum, and man abhors an intentional vacuum. The exigencies of life and the drive towards certitude are one in human nature; together they press in upon the intelligence when the will moves the intellect to assent. It is good for man to be certain; it is a kind of evil to remain forever suspended between opposite possibilities. The psychological peace following commitment is a good desired by the will and, in their own way, by the emotions. All this is sufficient to motivate the will to incline the intellect to an assent where being is not clearly present.[11] Conversely, the will can *want* the false to be true and thus block the intellect from considering the

The will and emotions move the intellect to assent where evidence is not present. The will so acts because it is a good to be certain; certitude brings a psychological peace that inclines the will to step in and force assent even though sufficient evidence is lacking.

---

[11] The discussion in the text is concerned, of course, with the influence of the will on the intellect in clearly speculative or theoretical issues. The influence of the will in practical matters is another issue. See Note 14.

evidence. This often occurs, not least in men who pride themselves on their "objectivity" and who are thus not alert to the danger which is one with human nature.[12]

The influence of the will is a nuisance and a source of error in speculative matters, but the will *must* be present acting on the intellect in practical matters. Facing material reality, man faces an order that is doubly contingent. It is contingent in its actual existence, because nothing in being except God must exist; it is contingent in its very materiality, because matter can exist under any form which it is prepared to receive. Although here and now matter may be determined and organized by the form of wood, the same matter tomorrow may be determined by the form of ashes as a result of a fire. Hence material things need not be, and need not be as they are. This double contingency blocks the human intellect from penetrating with absolute certitude a world which remains largely a mystery to the human mind. But it is in *this* world that man must act and make practical decisions even though he cannot possess intellectual certitude about them. Faced to the practical order, the intellect would hover forever between alternatives, none of which was up to the task of necessitating assent. The will must move the intellect in the practical realm, a realm wherein every decision is a risk.[13]

[12] It is well to recognize that *all* men are motivated, to a certain extent, by prejudice. Prejudice is not *necessarily* something evil. It simply means a "pre-judgment," a judgment we make even though all the evidence is not at hand. Without prejudices, in this sense of the term, man would not be able to act at all in the world, because certainty is restricted to but a small area of the knowledge any man possesses. For a discussion of this interpretation of prejudice, see Russell Kirk, *The Conservative Mind from Burke to Santayana* (Chicago: H. Regnery, 1953), Chapter I.

[13] Truth in the practical, prudential judgment is a conformity between the judgment and a righteously disposed will. If I act to the best of my ability in any given situation, if my action is motivated by understanding which has penetrated the facts so far I can penetrate them, if my action proceeds from a will rectified in the good, then my judgment is true, even though the situation speculatively affirmed is false. Dr. Simon gives the following example: A man sends his family on the train to the seashore for a vacation. His decision was motivated by the highest intentions. He judged, after scrutinizing the situation to the best of his ability, that a trip to the seashore by train *is a good* for my family. The train was wrecked and a child was killed. The judgment was *speculatively* false, but it was *prudentially* true because the head of the family acted

Diseased sensation, incomplete consciousness resulting from a lack of union between intellect and sensation, the drive of the will towards the good, the necessity to act without compelling evidence in the practical order—these are the causes of error.

When the intellect assents to a false proposition, the intellect does not assent to an act of being-true. Nonetheless, the intellect assents to *some* act of being. This act of being, in turn, must be intentional and cognitive because the man asserting a false proposition *means* to say something. In common speech, he knows what he is talking about, even though what he says is not true. The false proposition, therefore, is intentional, but it is not intentional in the way in which a true proposition is intentional. Every judgment states that an act of existing is united, in some manner, with a subject of being. Every judgment declares something to exist in some order of reality. In short, judgment universally *terminates* because the *term* of a relation is always implied in every relation and knowledge is thoroughly relational.

The false judgment terminates in that which is only the term of a relation. The true judgment terminates in a term which is also a subject of existence.

In the true judgment, we intend the term of the relation of knowledge *not as a term,* but as an independent reality. We *intend* [14] that what exists as an object of knowledge exists as a subject of being. And the object of knowledge *does* exist as a subject of being, because the act of existing of the judgment arises from and terminates in the physical existence the thing exercises in itself.

In the false judgment, we *intend* the term of the relation of knowledge *merely as a term.* What exists as an object of knowledge exists merely and solely *as an object, not as a subject.* Although the judgment remains relational, the relation has not been *referred* to extra-mental reality (because, ultimately, the relation is not caused by the extra-mental reality it is supposed to terminate in).

to the best of his ability and out of that fullness of knowledge which was at hand to him. The fact of contingency, as indicated in the text, blocks theoretical truth in practical matters. For a thorough discussion of the issue, see Yves Simon, *Nature and Functions of Authority* (Milwaukee: Marquette University Press, 1940), esp. pp. 22-29.

[14] "Intend" is used epistemologically, of course. It does not mean "wish" or anything belonging to the moral order.

In the false judgment, the intellect assents to the being of a form in a "subject" but the "subject" is a pseudo-subject. Merely the term of an act of knowledge, its ontological status is restricted to being a term and nothing more.

Unless the relation of knowledge can be *referred* to extra-mental reality by way of complete reflection to sensation, the intellect can never *intend* a term of its relation which term is also a subject of existence in its own right.[15]

To word it as tersely as possible: The being of the false judgment is a "being known to exist," which "to exist" exists solely as the *term* of the "being known." The being of a true judgment is a "being known to exist" which "to exist" exists as the very existence of a subject of being. *And this is known* because the "act of being known" is both related and *referred* (through reflection) to the "to exist" the thing exercises in itself.

Bibliography

Aristotle:
> *On induction: Prior Analytics*, I, 2, C. 23; *Posterior Analytics*, I, C. 18.

St. Thomas Aquinas:
> *On certitude and probability:* II-II, 70, a. 2 and a. 3; I-II, 105, a. 2, ad. 8; *In Hebr.*, c. 10, 1.3; *In Ioann.*, c. 8, 1.2;

Klubertanz, George, S.J., *The Philosophy of Human Nature* (New York: Appleton-Century-Crofts, 1953), Appendix O, pp. 428-431.

Maritain, J., *Formal Logic* (New York: Sheed & Ward, 1946), pp. 258-283. The logic of induction.

Newman, John Henry, *A Grammar of Assent* (London: Longman, Green, and Co., 1887), esp. Chapters I to III, and Chapter VII, pp. 3-19; 210-259. On probability and assent.

---

[15] See Francis Parker, "Realistic Epistemology," in *The Return to Reason*, ed. by John Wild (Chicago: H. Regnery Co., 1953), pp. 170-173. The finest treatment we know of on the being of false judgments.

Parker, Francis, "Realistic Epistemology," in *The Return to Reason*, ed. by John Wild (Chicago: H. Regnery Co., 1953), pp. 170-173. On the being of false judgments. Should be read by all students.

Phillips, R. P., D.D., *Modern Thomistic Philosophy* (Westminster: Newman Bookshop, 1935), Vol. II, pp. 8-16.

Simon, Yves, *Travaux d'approche pour une Théorie du Déterminisme in Études philosophique, École des Hautes Études* (Belgium, 1939).

—— *Prévoir et savoir* (Montreal: Éditions d'Arbre, 1944).

—— *Nature and Functions of Authority* (Milwaukee: Marquette University Press, 1940), esp. pp. 22-29 on practical knowledge and prudential truth.

Smith, Gerard, S.J., *Natural Theology* (New York: Macmillan, 1951), pp. 148-151, 251-252. On chance and Providence.

Phillips, R. P., D.D., *Modern Thomistic Philosophy* (Westminster: Newman Bookshop, 1935), Vol. II, pp. 8-16.

‹ III ›

Introduction to Epistemology
of Speculative Science

‹ 15 ›

Introduction to Epistemology
of Speculative Science

We have completed our thesis on the metaphysics and ontology of judgment and truth, which are—in truth—the heart of epistemology. Thus far this essay has attempted to penetrate the mystery of man's knowledge of being in its broadest sweep and in the light of the metaphysical and psychological principles functioning universally within human intellection. We have been discussing human knowledge. We shall now turn to certain kinds of human knowledge and analyze them in some detail.

(1) KNOWLEDGES ARE MANY

Knowledge is not one act; it is many. There are as many existentially distinct acts of knowledge as there *are* acts of knowledge. There are as many intentionally distinct acts of knowledge as there are things to know and ways in which they can be known. Since being is many, since knowers are many, it follows that knowledge itself is many. The plenitude and richness of being grounds the plenitude and richness of knowledge. The scope of human intellection is potentially infinite. Knowledges can be classified historically and then we look to the kinds of knowledge men have actually exercised. Knowledges can be classified according to their ends, and then final causality will be the principle of distinction. Knowledges can be classified according to the kinds of things understood, and then knowledges will be distinguished by their ob-

There are many valid principles for classifying and differentiating knowledges.

jects. Knowledges can be classified according to the ways in which the mind comes to grips with its object, and then method becomes the principle of division. Knowledges can be classified according to the level of perfection of the realities understood, and then the hierarchy of being and goodness will establish an order of value within human intellection.

The list is not complete. The ways in which the cake of intelligibility can be cut are potentially infinite.

If we restrict our consideration in this final section of our essay to scientific, speculative knowledge, it is because this kind of knowledge offers the greatest challenge to the epistemologist. We shall not treat practical knowledge formally, because—although it contains some epistemological issues—the subject is usually investigated in moral philosophy. We shall not treat aesthetic knowledge, because the question demands a training in the fine arts which cannot be presupposed in the American college student. What follows in this concluding chapter of our study is nothing more than an introduction to philosophical issues whose complete elucidation would demand a book all by itself.

Epistemology does not do the work of any science but its own; epistemology penetrates scientific knowledge already established.

Science has grown up largely unconscious of its own nature. It is the business of the scientist to do his own proper work, whatever it may be; as a scientist, he is not concerned with the metaphysics of his job. The philosopher has no right to tell the scientist *a priori* what to do or how to proceed in his chosen undertaking. The philosopher can only look at scientific knowledge as he finds it and give an account of it in terms of principles themselves fully philosophical.

(2) SPECULATIVE AND PRACTICAL SCIENCES

There is no one univocally valid way in which sciences must be ordered or classified. There are many valid principles of order, but perhaps the most obvious is that of distinguishing one science from another according to their respective goals: A science is called speculative if its end is simply the truth as known; a science is called practical if its end is knowledge which is productive or operative in some order. Metaphysics is a speculative science. Medicine is a practical science. The former simply looks to the truth of being; metaphysics does not serve or minister to operation, but sets before man an order to be understood. The latter science, medicine, understands, but it understands in order to operate; it looks to the truth about the healing of the human body and psyche and it is ordained totally towards that very art of healing. The goal of science is intrinsic to the science itself; it has nothing essentially to do with the personal end of the man possessing the science. To introduce personal motives into the finality of a science is to confuse two issues. A man might understand a speculative science such as metaphysics for a practical purpose; that is, he may want to teach the science and make his living in this way. A man may become a physician purely in order to know medicine; he may be fascinated by the subject and have no interest in setting up a practice. These personal ends, while crucially important from the ethical and religious point of view, do not change the inner finality of the science in question, a finality which is speculative or practical depending on the object of the science, not on the motives of the scientists.

The end of speculative science is the truth as known; the end of practical science is the truth as ordered to action.

(3) MATERIAL OBJECTS

Sciences can be distinguished according to their material objects. By material object we mean the thing or group of things understood in the science. Thus biology, concerning itself with living, organic things differs from logic which looks to the "being of reason."

Material object is the thing or things understood. Sciences can differ in material objects.

(4) FORMAL OBJECTS

Sciences can be divided according to their formal objects (or, "formal subjects," in the words of St. Thomas).

By formal object we mean the precise intelligible aspect under which the material object is grasped. From this point of view, sciences coinciding in the same material object differ in that they consider this material object from intrinsically distinct points of view.

(5) SCIENCE AND METHOD

Sciences can be differentiated according to the method they employ. Method implies two stages: (a) the hunt for meaning; (b) the penetration or judgment of meaning—the search for evidence and the weighing of evidence once discovered.

Discovery or induction is of two kinds: experiential and direct; experimental and rational. When the data to be penetrated by the science is given immediately in experience, the scientist simply renders explicit to rational consciousness what he already possesses implicitly. Data are given immediately in experience when the first principles are present to the man who is a scientist; that is, when being and sensation function together immediately within a judgment, when the judgment directly grasps being as sensed and perceived. Metaphysics and the philosophy of nature are the best examples of sciences proceeding experientially. However, some other sciences employ the method as well, particularly at the origin of their investigations. The negative norm for the experiential method is simply this: *Do we do anything* to the evidence before evaluating it? If we do something to the evidence, we are not proceeding according to the experiential method, but according to the experimental method.

For example, the chemist cannot evaluate his materials until he subjects them to tests, until he conditions them to the point where they can be penetrated by a judgment proper to his science. He experiments with reality before understanding it and his experimentation is integral to the process terminating in judgment. Before the bacteriologist can pass judgment on a virus, he must experiment; he must grow a culture; he must subject his culture to previously determined tests, and so on. Thus the experimental method is a selective or "abstractive" method; it concentrates on some facets within reality by isolating them from the whole. The experimental method is proper to most of the physical sciences. It is a less direct method than the experiential and therefore is less existential.[1]

Scientific method as the penetration into evidence or meaning is not merely twofold as is the method of discovery. There are as many methods of scientific penetration as there are sciences, and each science proceeds according to a method proper to itself. Metaphysics proceeds by way of judgment. The metaphysician penetrates the intelligible necessities of being which are revealed in all judgments. Experimental physics, on the contrary, proceeds by way of constructing mathematicized theories and hypotheses which are capable of explaining the data gathered experimentally and which are useful for the prediction of future events in the physical world. Mathematics proceeds deductively and abstractly. Given a set of mathematical axioms abstracted from real quantities, the mathematician can deduce from them an exhaustive set of conclusions: Given a mathematicized reality, the mathematician can abstract still further and make fresh deductions from his more highly abstracted axioms. In conclusion, scientific method cannot be determined *a priori*. We have to look at each science and scrutinize the method proper to it. Scientific method is not some monolithic yardstick as a number of popularizers of science would have the public believe. Method is as varied as is science.

(b) Method of penetration is intrinsic and proper to each science.

(6) SCIENCE AS A HABIT OF THE INTELLECT

Science can be divided from physical being. Science belongs to the order of knowledge, not the order of things. Nobody can point at a chair and say: "There is a

Science is a habit of demonstration and judgment.

[1] The distinction between an "experiential" and an "experimental" method is taken from: Henle, Robert, S.J., *Method in Metaphysics* (Milwaukee: Marquette University Press, 1951); and George Klubertanz, S.J., *The Philosophy of Human Nature* (New York: Appleton-Century-Crofts, 1953), pp. 385-410.

science." A kind of knowledge about the chair may be scientific, but not the chair itself. Thus the works of science, the technical products brought forth as a result of scientific understanding, are not themselves science. As a result, sciences are not distinguished from one another merely because certain things or principles are distinguished in reality. Although the objective structure of reality is the basis for the distinction of the sciences, the sciences are intrinsically distinguished from one another by means of the mind of man.

> The relation between a science and its subject is the same as that between a faculty or a *habitus* and its object. Now, properly speaking, the object of a faculty or a *habitus* is that under whose formal intelligibility *(ratio)* all things are referred to that faculty or *habitus;* as man and stone are referred to sight in that they are colored.[2]

Hence the subject or formal object of a science is that intelligibility or "meaning" under which everything in the science is investigated; this subject, in turn, is disengaged from things by the human intellect which is capable of making such a disengagement or distinction. Formally speaking, science is neither reality nor is it the mind: It is a unique way in which the mind sees reality.

(7) SCIENTIFIC GOALS

Scientific ideal today is not what it was for Aristotle and St. Thomas.

The meaning of the very word "science" has undergone a sweeping change in the last three hundred years or so. Today we spontaneously think of "science" as a method of recording and calculating physical phenomena in terms of mathematical theory. The modern ideal of science is largely practical or "demiurgical": Science is that which gives man mastery over the physical world. The classical and medieval scientific ideal was speculative, not practical: Scientific knowledge, at its highest, was an understanding of things in their causes. Unless otherwise indicated, the term "science" is used in this chapter in its older, traditional sense.

[2] *Summa Theologiae*, I, Q. 1, a. 7.

(8) SCIENCE AND CAUSALITY

Scientific knowledge is distinguished from nonscientific in that the former is knowledge through causes and the latter is not. Knowledge of facts and events is not called scientific in the traditional acceptation of the term. Factual knowledge may be trivial or it may be grand; it may be worth more than science, or it may be worth less—but it is not science itself. Scientific knowledge is knowledge of a fact in some one or more of the causes of the fact. To use Aristotle's famous example, a man knowing the fact of an eclipse is not said to be a scientist, but the man knowing the causes of the eclipse is said to be a scientist. Each science demonstrates or judges according to some cause. Where no cause is present in the mind as an explanation for the thing understood, the mind does not possess scientific understanding of the thing.

Science is knowledge through causes; mere knowledge of facts is not scientific.

(9) SCIENCE AND MATTER

Finally, sciences can be classified among themselves according to their relations to materiality. These respective relations to materiality govern the necessity possessed by the science. Knowledge is not considered scientific unless it is necessary knowledge, knowledge that must be as it is in some manner. Necessity in this connection begins with necessities inherent to material essence and concludes with necessities which are one with being itself.

Scientific knowledge is necessary; it must, in some sense, be as it is.

The necessary is dialectically and metaphysically opposed to the contingent—dialectically, because the necessary contradicts the contingent in concept; metaphysically, because ontological principles accounting for necessity are other than ontological principles accounting for contingency. If scientific knowledge is necessary knowledge, then it follows that the things known in science are themselves necessary, at least in the light in which they are known. Knowledge is *of* being; necessary knowledge is knowledge of that *in* being which is necessary.

Necessity is opposed to contingency.

Contingency: (a) existential—the finite need not be; (b) essential—things can change and thus cease being as they are.

Scientific knowledge is opposed to the contingent. There is a two-fold contingency in being: the contingency of finite existence and the contingency rooted in the structure of material nature. All things but God are existentially contingent, and since only one science—metaphysics—looks to God, this kind of contingency is without value in distinguishing sciences below metaphysics from one another. Other sciences are distinguished from one another according to the relations they bear to material essence. The contingency that is part of the natural world is one with the order of change or motion. When a thing changes, either accidentally or substantially, it ceases being what it was and becomes something else. Either it changes substantially and then wholly ceases being what it was, or it changes accidentally and acquires some new perfection and loses some old perfection. Change is the root of natural contingency.

Matter is the principle of change in composite essence; matter can be under any form and is therefore indifferent to the form it possesses.

Matter lies at the root of natural change. Matter is the principle permitting things to become other than they were. Whereas form is the principle of stability, matter —being in potency to all forms and thus indifferent to any one of them—is the principle of indetermination, of flux, of generation and corruption. The world around us attests to the truth of this axiom of Aristotelian cosmology. Matter prevents things remaining what they were; matter permits being to advance and it suffers being to decline.

Matter grounds change; change is one with natural contingency. Science is of the non-contingent. Hence sciences can be classified according to their lack of dependence on materiality.

If matter is the root of change, and if change is the root of natural contingency, and if the contingent is opposed to the necessary, and if science is of the necessary, then scientific knowledge is opposed to materiality. It follows that sciences can be classified according to the degree of independence from matter and change exhibited in them.

All sciences, since they deal with the necessary, remove themselves from any consideration of the individual as individual, because the principle of individuation is matter. Sciences can know the individual; indeed, sciences must know the individual, because only the individual exists. But sciences will not know the individual *as indi-*

vidual. As demonstrated in the discussion about judgment, the individual is grasped in sensation and held before the intellect by the phantasm; *man* then penetrates the individual according to some form or intelligibility to which his intellect is in act through the species which results from the action of the thing on his sensibility. Individuated matter, matter carved out in space and time, "these bones and this flesh," in the words of Aquinas, is —as such—foreign to human *conception.* Abstraction from the individuating material characteristics of finite being is common to all science and therefore cannot act as a principle differentiating one science from another.

All sciences abstract from individuated matter.

But matter can be considered not only as individuated, but as commonly sensible, universally capable of being contacted in sensation and perception. "Common sensible matter" is the technical phrase used to describe the matter that is bound up intrinsically with any material essence in its physical act of existing as a subject of being in the natural world: "flesh and bones" as opposed to "this flesh and these bones." Common sensible matter—qualified matter—falls under the universal scope of sensation and enters the nature of all material things. If we scrutinize all the objects which are understood by science, we can distinguish distinct kinds of scientific objects in relation to their dependence on, or independence from, sensible matter.

Common sensible matter is matter capable of being sensed and perceived. Scientific objects are related to common sensible matter in a three-fold way which bespeaks a three-fold degree of scientific independence from matter.

(a) There are objects of science depending on sensible matter both for their existence and for our understanding of them. These objects cannot exist apart from sensible matter, and if the scientist would understand them as they really exist, he must understand them as being in the sensible matter they need in order to exist at all. For example: dog, horse, elephant, squid, turkey, hen, smoke, mineral, tides, sand, the geological structure of the earth, sky, air—all these widely separated objects need sensible matter in order to exist, and if the scientist wants to understand and define them as they are in nature, then his understanding and his definitions must include the sensible matter entering their very essences as they are found in the natural world. This type of science gen-

(a) Objects depending on sensible matter for existence and understanding. Objects proper to philosophy of nature and natural sciences.

erically includes the philosophy of nature and the natural sciences; each in its own way looks to scientific objects on this same generic level.[3]

(b) There are objects of science depending on sensible matter for their existence, but not for their being understood by man. These objects cannot exist physically apart from sensible matter, but they can—curiously enough —be understood apart from the sensible matter they need in order to exist. Examples could be multiplied indefinitely: for example, line, number, triangle, square, rhombus, and so on. All these realities need sensible matter in order to exist: the triangle existing in the natural world

---

[3] The professional philosopher will note that I have not utilized the traditional "three degrees of formal abstraction." Although a thorough treatment of the question is precluded by the nature of a textbook, it might be advisable to defend our departure from this traditional distinction by noting: (a) St. Thomas *never* speaks of "three degrees of formal abstraction." So far as I am aware, the distinction is first used by Cajetan in his *In De Ente et Essentia,* Prooemium, Q. 1, n. 5, although the doctrine may have antecedents in late medieval scholasticism. (b) For St. Thomas, the abstraction of a *form* is proper to mathematical science. Sciences of nature use the abstraction of a *total* essence (that is, a complete essence: matter and form) from existing, material things. Metaphysics proceeds by *separation,* an act of judgment, which, while a *distinction,* is an "abstraction" only metaphorically. (c) St. Thomas' *triplex distinctio* is able to distinguish the intentional acts whereby scientific habits can be distinguished generically, and it is able to distinguish the degree of *necessity* found in generic levels of science. However, it is not an adequate principle for distinguishing one specific science from another if these sciences exist on the same level of scientific necessity, and if these sciences are disengaged by way of the same intentional act of the intellect. For example, both the philosophy of nature ("cosmology") and geology bear on objects needing sensible matter for being and being understood. Both sciences are one in that they confront objects presenting the least degree of scientific necessity because closest to the order of matter. Both sciences grasp their objects by abstracting intelligibilities which are intrinsic to total or complete essences. Nonetheless, the one science is clearly not the other. How are they distinguished specifically? The Cajetanist "three degrees of abstraction" cannot settle the issue. It is necessary to introduce some new principle, a principle of methodology, which, while not affecting the generic level of necessity or the generic structure of the intentional act employed, is able to distinguish the one science from the other. In the instance in question, the sciences can be distinguished methodologically in that the one employs an experiential and the other an experimental method. (d) The traditional "three degrees of abstraction" are utterly unable to place St. Thomas' philosophy of man within the hierarchy of science. If man is understood the way in which the traditional "philosopher of nature" understands him, then the most important truths about man can never be known; that is, the spirituality of his soul, the subsistence of his soul, the immortality of his soul. To the traditional philosopher of nature,

exists in chalk, wood, smoke, steel, iron, or some other kind of matter which can be sensed. But in the science of geometry, the triangle and its properties are understood without adverting to this sensible matter. Within the mind of the geometrician, the triangle is stripped of all sensible qualities. So, too, with all objects of this kind. This class of scientific objects belongs to mathematics.

(c) There are objects of science depending on sensible matter neither for their existence nor for our understanding of them. These objects can and do exist apart from sensible matter and if they are to be understood as they

(c) Objects depending on matter neither for existence nor for our understanding of them: metaphysics.

"being" is a "being material." This follows from the nature of the abstraction employed: To abstract a total or whole essence is to understand things as matter-form composites; it is to see form as an act of matter and nothing else. But in order to grasp the spirituality of the human soul, a philosopher must *separate* being from material being: he must judge that *to be* is not necessarily *to be material.* In short, he must understand that being is rendered being through the exercise of existence, not through the possession of material substantiality. The philosopher of man is forced to make this separation when he confronts the human soul, because, for the first time, he grasps a principle which *is being without being material.* The philosophy of man, therefore, crosses into the metaphysical and demands the metaphysical for its *own* achievement. Nonetheless, the philosophy of man is not metaphysics because man—as a composite nature—is an essence, and metaphysics is not the science of any given essence. In short, the unity of the philosophy of man cannot be explained in the light of the Cajetanist doctrine. In all probability the question never occurred to Cajetan because: (a) he seems to have taken no cognizance of what St. Thomas had to say about *separation;* (b) he misunderstood his master on the subsistence and immortality of the human soul. For Cajetan, the immortality of the soul was only probable on philosophical grounds. For St. Thomas, it is nothing other than a corollary from his metaphysics of being. (The *real* problem for St. Thomas is not, Is the soul immortal? The real problem is, *Could* God annihilate the soul once it is in being?) For the position of Cajetan, its historical antecedents and literature dealing with the question: See E. Gilson, *History of Christian Philosophy in the Middle Ages* (New York: Random House, 1955), pp. 409, 800-801.

For literature defending our general point of view: See L.-B. Geiger, O.P., *La participation dans la philosophie de s. Thomas* (Paris: Vrin, 1942), pp. 317-341, and "Abstraction et séparation d'après saint Thomas," *Revue des Sciences Philosophiques et Theologiques,* Vol. XLVIII (1948), pp. 328-339; D. J. Robert, O.P., "La Métaphysique, science distinct de toute autre discipline philosophique selon s. Thomas d'Aquin," *Divus Thomas* (Piacenza), Vol. L, 1947, pp. 206-223; L. M. Regis, "Un livre . . . La philosophie de la nature. Quelques apories," *Etudes et Recherches. Philosophie,* Vol. I, p. 141, pp. 138-140.

For literature defending the opposite point of view: See J. Maritain, *Short Treatise on Existence and the Existent* (New York: Pantheon, 1948), tr. by L. Galantiere and G. Phelan, pp. 28-40, Note 14; M. V. Leroy, O.P., "Abstractio et separatio d'apres un texte controversé de s. Thomas," *Revue Thomiste,* Vol. XLVIII, 1948, pp. 51-53.

actually exist or can exist, they must be understood as being separated or capable of being separated from the material order. Such objects are of two kinds: those which can exist in sensible matter but that need not exist in sensible matter—such as being, act, potency, truth, beauty, goodness, and so forth; and those which cannot exist in matter—such as the angels, the human soul considered intrinsically as a principle of spiritual subsistence, and finally: God. Both are proper to metaphysics.

A triple ascent from matter and motion grounding a hierarchy of sciences.

When these kinds of objects are viewed with reference to their withdrawal from the sensible order, you will notice that the first order involves a double affirmation; the second, an affirmation and a negation; the third, a double negation:

(a) Yes: they need sensible matter for existence.
Yes: they need sensible matter for being-understood.

(b) Yes: they need sensible matter for existence.
No: they do not need sensible matter for being-understood.

(c) No: they do not need sensible matter for existence.
No: they do not need sensible matter for being-understood.

This triple ascent from dependence on sensible matter yields a triple order of necessity in speculative sciences; beginning with a relatively inferior necessity, the hierarchy ends with a necessity altogether passing the order of material contingency.

Three ways of distinguishing scientific objects with reference to matter correspond to three distinct acts of the intellect.

(10) SCIENTIFIC DISTINCTION

Since the intellect can distinguish three distinct kinds of scientific objects (in relation to matter), then it follows that there must be three distinct intellectual acts corresponding to the three distinct types of sciences.

Affirmative judgments not acts of distinction.

It is clear that man cannot distinguish one thing from another thing when he judges affirmatively: an affirmative judgment simply declares something to exist or to exist in a given way. The affirmative judgment does not discriminate between realities, does not distinguish one thing from another. Therefore, although the crown of all science is affirmative knowledge—knowledge of being in some order—affirmative judgments are without value in distinguishing one body of scientific objects from another.

Man distinguishes in judgment only when he denies, when he negates. This kind of distinction is really a *separation* because, in every true negative judgment, the intellect separates things or principles actually separated or capable of being separated in existence. In reality, the being of a man is separated from the being of a horse: the one is not the other. When the judgment reiterates this existential distinction, when the judgment declares that "man is not a horse," the intellect has truly separated things that are really separated. The negative judgment is the only valid way in which man can distinguish objects in the act of judgment. Since metaphysics is the science of the act of being, the metaphysician proceeds by way of separation: He denies that being is necessarily linked with material being; he denies that the good, the true, the beautiful, the actual are one with the intrinsic structure of material essence. "Being," he says, "is not necessarily being this or that." Although all sciences use negative judgments to a certain extent, and although metaphysics uses affirmative judgments and finds its full perfection in the affirmative that God exists as the Cause of being, separation is uniquely proper to metaphysics in the sense that the metaphysician can get at his formal object—being as being—only by constantly separating it from the material and essential conditions in which it is presented to him in sensation.

Distinction on level of judgment is separation in a negative judgment.

Only metaphysics bears on things in the light of their existence. All other sciences are concerned with essential aspects of reality and, although they look to existence, they look to it as a fact, not as an act. The other sciences distinguish objects by way of abstraction, not separation.

To abstract is to consider some aspect of reality in isolation from the existential conditions or things in which that aspect has being. If I abstract the nature of "circle" from a baseball, I consider it in isolation from the baseball in which it exists. To abstract is not to falsify, be-

The mind can distinguish by abstraction; that is, by considering one segment of reality without adverting to the existential conditions or things in which it has being. Abstraction is proper to simple understanding.

cause abstraction is not separation; *it is not judgment.* If I *judged* that "circle" existed in physical existence the way in which it existed in my mind, then I would be guilty of a false judgment: that is, to judge that "The ball is not circular" is to judge falsely. But abstraction is not judgment. The intellect merely considers the form or nature of circle without adverting to the ball in which it exists. The mind analyzes or contemplates some segment of reality without saying anything about its existential status. Abstraction belongs, therefore, to the order of simple understanding rather than to the order of judgment.

The abstraction we are talking about is *scientific* abstraction; it is a conscious act of discrimination. It is not the preconscious act of the agent intellect illuminating the species in the phantasm. Once the intellect is actualized by a species, the intellect can—as shown in earlier chapters—proceed to either simple understanding or judgment. If the mind does proceed to simple understanding, it will penetrate some essential aspect of reality, which penetration or "insight" will be expressed in a concept or definition. All concepts and definitions are the products of one of two ways in which the intellect can abstract the order of essence.

Abstraction is either: (a) The abstraction of a complete essence from the particular things possessing that essence—"the abstraction of a *whole*," in the words of St. Thomas; (b) Or the abstraction of some form from the sensible matter in which it exists—"the abstraction of a *form*," in the words of St. Thomas.

Abstraction of a universal nature from the thing sharing the nature.

(a) In physical existence, John, Paul, and James all possess the nature of man. The mind consciously abstracts this nature from the individuals possessing it in order that the mind might understand the nature in its universality. This kind of abstraction is common to all the sciences and is found quite widely on the pre-scientific order as well. Although common to all the sciences, it is proper to the sciences of nature.

Abstraction of a form from the sensible matter in which it exists.

(b) The second kind of abstraction is the abstraction of some form from the sensible matter in which it exists.

The mind does not consider an essence in isolation from the individuals in which it exists. The mind rather abstracts certain forms that in reality depend on sensible matter for existence; once abstracted, the mind considers these forms in and for themselves. This kind of abstraction is proper to the mathematical sciences.

This brief introduction to the philosophy of the speculative sciences by no means exhausts the epistemological problems science presents to the philosopher. We might ask ourselves, for instance, precisely how is the separation of being from matter and motion made by the metaphysician? How are the diverse sciences on the level of nature *specifically* differentiated from one another? How is it possible for man to apply the mathematical to the physical order and thus harness nature to his own ends? What caused the great shift from a contemplative to a demiurgical ideal of science at the time of the Enlightenment? How is science related to history and what is the order between them? An introduction to epistemology has no right to probe these issues. They are raised merely to warn the reader and, perhaps, to encourage him. The search for philosophical truth shall never end this side of paradise.

Suggested Texts for Discussion

Now we must understand that when habits or powers are distinguished according to their objects, they are not distinguished according to just any differences of objects, but according to those which essentially characterize the objects as objects. For instance, to be either an animal or plant is accidental to a sensible thing as sensible; and so the distinction of the senses is not taken from this difference, but rather from the difference of color and sound. Consequently, the speculative sciences must be distinguished according to the differences among objects of speculation precisely as objects of speculation. Now an object of this kind—that is to say, an object of a speculative power—possesses one characteristic on the side of the intellectual power and another on the side of the habit of science perfecting the intellect. On the side of the intellect it belongs to it to be immaterial, because the intellect itself is immaterial. On the side of the habit of science it belongs to it to be necessary, because science is of the necessary, as it proved in the *Posterior Analytics.* Now whatever is necessary, is as such immobile; for, as is said in the *Metaphysics,* everything which is moved, in so far as it is moved, can be or not be, either absolutely or in a certain respect. Therefore, separation from matter and motion, or connection with them, essentially belong to an object of speculation, which is the object of speculative science. Consequently the speculative sciences are distinguished according to their disposition *(ordinem)* with reference to separation from matter and motion.

Now there are some objects of speculation which depend on matter with respect to their existence, for they can only exist in matter. And there is a distinction among these. Some depend on matter both with respect to their existence and their concept. This is the case with those whose definition contains sensible matter and which, therefore, cannot be understood without sensible matter; as, for instance, it is necessary to include flesh and bones in the definition of man. Physics or natural science studies things of this sort. There are some objects of speculation, however, which although depending on matter with respect to existence, do not depend on it with respect to their concept, because sensible matter is not included in their definitions. This is the case with lines and numbers—the sort of things mathematics studies. There are still other objects of speculation which do not depend on matter with respect to their existence because they can exist without matter. This is true, whether they never exist in matter, e.g., God and the angels, or whether they exist in matter in some things and in others do not, e.g., substance, quality, being, potency, act, one and many, and the like. Theology or divine science (so called because God is the principal thing known in it) deals with all these. (St. Thomas Aquinas, *Commentary on the De Trinitate of Boethius,* Q. 5, a. 1, tr. by Armand Maurer, C.S.B. in *The Division and Methods of the Sciences* [Toronto: The Pontifical Institute of Mediaeval Studies, 1953], pp. 6-8.

We must realize that, as the Philosopher says, the intellect has two operations, one called the "understanding of indivisibles," by which it knows *what* a thing is; and another by which it composes and divides, that is to say, by forming affirmative and negative enunciations. Now these two operations correspond to two principles in things. The first operation has regard to the nature itself of a thing, in virtue of which the known thing holds a certain rank among beings, whether it be a complete thing, as some whole, or an incomplete thing, as a part of an accident. The second operation has regard to a thing's act of existing (*esse*) . . .

Now, since the truth of the intellect results from its conformity with the thing, clearly in this second operation the intellect cannot truthfully abstract what is united in reality, because the abstraction would signify a separation with regard to the very existence of the thing. For example, if I abstract man from whiteness by saying, "Man is not white," I signify that there is a separation in reality. So if in reality man and whiteness are not separated, the intellect will be false. Through this operation, then, the intellect can truthfully abstract only those things which are separated in reality, as when we say, "Man is not an ass."

Through the first operation, however, we can abstract things which are not separated in reality; not all, it is true, but some. For since everything is intelligible in so far as it is in act, as the *Metaphysics* says, we must understand the nature itself or the quiddity of a thing either inasmuch as it is a certain act (as happens in the case of forms themselves and simple substances); or by reason of that which is its act (as we know composite substances through their forms); or by reason of that which takes the place of act in it (as we know prime matter through its relationship to form, and vacuum through the absence of a body in place). And it is from this that each nature is given its definition . . .

Accordingly, in its various operations the intellect distinguishes one thing from another in different ways. In the operation by which it composes and divides, it distinguishes one from another by understanding that the thing does not exist in the other. In the operation, however, by which it understands what a thing is, it distinguishes one from the other by knowing what one is without knowing anything of the other, either that it is united to it or separated from it. So this distinction is not properly called separation, but only the first. It is correctly called abstraction, but only when the things, one of which is known without the other, are one in reality. For if we consider animal without considering stone, we do not say that we abstract animal from stone.

It follows that since, properly speaking, we can only abstract things united in reality, there are two sorts of abstraction corresponding to the two modes of union mentioned above, namely, the union of part and whole, and the union of form and matter. The first is that in which we abstract form from matter, and the second is that in which we abstract a whole from its parts.

Now that form can be abstracted from some matter, the intelligibility of whose essence does not depend on matter of that sort; but the intellect cannot abstract form from the sort of matter on which the intelligibility of the essence depends. Consequently, since all accidents are related to substance as form to matter, and since the nature of every accident is to depend on substance, any accidental form cannot possibly be separated from substance. Accidents, however, befall substance in a definite order. Quantity comes from quality, then passions and motion. So quantity can be considered in substance before the sensible qualities, in virtue of which matter is called sensible, are understood in it. Quantity, then, does not depend on sensible matter with regard to the nature of its substance, but only on intelligible matter. For, after accidents have been excluded, substance remains intelligible only to the intellect, because the sense powers do not reach a comprehension of substance. And it is mathematics, which considers quantities and the properties of quantities, such as figures and the like, which treats of abstract entities of this sort.

Furthermore, we cannot abstract a whole from just any parts whatsoever. For there are some parts on which the nature of the whole depends, that is, when to be such a whole is to be composed of such parts. It is in this way that a syllable is related to letters and a mixed body to the elements. Parts of this sort, which are necessary for understanding the whole because they enter into its definition, are called parts of the species and of the form. . . . And this sort of abstraction is the abstraction of the universal from the particular.

So there are two abstractions of the intellect: One which corresponds to the union of form and matter or accident and substance. This is the abstraction of form from sensible matter. The other corresponds to the union of whole and part; and to this corresponds the abstraction of the universal from the particular. This is the abstraction of a whole, in which we consider a nature according to its essential character, in independence of all parts which do not belong to the species but are accidental parts. . . .

However, in the case of those things which can exist separately, separation rather than abstraction obtains . . .

We conclude that in the operation of the intellect there is present a threefold distinction: One with respect to the operation of the intellect composing and dividing, which is properly called separation; and this belongs to divine science or metaphysics. There is another with respect to the operation by which the quiddities of things are formed, which is the abstraction of form from sensible matter; and this belongs to mathematics. And there is a third with respect to the same operation which is the abstraction of the universal from the particular; and this indeed belongs to physics and to all the sciences in general, because in every science we disregard the accidental and consider what is essential. (*Ibid.*, Q. V., a. 3, pp. 26-32).

Bibliography

Aristotle:
   Prior Analytics, I, 2, C. 23; *Posterior Analytics*, I, C. 18.
St. Thomas Aquinas:
   In Librum Boethii de Trinitate Questiones Quinta et Sexta, Nach dem Autograph herausgegeben von Paul Wyser, O.P. (Fribourg: Societé Philosophique, 1948). English translation in, *St. Thomas Aquinas: The Division and Methods of the Sciences*, ed. by Armand Maurer, C.S.B., esp. Q. 5, a. 1 (pp. 6-8) and Q. 5, a. 1 (pp. 26-32).
   In I Eth., 1. 1, nn. 1-2; *In Meta.*, Prooemium; *In I Phys.*, 1. 1, nn. 1-3; *S. T.*, I, 40, 3; I, 85, 1, ad. 1 and ad. 2; *In I Post Anal.* 1. 2, nn. 2-3; *In III De Anima*, 1. 10, n. 745; *De Ente et Essentia*, 2.

Allers, Rudolf, "On Intellectual Operations," *The New Scholasticism*, January, 1952, pp. 1-36.
Geiger, L. B., *La Participation dans la Philosophie de Saint Thomas* (Paris: J. Vrin, 1942), pp. 317-341.
―――― "Abstraction et séparation d'après s. Thomas. *In de Trinitate*, q. 5, a. 3", *Revue des sciences philosophiques et théologique*, Vol. XLVIII, 1948, pp. 328-39.

Henle, Robert, S.J., *Method in Metaphysics* (Milwaukee: Marquette University Press, 1951).

Klubertanz, George, S.J., *The Philosophy of Human Nature* (New York: Appleton-Century-Crofts, 1953), pp. 385-410.

Leroy, M. V., "Abstraction et separation d'après un texte controversé de s. Thomas," *Revue Thomiste*, Vol. XLVIII, 1948, pp. 51-3.

Maritain, Jacques, *Distinguer pour unir ou les Degres du Savoir* (Paris: Desclée de Brouwer, 1946), pp. 44-133.

—— *Short Treatise on Existence and the Existent*, trans. by L. Galantière and G. Phelan (New York: Pantheon, 1948), pp. 28-40, Note 14.

—— *Philosophy of Nature*, trans. by Imelda Byrne (New York: Philosophical Library, 1951).

Maurer, Armand, "Form and Essence in the Philosophy of St. Thomas," *Mediaeval Studies*, Vol. IV, 1951, pp. 165-176.

Owens, Joseph, *The Doctrine of Being in the Aristotelian Metaphysics* (Toronto: Pontifical Institute of Mediaeval Studies, 1951).

Regis, L. M., O.P., "Un libre . . . La philosophie de la nature. Quelques apories," in *Etudes et Recherches. Philosophie.* Cahier I (Ottawa, 1936), pp. 127-156.

Robert, J. D., "La métaphysique, science distincte de toute autre discipline philosophique selon s. Thomas d'Aquin," *Divus Thomas* (Piacenza), Vol. L, 1947, pp. 206-23.

Simon, Yves R., "Maritain's Philosophy of the Sciences," *The Maritain Volume of the Thomist* (New York: Sheed & Ward, 1943), pp. 85-102.

General Bibliography

Primary Sources

Aristotle:
> *The Works of Aristotle Translated into English,* 11 vols., ed. by W. D. Ross and others (Oxford: Clarendon Press, 1928-1931).
>
> *The Basic Works of Aristotle,* ed. by Richard McKeon (New York: Random House, 1941).

Cajetan:
> *In De Ente et Essentia,* ed. by P.M.-H. Laurent (Taurini: Marietti, 1934).
>
> *Commentarium in Summa Theologiae,* ed. Leonina XIII P.M. (Romae: Apud Sedem Commissionis Leoninae, 1934).

Descartes:
> *A Discourse on Method,* tr. by J. Veitsch (La Salle, Illinois: The Open Court Publishing Co., 1946).
>
> *The Meditations,* tr. by J. Veitsch (La Salle, Illinois: The Open Court Publishing Co., 1946).
>
> *The Principles of Philosophy,* tr. by J. Veitsch (La Salle, Illinois: The Open Court Publishing Co., 1946).

John of St. Thomas:
> *Cursus Philosophicus,* 3 vols., ed. Reiser (Turin: Marietti, 1930).
>
> *Cursus Theologicus,* 4 vols., ed. Solesme (Paris: Desclée de Brouwer et cie., 1931).

Kant:
> *Critique of Pure Reason,* tr. by Norman Kemp Smith (London: Macmillan and Co., 1934).

Plato:
> *The Dialogues of Plato,* 5 vols., tr. by B. Jowett, M.A. (Oxford: Clarendon Press, 1871).
>
> *The Sophist,* ed. by Francis M. Cornford (London: Rutledge and Keegan, Ltd., 1951).

Thomas Aquinas:
> *Opera Omnia,* 34 vols. ed. by E. Frette and P. Mare (Paris: Vivès, 1872-1880).

S. Thomae de Aquino Ordinis Praedicatorum Summa Theologiae, cura et studio Instituti Studiorum Medievalium Ottaviensis ad. textum S. Pii. PP. V iussu confectum recognita. Vols. 1-4, 1941-1944 (Ottawa: Impensis Studii Generalis O. Pr.*.)

S. Thomas de Aquino Doctoris Angelici Summa Contra Gentiles, Editio Leonina Manualis (Romae: Apud Sedem Commissionis Leoninae, 1934).

S. Thomae Aquinatis Opuscula Omnia, 5 vols., ed. by P. Mandonnet (Paris: P. Lethielleux, 1927).

Scriptum super Libros Sententiarum Magistri Petri Lombardi, 4 vols., ed. by P. Mandonnet and F. Moos (Paris: P. Lethielleux, 1929-1947).

In Metaphysicam Aristotelis Commentaria, ed. by P. Fr. M.-R. Cathala (Taurini: Marietti, 1926).

In Aristotelis librum de Anima commentarium, ed. by A. M. Pirotta, O.P. (Taurini: Marietti, 1925).

Questiones Disputatae, 5 vols., (Romae: Domus Marietti, 1942).

Le "De Ente et Essentia" de s. Thomas d'Aquin, ed. M.-D. Roland-Gosselin (Bibliothèque Thomiste, Vol. VIII, Kain: Le Saulchoir, 1926).

In Librum Boethii de Trinitate Questiones Quinta et Sexta, Nach dem Autograph Cod. Vat. lat. 9850 mit Einleitung herausgegeben von Paul Wyser, O.P. (Fribourg: Société Philosophique, 1948).

St. Thomas Aquinas, The Division and Method of the Sciences, ed. by Armand Maurer, C.S.B. (Toronto: The Pontifical Institute of Mediaeval Studies, 1953).

Truth, tr. by Robert W. Schmidt, S.J., in 3 vols. (Chicago: Henry Regnery Co., 1954).

Secondary Sources

Allers, Rudolf, "On Intellectual Operations," *The New Scholasticism,* January, 1952, pp. 1-6.

Anderson, James, *The Cause of Being* (St. Louis: Herder, 1952).

Ardley, Gavin, *Aquinas and Kant, The Foundations of the Modern Sciences* (London and New York: Longmans, Green and Co., 1950).

Bergson, Henri, *Creative Evolution* (New York: The Modern Library, 1944).

Brooks, Cleanth, "The Language of Paradox," *Critiques and Essays in Criticism,* ed. by Robert W. Stallman (New York: Ronald Press Co., 1949), pp. 66-80.

Chesterton, Gilbert Keith, *Orthodoxy* (New York: Lane, 1919).

Coffey, Brian, "The Notion of Order According to St. Thomas Aquinas," *The Modern Schoolman,* Vol. XXVII, No. 1, pp. 1-18.

Collins, James, *The Existentialists* (Chicago: Henry Regnery, 1952).

―― *A History of Modern European Philosophy* (Milwaukee: Bruce Publishing Co., 1954).

Dalbiez, Roland, *Psychoanalytical Method and the Doctrine of Freud*, tr. by Joan Rivière (London: Allen and Unwin, 1931).

Duhem, Pierre, *Essai sur la notion de Théorie physique de Platon à Galilée* (Paris: Annales de philosophie crétienne, 1908).

―― *Le Système du Monde. Histoire des doctrines cosmologiques de Platon à Copernic*. 5 vols. (Paris, 1913-17).

Eddington, Sir Arthur, *Nature of the Physical World* (New York: Macmillan, 1929).

Finance, Joseph de, *Etre et Agir dans la Philosophie de S. Thomas* (Paris: Beauchesne et ses Fils, 1945).

Freud, Sigmund, *Introductory Lectures on Psycho-Analysis*, tr. by Joan Rivière (London: Allen and Unwin, 1931).

Geiger, L. B., *La Participation dans la Philosophie de Saint Thomas* (Paris: J. Vrin, 1942).

―― "Abraction et séparation d'apres s. Thomas," *Revue des sciences philosophiques et théologique*, Vol. XLVIII, 1948, pp. 328-339.

Gilson, Etienne, *Le réalisme méthodique* (Paris: P. Téqui, 1935).

―― *The Spirit of Mediaeval Philosophy*, tr. Downes (New York: Sheed and Ward, 1936).

―― *Réalisme thomiste et critique de la connaissance* (Paris: J. Vrin, 1939).

―― *Le Thomisme, cin. ed., Études de philosophie médiévale*, Vol. I (Paris: J. Vrin, 1945).

―― *L'être et l'essence* (Paris: J. Vrin, 1948).

―― *Being and Some Philosophers* (Toronto: Pontifical Institute of Mediaeval Studies, 1949).

―― *History of Christian Philosophy in the Middle Ages* (New York: Random House, 1955).

―― "La notion d'existence chez Guillaume d'Auvergne," *Archives d'Histoire Doctrinale et Littéraire du Moyen Age*, Vol. XXI, 1946, pp. 62-64.

―― "Les principes et les causes," *Revue Thomiste*, Vol. LX, 1952, pp. 54-72.

―― "Cajétan et l'existence," *Tijdschrift voor Philosophie*, Vol. 15, 1953, pp. 267-286.

Guardini, Romano, *Das Ende der Neuzeit* (Zurich: Verlag Hesse, 1949).

Heisenberg, Werner, "Mann: Natur: Technik," *Münchener Katholische Kirchenzeitung*, No. 48 (Nov. 29, 195).

Henle, Robert, S.J., *Method in Metaphysics* (Milwaukee: Marquette University Press, 1951).

Hoenen, Peter, S.J., *Reality and Judgment According to St. Thomas Aquinas* (Chicago: H. Regnery Co., 1952).

Holloway, M., "Abstraction from Matter in Human Cognition," *The Modern Schoolman,* Vol. XXIII, 1946, pp. 120-130.

Jung, C. G., *Archetypes and the Collective Unconscious, The Collected Works,* Vol. 9 (London: Rutledge and Kegan Paul, 1953).

Kennard, George V., S.J., *The Intellect Composing and Dividing According to St. Thomas Aquinas.* Unpublished dissertation, St. Louis University, 1948.

Kirk, Russell, "York and Social Boredom," *The Sewanee Review,* Winter, 1953, pp. 114-128.

Kline, Morris, *Mathematics and Western Culture* (London: George Allen and Unwin, Ltd., 1954).

Klubertanz, George P., S.J., *The Discursive Power* (Saint Louis: The Modern Schoolman, 1952).

—— *The Philosophy of Human Nature* (New York: Appleton-Century-Crofts, 1953).

—— "The Unity of Human Operation," *The Modern Schoolman,* Vol. XXVII, 1950, pp. 75-108.

Leroy, M. V., "Abstraction et séparation d'après s. Thomas," *Revue des sciences philosophiques et théologiques,* Vol. XLVIII (1948), pp. 328-339.

Lonergan, Bernard, S.J., "The Concept of *Verbum* in the Writings of St. Thomas Aquinas," *Theological Studies,* VII, n. 1-4.

Maritain, Jacques, *Distinguer pour unir, ou les degrés du savoir* (Paris: Desclée de Brouwer, 1946).

—— *The Philosophy of Nature* (New York: The Philosophical Library, 1951).

—— *Science and Wisdom,* tr. by B. Wall (New York: C. Scribner's Sons, 1940).

—— *A Preface to Metaphysics,* tr. by E. I. Watkin (New York: A Preface to Metaphysics, 1940).

—— *Existence and the Existent,* tr. by L. Galantiere and G. B. Phelan (New York: Pantheon Books, Inc., 1949).

—— "The Conflict of Methods at the End of the Middle Ages," *The Thomist,* October, 1954, pp. 527-538.

Mascall, E. L., *Existence and Analogy* (London: Longmans, Green, and Co., 1949).

Maurer, Armand, "Form and Essence in the Philosophy of St. Thomas," *Mediaeval Studies,* Vol. 12, 1951, pp. 165-176.

Muller-Thym, Bernard, J., "The 'To Be' Which Signifies the Truth of Propositions," *Proceedings of the American Catholic Philosophical Association,* Vol. XVI, 1940, esp. pp. 234-245.

—— "The Common Sense, Perfection of the Order of Pure Sensibility," *The Thomist,* Vol. II, 1940, pp. 336-361.

—— "Of History as a Calculus Whose Term is Science," *The Modern Schoolman,* Vol. XIX, No. 3, pp. 42-48.

Newman, John Henry, *A Grammar of Assent* (London: Longmans, Green, and Co., 1887).

Nicholl, Donald, *Recent Thought in Focus* (London: Sheed and Ward, 1952).

Owens, Joseph, *The Doctrine of Being in the Aristotelian Metaphysics* (Toronto: Pontifical Institute of Mediaeval Studies, 1951).

—— "Theodicy, Natural Theology, and Metaphysics," *The Modern Schoolman*, V. XXX, 1951, pp. 126-137.

—— "The Causal Proposition—Principle or Conclusion," *The Modern Schoolman*, V. XXXIII, n. 1-3, 1955.

—— "The Object of Metaphysics," *The New Scholasticism*, V. XXVIII, n. 4, 1955.

Parker, Francis, "Realistic Epistemology," in *The Return to Reason*, ed. by J. Wild (Chicago: H. Regnery Co., 1953).

Phelan, Gerald B., "Verum sequitur esse rerum," *Medieval Studies*, V. I, n. 1.

—— "A Note on the Formal Object of Metaphysics," *Essays in Modern Scholasticism* (Westminster: The Newman Press, 1944).

—— "The Existentialism of St. Thomas," *Proceedings of the American Catholic Philosophical Association*, V. XXI, 1946, pp. 25-39.

—— "Being and the Metaphysicians," *From an Abundant Spring; the Walter Farrel Memorial Volume of the Thomist* (New York: Sheed and Ward, 1952).

Philippe, M. D., "Abstraction, addition, séparation dans la philosophie d'Aristote," *Revue Thomiste*, Vol. 32, 1948, pp. 461-479.

Phillips, R. P., D.D., *Modern Thomistic Philosophy* (Westminster: Newman Bookshop, 1935).

Poincaré, Henri, *The Foundations of Science*, tr. by G. Halstead (New York: Harcourt, Brace and Co., 1940).

Rahner, Hugo, S.J., "Der spielende Mensch," *Eranos Jahrbuch*, Vol. XVI, 1949.

Régis, L. M., O.P., "Un libre . . . La philosophie de la nature. Quelques apories," *Etudes et Recherches. Philosophie.* Cahier I (Ottawa: 1936), pp. 127-156.

—— *St. Thomas and Epistemology*, The Aquinas Lecture, 1945, (Milwaukee: Marquette University Press, 1946).

Robert, J. D., "La metaphysique, science distincte de toute autre discipline metaphysique selon saint Thomas d'Aquin," *Divus Thomas* (Piacenza), Vol. L, 1947, pp. 206-222.

Russell, Lord Bertrand, *Library of Living Philosophers: Bertrand Russell.* (Evanston: North Western University Press, 1944).

Ryan, Edmund J., C.PP.S., *The Role of the Sensus Communis in the Philosophy of St. Thomas Aquinas* (Carthagena, Ohio: Messenger Press, 1951).

Sertillanges, A. D., *The Foundations of Thomistic Philosophy*, tr. by G. Anstruther (St. Louis: Herder, 1931).

Smith, Gerard, S.J., "A Date in the History of Epistemology," *The Thomist* (The Maritain Volume), Vol. V, January, 1953, pp. 246-255.

—— "Avicenna and the Possibles," *The New Scholasticism*, Vol. XVII, No. 4, 1943, pp. 340-357.

—— "Before You Start Talking About God," *The Modern Schoolman*, Vol. XXII, No. I, pp. 24-43.

—— *Natural Theology* (New York: Macmillan, 1951).

Simon, Yves R., *Introduction à l'ontologie du connaître* (Paris: Desclée de Brouwer, 1934).

—— *Critique de la connaissance morale* (Paris: Labergerie, 1934).

—— *Prevoir et savoir* (Montreal: Editions de l'Arbre, 1944).

—— *Nature and Functions of Authority* (Milwaukee: Marquette University Press, 1940).

—— "Maritain's Philosophy of the Sciences," *The Maritain Volume of the Thomist* (New York: Sheed and Ward, 1943).

Simonin, R. P., "La notion d'intentio," *Revue des sciences philosophiques et théologiques*, July, 1930, pp. 450-471.

Tate, Allen, "Tension in Poetry," *Critiques and Essays in Criticism*, ed. by R. W. Stallman (New York: Ronald, 1939), pp. 55-66.

Taylor, F. Sherwood, *The Alchemists, Founders of Modern Chemistry* (New York: Harcourt, Brace and Co., 1949).

Turner, Vincent, S.J., "Preliminaries to Theism," *The Dublin Review*, No. 452, 1951, pp. 12-27.

Van Steenberghen, Fernand, *Epistemology*, (New York: Wagner, 1949).

Voegelin, Eric, *The New Science of Politics* (Chicago: The University of Chicago Press, 1952).

Wilhelmsen, Frederick D., "Meditation on Nothing," *The Downside Review*, No. 228, 1954, pp. 135-145.

—— "The Philosopher and the Myth," *The Modern Schoolman*, Vol. XXXII, 1954, pp. 39-55.

Zedler, Beatrice, "St. Thomas and Avicenna in the 'De Potentia Dei'," *Traditio*, Vol. VI, 1948, pp. 105-159.

Name Index

Subject Index

A

Abstraction, double, of critical philosophy, 26-28

Abstraction, from existence, 99-100, 141

Abstraction, scientific, 142, 197-98

Action, 58-59, 61-62, 93-95, 159-60

Apprehension, simple (*see* Understanding, simple)

Aristotelianism, 18

Assent, 157-63

Assumption, 19-22

B

Being, first principle of, 15, 18-24, 41, 44-53, 65, 99

"Being," meaning of, 59-62

Body, 22-23, 31

C

Certitude, 165-66

Certitude, common, 173

Certitude, metaphysical, 167-68

Certitude, moral, 170-71

Certitude, physical, 168-70

Certitude, scientific, 173

Certitude, subjective, 171-72

Civilization, 54-56

Cogito, 12-15, 17-19, 26, 39, 41

Communication, 55-56, 115

Concept, 29-30, 61-62, 66, 106

Conformity, 140-41, 146, 148, 150-52

Consciousness, 101-02, 106-07, 111, 129, 143, 145-48, 158-59, 161-66

Contradiction, principle of, 44-46, 48-49, 51-52

Copula, 62

Creature, 135-38

Criteriology, *v*

Critical problem, 4, 6, 8, 14-15, 22, 26-27, 30-31, 38-41

Critique of knowledge, 14-15, 17-19, 22-24, 26-28, 31, 33, 38-42

D

Deduction, 10

Doubt, Cartesian, 8, 11-14, 27-28

Dreams, 31-33

E

Epistemology, *v-vi*, 3-6, 8, 15, 17-18, 90-91, 147

Error (*see* Falsity)

Essence, 29-30, 58-62, 134-35, 138-39, 141-42 (*see also* Nature)

Evidence, 20-22, 28-31, 33-34, 159-61, 167

Existence, act of, 60-62, 66-71, 80-81, 93-99, 136-40, 158

Existence, intentional, 80-83, 98-99, 143, 147-48, 153, 162-63, 179-80

Existence, knowledge of, 18-20, 27-31, 45-52, 66-70, 101, 160-61, 165

Experience, 127-29

F

Falsity, 77, 140-42, 165, 175-80

Form, 93-95, 97-98, 129-31, 147-48, 150-52, 160-61

G

God, 12-13, 50, 90-91, 135-38, 140

Grammar, 53-62

213